DORSET VILLAGES

Dorset Villages

ROLAND GANT

ROBERT HALE · LONDON

ISBN 0 7091 8135 3

Robert Hale Limited
Clerkenwell House,
Clerkenwell Green,
London, EC1

PRINTED IN GREAT BRITAIN BY
CLARKE, DOBLE & BRENDON LTD.
PLYMOUTH AND LONDON

Contents

Illustrations

Evershot—detail of brass to William Grey (d.1524)
Leigh—village cross
Whitchurch Canonicorum: the shrine of St Wite
Wynford Eagle church with (inset) 'The Honour of the Eagle'
    perched on the porch gable of Wynford Eagle Manor (1630)
St George, Reforne, Portland
Thatching at Turner's Puddle
Thatching at Burton Bradstock
Portland—old Lower Light

Between pages 128 and 129

Cerne Abbas, looking up Abbey Street to Abbey Farm
Creech Grange Arch
Portland: the entrance to the Verne Prison across the artificial
    ravine (1860–67)
Burton Bradstock
Burton Bradstock
Entering Abbotsbury on the Bridport road
Abbotsbury
St Catherine's Chapel, Abbotsbury
Abbotsbury Tithe Barn
Little Bredy
Little Bredy, where the Bride rises in the grounds of Bride Head
    House

Between pages 160 and 161

Winterborne Came: this farm building under Came Down was
    Roland Gant's study in 1941
Plush: a font put out to grass as a bird-bath
Hilfield: a cavalry near the Franciscan Friary
Plush: not a kiln or a bake-oven but a hydraulic ram in a farm
    water-system
Piddletrenthide, lying just under the snow-line when this photo-
    graph was taken
Portland—Easton's main street, known as 'Wakeham'
Hilfield church
Toller Fratrum church

Hermitage—the church bellcote with a ball on top
Studland church
The Cobb, Lyme Regis
The Smugglers' Inn, Osmington Mills
West Bay Harbour and E. S. Prior's 1885 Bay House Hotel
West Bay: retailer of local history and local fish, Des Gape
Little Bredy church

Photographs by Roland and Alasdair Gant

MAP

Acknowledgements

I am grateful to many people for information and help while I was preparing this book and I cannot mention them all by name. I should like to thank in particular the following: Amanda, Betty and the late Kenneth Allsop, Reginald Charles, John Eastwood, Desmond Gape, Robert Gittings, Allen Hiscock, George Millar, Victor Montagu, Michael Shaw, Monique and Hugh Stevens, the late Sylvia Townsend Warner and staff of the Dorset County Library in Blandford, Bridport, Dorchester, Sherborne and Sturminster Newton.

I am indebted to the following books, their authors and publishers and for permission to quote extracts: *Dorset: a Shell Guide* by Michael Pitt Rivers (Faber); *Purbeck: the Ingrained Island* by Paul Hyland (Gollancz); *Purbeck Island* by Rodney Legg (Dorset Publishing Company); *Guide to Prehistoric and Roman Monuments in England and Wales* by Jacquetta Hawkes (Chatto and Windus); *Portrait of Dorset* by Ralph Wightman (Robert Hale); *Dorset Up Along and Down Along* edited by M. R. Dacombe (Friary Press, Dorchester); *Dorset.* Royal Commission for Historical Monuments, 4 vols (H.M.S.O.); *Young Thomas Hardy* and *The Older Hardy* by Robert Gittings (Heinemann Educational Books); *The Place-Names of Dorset* by Anton Fägersten (E.P. Publishing); *Dorset (The Buildings of England)* by John Newman and Nikolaus Pevsner (Penguin Books); a letter published in the correspondence columns of *The Times*—The Lord Wynford of Wynford Eagle and Times Newspapers Ltd.

Nadia and Alasdair not only helped with photographs and criticism but put up with both my inconvenient absence and my distracted presence—a special thank-you to them both.

R.G.

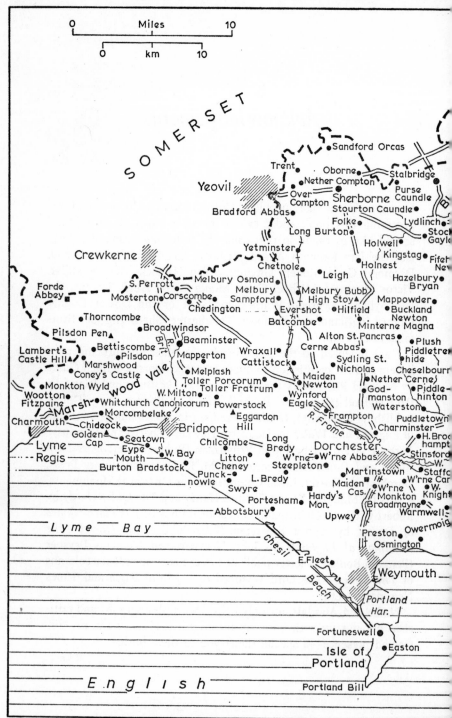

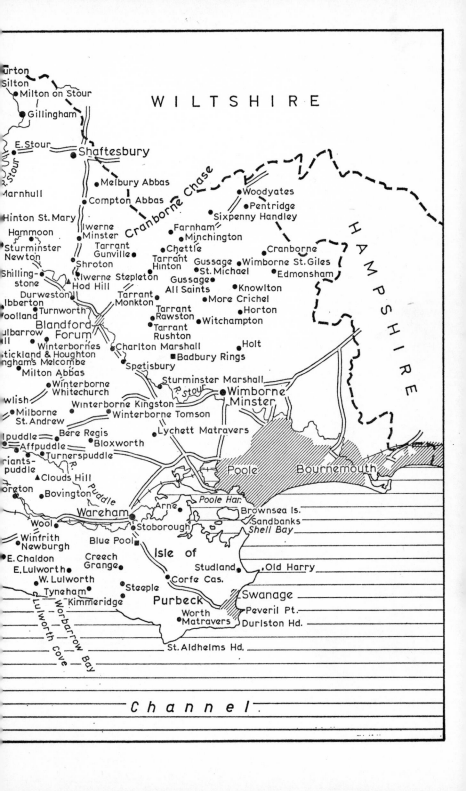

I

How to Invade Dorset

THE stranger, making his way south-west from Salisbury to Blandford Forum, may think he has entered a never-never maze. Hampshire has been left nearly twenty miles back at Lobscombe Corner,
where the A343 road from Andover joins the A30 from Stock-
bridge at the Wiltshire border. And yet the western border of
Wiltshire at the opposite end of the county also gives way to
Hampshire where the road slices across three or four miles of the
northern tip of a narrow Hants enclave in Wilts. A sudden change
in the landscape adds to an impression that here was some past
'battle of the bulge'. Rolling pasture and arable land give way to
a swell of gorse and scrub that has long been doing its best to
throw green spray over the hulks of Nissen huts abandoned years
ago by their crews. Ivy munches its way up the brick pillars of a
tower that held the water to make the tea to give to the troops.
But the last missile fired in anger was most likely from a sling or
bow.

Early in the seventh century AD Bokerley Dyke, a massive defen-
sive earthwork, was raised along four miles of what is still the
Dorset boundary. At its northern end was the dense forest of
Cranborne Chase, and at the southern extremity lay inhospitable
heathlands. The dyke blocked the Salisbury–Dorchester Roman
road, was strengthened from time to time and for nearly two
centuries protected the British peoples of Dorset from the Saxons.
The coast was too difficult for them to invade by sea in force, but
in 875 the Danes took Wareham and laid waste the surrounding
lands, until King Alfred drove them out of all Wessex.

At Bokerley Junction, where the A354 from Salisbury sweeps

in a wide curve out of that sprig of Hampshire, one green sign proclaims 'Dorset' and another announces "Woodyates'. There is not much sign of a village, for there is no church, and the great coaching-inn that was used for staging horses between Salisbury and Dorchester, and which was once kept by Robert Browning's great-grandfather Thomas, has now vanished completely. But stop at Woodyates all the same because here the history of centuries can be walked on and through.

Early one mid-May morning I walked beside, along and across Bokerley Dyke. To the east the sun was half tomato and half lemon as it rose through the mist that lay like fleece in the hollows and in the deeper parts of the ditch which is on the Hampshire side and is often eighteen feet from top to bottom so that one can imagine the steepness and strength of the fortifications as they were fifteen hundred years ago. I felt strongly what it must have been like to patrol the dyke, watching for reconnoitring Saxons in the early morning mist and peering suddenly and suspiciously at the brambles behind which something rustled and moved and then moved again and was seen to be a hare bounding off into the damp whiteness. To one side I saw some beehives, standing unexpected and like ancient, shrunken bathing-machines in a grassy glade. No sound of bees at that time, only the steady dripping from the branches of the silver birches. Then that frontier sensation surged back as a helicopter clattered and glittered along in the sunshine a couple of hundred feet up. I instinctively looked around me for the nearest cover—a threatened Briton to the marrow.

Less than a mile down a narrow one-way road, the first turning to the left as you come into Dorset, is Pentridge, its name derived from the Celtic *pen* which is 'hill' and *twrch* meaning 'boar'. This hill of the boars was first set down as 'Pentric' eighty years before the birth of King Alfred in AD 849. A mile to the south-east, on Oakley Down, Alfred's father Aethelwulf defeated the Danes in 851 in what the Anglo-Saxon Chronicle recorded as "the greatest slaughter of a heathen host".

A thousand years later Tess walked slowly beside Alec d'Urberville's gig, from which she had stepped down after wiping his kiss from her cheek: ". . . in this manner, at a slow pace, they advanced towards the village of Trantridge. . . . A few minutes later the chimneys of The Slopes appeared in view, and in a snug nook to the right the poultry-farm and cottage of Tess's destination."

Because Pentridge, or 'Trantridge' as Thomas Hardy called it in *Tess of the d'Urbervilles* and *Jude the Obscure*, can only be reached and left by the one road, it has changed little apart from the rebuilding in the nineteenth century of the church, dedicated to the eighth-century Celtic saint Rumbold who took the Gospel to the then heathen Low Countries. It is a long, narrow, stone and flint building with no aisles and a square tower surmounted by a chunky spire. St Rumbold's has settled very comfortably into a churchyard unmarred by fussy tidiness within the rusty undulations of a pretty iron fence that has a fastening on the gate which looks so complicated that the first time I went there I climbed over it. On the way out I discovered that it did not in fact close at all. The gateway of the porch is a rustic affair artfully fashioned of branches.

On the south wall of the nave there is a tablet, "To the memory of Robert Browning of Woodyates in this parish who died November 25 1746 and is the first known forefather of Robert Browning the poet. He married Elizabeth Pethebridge who died 1759, and their son Thomas, born 1721 of Woodyates Inn was the poet's great-grandfather. This tablet was erected by some of the poet's friends and admirers 1902."

Thomas and Jane Browning had their elder son baptized 'Robert' on 12th September 1749 in Pentridge Church. When he was twenty, he went to London to work in the Bank of England. His first child was, in turn, called Robert, and so was that Robert's son. The poet always described Pentridge as the cradle of his family.

King George III used to lunch at the Woodyates Inn on his way to Weymouth where he spent his summers, and one who sought to be king, who had, the previous century, raised his standard and an army of simple and untrained Dorset men against the forces of King James II also passed this way, but it was no royal progress: in 1685 the Duke of Monmouth, in flight after his defeat at Sedgemoor, abandoned his horse, ironically, at the staging-inn of Woodyates and went on foot disguised as a shepherd but was soon flushed from the ditch where he was hiding a few miles away, near Horton. He was beheaded in London on Tower Hill, and the Reign of Terror of Judge Jeffreys and the Bloody Assizes gathered up Monmouth's supporters for the gallows or transportation.

The country around Pentridge is a treasurescape for archæologists, rich even for Dorset (so rich a county in prehistoric sites), with barrows, tracks and ditches that proliferate and invite one to spend some time walking there. About a mile north of Pentridge there are two parallel banks some eighty-five yards apart that run for over six miles from Bokerley Dyke to Thickthorn Down. Known as 'the Dorset Cursus,' it crosses Ackling Dyke, the Roman road running from Badbury Rings near Wimborne Minster to Old Sarum, the forerunner of present-day Salisbury. Four miles of the dyke are extremely well preserved, and to walk along the agger, or causeway, from Oakley Down to Gussage Hill is to get a vivid idea of how the Roman legions moved across the country. It is one of the finest stretches of Roman road in Britain. The Cursus and Ackling Dyke cross on Wyke Down, and groups of long barrows lie at either end of the Cursus which is over three times as long as the more familiar one at Stonehenge. It is generally thought to have been some sort of ceremonial route to the long barrows.

From Penbury Knoll, a little less than a mile to the south-east of Pentridge, on a clear day you will get an idea of what this district holds. In addition to Bokerley Dyke, Ackling Dyke, long barrows, round barrows and Celtic fields, just to the north and over the county border with Hampshire there is Bronze Age Grim's Ditch, or 'Grimsdyke,' as a local filling-station usefully marks the location. Merely to walk there is exhilarating in any season—when the larks are singing above the short turf or when the fine rain is driving, but it is well worth carrying a large-scale map to know exactly what lies there.

If you are walking, you might as well go down the other side of Penbury Knoll as well and along to Cranborne, about two and a half miles to the south-west.

Formerly an important market town, Cranborne's importance has dwindled but certainly not into decay. Though the town was once a centre of power and of an often suspect justice that dealt summarily with a frequently understandable lawlessness, you could easily pass through without being aware of the turmoil of times past. Over four hundred years ago John Leland wrote of Cranborne as having "a praty thorroghfair, and for one streat meatly well builded. There rennith a fleting bek thorrogh it, and passid down thorrogh the streat self on the right hand." It is still meetly built, although now many houses are of red brick, mingling with the older ones of cob and timber, and the little River Cran, or Crane, still flows through on its way to the Moors River at Verwood.

I have often come across something unusual or specially memorable in Cranborne. Once I came out of narrow Swan Street into the small Square at the end of an April afternoon when I could almost see the beech trees unfolding in the suddenly warm sunshine: through the completely deserted Square clopped a roan gelding bearing on his back a young girl with long dark hair who carried in the crook of her arm an enormous bunch of daffodils. On another occasion I drove slowly through thick mist from Wyke Down early one November morning, and below the beeches to the left of the road their leaves, layer on layer, glowed in the milky haze with a colour that russet gets nowhere near describing.

In AD 980 a Benedictine priory was founded here to which Tewkesbury was subordinate, but a hundred years later, when the Abbey of Tewkesbury was rebuilt, the roles were reversed, and Cranborne became a cell of the Abbey. Nothing now remains of the priory, which had declined until there were only two monks left at the time of the Dissolution, but its former importance and the original size of the parish (forty miles in circumference) explain the largeness of the church.

According to a manuscript in the Ashmolean Museum, a college of six monks was established at Cranborne in memory of six Britons killed in battle there. In the records of Tewkesbury Abbey is recorded that

> . . . about the year 930, in the reign of King Athelstan, there lived a noble knight named Aylward Sneaw or Snow, so called from his fair complexion, who, being mindful of his death, founded a Monastery in honour of God, our Lord Jesus Christ and His Mother and Saint Bartholomew, in his demesne at Cranborn. Having collected there some brethren under an Abbot, who should strictly obey the rule of St Benedict, he made the Priory of Tewkesbury, of which he was patron, entirely subordinate to the Church of Cranborn.

The Abbey was established by 980 and was recorded in 1086 in the Domesday Book as a very important monastic foundation, but in 1102 Giraldus the Abbot and his fifty-seven monks were moved to Tewkesbury. It was then that Cranborne became a priory and cell of Tewkesbury, and in 1339 the Prior was even ordered by Edward III to take an armed force to repel some new would-be invader of Dorset. At the Dissolution of the Monasteries both Tewkesbury and Cranborne were surrendered to Henry VIII in 1540, and in 1703 what remained of the priory buildings were finally demolished.

The centuries' progress is well marked in the stone and flint church. The doorway in the north porch is Norman, the nave Early English, and on the south wall there are paintings of the fourteenth century or possibly earlier, which were discovered under the lime-wash in 1870. One is of St Christopher carrying a child while his leg is being bitten by a fish, and next to him is the Tree of the Seven Deadly Sins which, a piece of medieval male chauvinism, grows out of the head of a woman. To the right of this is Christ in Majesty with figures kneeling in worship. The font is of about 1240, octagonal and of Purbeck marble. It was moved about the church a bit during the extensive but by no means disastrous nineteenth-century restoration, and again in 1970 to its present position near the south door. There it looks in its right place and solidly at rest at last. It is an object that merits slow inspection, to walk around slowly and then to sit and contemplate the austere beauty of the shape and the two shallow pointed arches incised on each of the sides and left blank. Perhaps this inspired the carver of the fifteenth-century oak pulpit to leave the arches blank there too. But on the pulpit are carved emblems of the chase—a hawk catching a hare, a hound and a crowing cock. The monogram 'TP' is probably that of Thomas Parker, Abbot of Tewkesbury and Cranborne, 1381–1421.

A monument to John Elliott, who died in 1641, depicts a boy with a posy of flowers, resting his elbow on a skull. Apparently he spoke seven languages but died at the age of seven, said to have choked on a fish-bone. Any connection with the fish that took such a dislike to the child-carrying St Christopher on the wall?

The south-aisle wooden reredos was carved by the Reverend F. M. Fisher, Vicar 1888–1910, who also carved the altar and the screen. I often admire the delicacy and obvious loving care with which the representations of artichokes, cuckoo-pint, poppies and ball-flowers are carved. There is a window in the south wall to the memory of the good Vicar, and also one to John Tregonwell, who died in 1885, son of Lewis Tregonwell who in 1810 built a house by the sea at a spot that became Bournemouth.

A gravestone caught my attention in the churchyard. In memory of Abel Brewer (d. 1879), it is in the form of a Celtic cross decorated with ultramarine and terracotta tiles bearing a six-petalled flower-design. Was Abel Brewer not a brewer but a tiler or mason? I have never seen a similar headstone lending such a Byzantine dash to a lean, grey and mossy company.

Hidden behind the church is the grey stone manor that is one of the loveliest in Dorset or possibly in England. Early in the thirteenth century King John had a hunting-lodge built here for his use when hunting in Cranborne Chase. The present house was built early in the reign of James I, who was entertained there by Robert Cecil, to whom the manor and the rights of Cranborne Chase had been granted by Queen Elizabeth I. The King had great faith in Cecil's loyalty and advice and created him Viscount Cranborne in 1604 and Earl of Salisbury in 1605. He was frequently called 'the crook-backed earl', but James, who was no giant himself, nicknamed him 'my little beagle' because of the efficiency with which he tracked down conspirators. Cecil wanted to make his house literally fit for a king, and so he had a tower heightened and another built to match it; wings were added to the house (they were later pulled down), and two arcaded loggias were built in the north and south fronts. The house is not open to the public but can be seen through the gateway in the church-yard wall at the end of an avenue of lime trees. But the gardens are open to the public on the first Saturday and Sunday of each spring, summer and early autumn months and on Bank Holidays and certain other advertised days. The first Earl had his gardens planned by Mounten Jennings and John Tradescant, who laid out for him his gardens at Hatfield. Its seventeenth-century style garden is divided into several courts with orchard, mount and kitchen garden which have been preserved largely through neglect.

During the Civil War the second Earl supported Parliament, and as a result the Royalist troops quartered in Cranborne in

1643 saw it as an enemy-owned house that Cromwell could knock about a bit. Considerable damage was done to the house, and cavalry trampled and grazed over the flowerbeds, but without obliterating the over-all design. The Cecils then abandoned Cranborne for a couple of centuries to concentrate on their house at Hatfield, closer to London and the source of power. In 1863 the second Marquess of Salisbury had the house and gardens restored, and a century later Viscount (now the sixth Marquess) and Viscountess Cranborne had the garden replanted within the original design and framework and a carefully planned conformation to the artistic context of the whole. The north court, which is flanked by the house, is dominated by white flowers, particularly white roses like those which cover the mellow brick lozenge-plan lodges. The south court is paved and has contrasting panels of coloured pebbles and turf and wide flowered borders. The mount is now composed of a pattern of box-bordered beds and ablaze with a variety of colours. A pre-seventeenth-century atmosphere is strongest in the herb garden, reached through two other enclosures, where the air between its walls is—in summer—aromatic and alive with the continuo of bees. Medieval too is the mingling of fruit-trees and flowers along the path to the church.

The Cranborne Garden Centre is open daily and on Sunday afternoons throughout the year. There one can buy for one's own garden most of what is growing in the Manor Gardens, from the 'old-fashioned' roses in which they specialize to a pot of chives. There is a gift-shop which has no hint of 'gyftte shoppe' about it but has a wide range of baskets, trugs, glass paperweights containing dried flowers, books and country-made useful and decorative objects of all kinds. Whenever I have called there, whether for bags of peat, cedarwood trellis, fertilizer or bush-roses, I have always come away with those small and long-thought-about gifts which are taken home and put away for Christmas or birthday and are usually only found some time after the event for which they were bought has passed.

Over the Jacobean south porch of the manor stand figures of Justice and Mercy, and in the house is a room which was a dungeon. The Manor was the seat of the Chase Court which sought to impose order in the past on the thickly-wooded 700,000 acres that stretched along Dorset's eastern border and into Hampshire and Wiltshire. It was notorious for its lawlessness. Hungry men, professional poachers and gentlemen poachers seeking nocturnal thrills, robbers, highwaymen and smugglers passing inland the goods illegally landed at Swanage and Poole—all thrived here, barely checked by the fear of death by bullet or club, mutilation by man-traps or prison and transportation. The stories of Cranborne Chase, ruled by its own laws and at the same time a haven for the lawless, still stand as thick as the trees that once kept the outside world at bay. The Sheaf of Arrows Inn is a reminder of the years of hunting, and so are the antlers that hang beside the door of a former chapel. Not only did King John, James I and Charles I come to Cranborne for the hunting but Charles I returned there when he was more quarry than hunter, on his way from Exeter and Chard and heading towards the second battle of Newbury of 27th October 1644. And through the visits of kings in peace and war, and the occupation by soldiers in the English Revolution, the ordinary people of Cranborne went about the business of daily living. They still do: you will get the aroma of real bread as you pass Noble's bakery—except that you most likely will not pass it but call in. And that fictional past that Hardy brought alive in the Flower-de-Luce Inn at Chaseborough is barely changed, as you will find if you sit in the bar of the 'Fleur-de-Lys' which dates from the sixteenth century. Everywhere the visitor is reminded that this 'settlement on the cranes' stream' has been there a very long time.

2

Pleasures of the Chase

THE term 'Chase' denotes hunting rights over a district but does not include ownership. When a 'Chase' passed to the monarch, it became a 'Forest', as Cranborne did when King John married an heiress of the House of Gloucester, whereby he gained the Chase as well—which did not deter him from swiftly divorcing his wife. On King John's death, the Forest returned to the earls of Gloucester, and Cranborne reverted to being a Chase. But, Forest or Chase, it remained what Thomas Hardy called ". . . one of the few remaining woodlands in England of undoubted primeval date, wherein Druidical mistletoe is still found on aged oaks, and where enormous yew trees, not planted by the hand of man, grew as they had grown when they were pollarded for bows".

It was Parliament rather than hunting monarchs which finally brought order to the turbulent Chase. An Act of 1830 brought about its disafforestation, which meant, of course, not the wholesale felling of trees but the abolition of hunting rights in the Chase and erstwhile Royal Forest. Just before then it was estimated that between twelve and twenty thousand deer still remained within the hundred-mile circumference of the Chase. The land itself underwent some taming, and there are many fields now where formerly there were trees and thickets, yet there is the sense that the former wildness has not been completely dissipated.

There is a very compact and civilized village less than three miles from Cranborne—but remember that Wimborne St Giles is *not* close to Wimborne Minster but about ten miles distant. Some careful map-reading is necessary around here so as not to miss the turnings. If you get one of the right ones first time, you may see a signpost that states "MONKTON UP WIMBORNE and 6d HANDLEY 4¼". But do not follow it now, just note the unusual name of the second village and pray that total metrication does not intervene before you visit it.

As Wimborne is built in a marshy valley where the River Allen runs under a bridge at one end of the village and into the park of St Giles House, there is a feeling of being sheltered here by the beech-crowned downs of Cranborne Chase as well as by the tall trees in the park with a profusion of mistletoe (also Druidical?) growing to the very tops. On the Allen is a well-preserved seventeenth-century brick mill-house, opposite the village stocks that stand on a plot of greensward by the road. They are shielded from the rain, as their tenants surely were not, by the kind of small, steeply-pitched roof on posts that protects wells and lych-gates.

Wimborne St Giles has been owned for hundreds of years by the Ashleys, later Ashley Coopers and, since 1672, earls of Shaftesbury. The Anthony Ashley who was Clerk to Elizabeth I's Privy Council is said to have introduced the cabbage to England. In that respect he is perhaps a doubtful benefactor, but he was a true and well-remembered one for the row of almshouses built in 1624 beside the church and overlooking the wide village green. They are of red brick and single-storey, with a two-storeyed centre block with a three-bay stone arcade. On the back of the door by which one passes through this centre block I found a sun carved into the black oak, and in the arcade itself lay a broken marble pillar topped by an urn. Coming out at the back of the almshouses, I found myself in modest garden plots, all beansticks, wilting potato haulms and sly up-and-coming dock leaves. I had half-expected a courtyard, but these gardens, surrounded by ancient walls and the back of the church, must be exactly what Sir Anthony intended for the eleven old widows who lived there.

The architect of the main part of the present church, built in 1732, may have been one of the Bastard brothers of Blandford, but naturally the Victorians had a go at 'improving' this Early Georgian church, and G. F. Bodley remodelled it in 1886–7. After it was badly damaged by fire in 1908, Sir Ninian Comper set about him with great energy and sometimes mistakenly. Newman and Pevsner's comment cannot be bettered: "He [Comper] put in tall, round piers to separate his aisle from the eighteenth-century nave and also to create a south aisle. This was bound to be preposterously narrow, and the whole conceit shows up Comper at his most wilful." They wonder if the hexagonal sphere by the feet of the early-seventeenth-century effigies of Sir Anthony Ashley and his wife is a motif connected with his interest in sea-charts, but there is another theory that it represents the sire of the English cabbage race! The canopy over the figures is wearisomely elaborate, and on the floor beside them is the kneeling figure of their only child, Anne, who later married Sir John Cooper of Rockbourne and became the mother of Sir Anthony Ashley Cooper, later first Earl of Shaftesbury.

In a fragment of autobiography Shaftesbury wrote:

My birth was at Wimborn St Gyles in the county of Dorsett, on the 22nd day of July 1621, early in the morning; my parents on both sides of a noble stock, being of the first rank of gentry in those counties where they lived. My mother's name was Anne, the sole daughter and heir of Sir Anthony Ashley, knight and baronet, lord of the manor and place where I was born: my father, Sir John Cooper, knight and baronet, son of Sir John Cooper, of Rockborn in the county of Hamshyre. I was christened by the name of Anthony Ashley, for, notwithstanding my grandfather had articles with my father and his guardians that he should change his name to Ashley, yet, to make all sure in the eldest, he resolved to add his name, so that it should not be parted with.

In 1651 he laid the first stone of St Giles House. Built to the plans of an unknown architect in the style of Inigo Jones, extensive alterations were made in the mid-eighteenth century and in Victorian times two Italianate towers were added. The interior has remained largely unchanged from the mid-eighteenth century, with a chimneypiece, ceiling and other features retained from the seventeenth century. There is an Ionic garden temple, an ornamental gateway of the eighteenth century and a shell grotto which has to be seen to be believed. Unfortunately, the last time I was in Wimborne St Giles the house and park were closed to the public, and I was told that the house was being extensively repaired. I walked a little way into the park on a damp day in early winter when the fallen leaves, overgrown paths and general air of desertion and decay lent a brooding 'Gothick' air to this setting for a production of *The Sleeping Beauty*.

Sir Anthony Ashley Cooper may have known from the start what kind of house he wanted and proceeded in a direct line to getting it built, but there was less continuity in the architecture of his own life. He was one of the Members of Parliament for Tewkesbury in 1640, was a Royalist for two years, went over to the Parliamentarians and sat as a Wiltshire Member in the Barebones Parliament. He was appointed one of Oliver Cromwell's Council of State, then, from 1655, opposed Cromwell and at the Restoration became Lord Lieutenant of Dorset, Chancellor of the Exchequer and Privy Councillor and was raised to the peerage as Baron Ashley of Wimborne St Giles. He was a member of the 'Cabal' Ministry comprised of Clifford, Ashley, Buckingham, Arlington and Lauderdale, and he was created Earl of Shaftesbury in 1672. Then he ran into trouble by ill-judging the sides he should back, was imprisoned in the Tower of London a couple of times—the second on a charge of treason, fled to Holland and died there in 1682.

It was not this eloquent and gifted opportunistic politician who gave his name to Shaftesbury Avenue in London but the seventh earl (1801–85), champion of the poor, Chairman of the Ragged School Union and one of the most loved of British social reformers. How many of the millions of visitors to Piccadilly Circus, and how many Londoners themselves know that the statue of Eros, *bury*ing his *shaft* in the ground in the direction of Shaftesbury Avenue, commemorates him.

But to come back for a moment to the first earl: John Dryden satirized him as 'Achitophel' and the two lines which are most frequently quoted may as well be quoted again because they give a brilliant contemporary portrait of him:

> For close designs and crooked counsels fit,
> Sagacious, bold and turbulent of wit. . . .

But it was not all plotting at St Giles, or if it was, it was leavened by some merriment—which may, of course, have been part of a softening-up of the guests. There is a story that Charles II on a visit was holding his own with some hard-drinking companions in the cellar and knighted one of them on the spot. This was Sir Edward Hooper of Boveridge of whom there is a (perhaps fittingly) recumbent effigy in Cranborne Church.

That road signposted 'MONKTON UP WIMBORNE and 6d HANDLEY' leads over the A354 to a village which was largely rebuilt after a great fire in 1892, in which nearly two hundred people were rendered homeless and destitute. In a contemporary account it was said that the fire which raged through Handley was started by sparks from the wheelwright's fire. It was 20th May in a very dry spring, and a high wind tossed the burning thatch into the air and spread the fire.

A former curate of the parish was sent by the bishop to enquire into the matter. As he passed up the ruined street, he met an old parishioner and asked for particulars. At the end of her graphic story, he asked what the vicar was doing about it. The old lady sniffed contemptuously—"The Passon," she said. "He's no sense. What d'ye think his text was on Sunday? 'We went through fire and water, but Thou has brought us to a wealthy place.' It's true there was fire enough, but there wer'n't no watter to put it out. And I ask you, Sar!"—with a dramatic gesture towards the smoul-dering ruins around her—"Would you call this 'a wealthy place'?" This sad catastrophe aroused much general interest and sympathy, and gifts of all sorts came pouring in. In fact, so much clothing was sent that it was said you could, for a long time, tell a man from our parish because he usually wore two if not three waist-coats. A great deal of money was collected, so much that when all claims had been met, at least £1,000 was left over. Unfortunately so much squabbling arose about the further spending of this big balance that it was put into chancery, where it has remained ever since.

The name of the village is derived from the two former hundreds, Sexpena and Hanlege, which were, according to *The Place-Names of Dorset*, ". . . from the thirteenth-century onwards . . . mostly mentioned together and seem at a fairly early date to have been united or confused . . . perhaps owing to the fact that they both belonged to the abbess of Shaftesbury". The names themselves probably came from the combination of the Old English 'Saxons' hilltop' and 'a high clearing'.

Sixpenny Handley is a somewhat sprawling village. The church was heavily restored in 1877, and there is some unfortunate brick facing on the inside walls, but it has retreated obligingly into the background under coats of whitewash. A seated Christ in Glory has been weathered almost beyond recognition to an austere majesty. The Purbeck marble font is of the twelfth century, and there are some gigantic Norman gargoyles on the tower. In the north of the churchyard a tombstone is inscribed: "This stone was the cover of the tomb which was removed to afford space for the enlargement of the church in 1879. When deer-stealing was prevalent, the deer-stealers used to remove it to place in the tomb the deer they had taken till they had an opportunity to remove them." One of the lawless inhabitants of Sixpenny Handley, who may have been involved in deer-stealing but is remembered more for his dealings in more valuable game, was Isaac Gulliver, a notorious Dorset king among smugglers. Gulliver's travels were concentrated between the coast and Cranborne Chase. He was never caught, was married in the church in 1768, was for a time landlord of a local inn and died a rich man.

In his autobiographical writings the first Earl of Shaftesbury described how the local landowners used to meet each week at the Sixpenny Handley bowling-green. Of the year 1639, he wrote:

The eastern part of Dorsetshire had a bowling-green at Hanley, where the gentlemen went constantly once a week, though neither the green nor accommodation was inviting, yet it was well placed for to continue the correspondence of the gentry of those parts. Thither resorted Mr Hastings of Woodland, Sir Gerard Nappeir, Mr Rogers, Sir William Uvedall, Mr Carent of Woodyats, Mr Okeden, Mr Butler, father and son, and Mr Edward Hooper of Boryads [the same Edward Hooper of Boveridge who was later dubbed at a cellar wine-bibbing by the Merry Monarch], Mr Ryves of Raynston, Mr Holles, Mr Chafin of Chettle, Mr Hussey of Edmondsham, Mr Ernley, Mr Arney, Sir George Moreton, and myself, with several others. . . .

His brilliant pen portrait of the first of these gentlemen takes us straight into the mid-seventeenth century, and the manners of the preceding one:

Mr Hastings, by his quality, being the son, brother and uncle to the earls of Huntingdon, and his way of living had the first place amongst us. He was peradventure an original in our age, or rather

the copy of our nobility in ancient days in hunting and not warlike
times: he was low, very strong and very active, of a reddish flaxen
hair, his clothes always green cloth, and never all worth when new
five pounds. His house was perfectly of the old fashion, in the
midst of a large park well stocked with deer, and near the house
rabbits to serve his kitchen, many fish-ponds, and great store of
wood and timber; a bowling-green in it, long but narrow, full of
high ridges, it being never levelled since it was ploughed; they
used round sand bowls, and it had a banqueting house like a stand,
a large one built in a tree. He kept all manner of sport hounds that
ran buck, fox, hare, otter, and badger, and hawks long and short
winged; he had all sorts of nets for fishing: he had a walk in the
New Forest and the manor of Christ Church. This last supplied him
with red deer, sea and river fish; and indeed all his neighbours'
grounds and royalties were free to him, who bestowed all his time
in such sports, but what he borrowed to caress his neighbours'
wives and daughters, there being not a woman in all his walks of
the degree of a yeoman's wife or under, and under the age of
forty, but it was extremely her fault if he were not intimately
acquainted with her. This made him very popular, always speaking
kindly to the husband, brother or father, who was to boot very welcome to his house, whenever he came; there he found beef pudding
and small beer in great plenty, a house not so neatly kept as to
shame him or his dirty shoes, the great hall strewed with marrow-
bones, full of hawks' perches, hounds, spaniels, and terriers, the
upper sides of the hall hung with the fox-skins of this and the
last year's skinning, here and there a polecat intermixed, guns and
keepers' and huntsmen's poles in abundance. The parlour was a
large long room as properly furnished; on a great hearth paved with
brick lay some terriers and the choicest hounds and spaniels; sel-
dom but two of the great chairs had litters of young cats in them
which were not to be disturbed, he having always three or four
attending him at dinner, and a little white round stick of fourteen
inches long lying by his trencher that he might defend such meat
as he had no mind to part with to them. The windows, which were
very large, served for places to lay his arrows, crossbows, stone-
bows and other such like accoutrements; the corners of the room
full of the best chose hunting and hawking poles; an oyster-table
at the lower end, which was of constant use twice a day all the
year round, for he never failed to eat oysters before dinner and
supper through all seasons. The neighbouring town of Poole supplied him with them. The upper part of this room had two small

tables and a desk, on the one side of which was a church Bible, on the other the Book of Martyrs; on the tables were hawks' hoods, bells and such like, two or three old green hats with their crowns thrust in so as to hold ten or a dozen eggs, which were of a pheasant kind of poultry he took much care of and fed himself; tables, dice, cards and boxes were not wanting. In the hole of the desks were store of tobacco pipes that had been used. On one side of this end of the room was the door of a closet, wherein stood the strong beer and the wine, which never came thence but in single glasses, that being the rule of the house exactly observed, for he never exceeded in drink or permitted it. On the other side was a door into an old chapel not used for devotion; the pulpit, as the safest place, was never wanting of a cold chine of beef, pasty of venison, gammon of bacon, or great apple-pie with thick crust extremely baked. His table cost him not much, though it was very good to eat at, his sports supplying all but beef and mutton, except Friday, when he had the best sea-fish as well as other fish he could get, and was the day that his neighbours of best quality most visited him. He never wanted a London pudding, and always sung it in with "my part lies therein-a". He drank a glass of wine or two at meals, very often syrup of gilliflower in his sack, and had always a tun glass without feet stood by him holding a pint of small beer, which he often stirred with a great sprig of rosemary. He was well natured, but soon angry, calling his servants bastard and cuckoldy knaves, in one of which he often spoke truth to his own knowledge, and sometimes in both, though of the same man. He lived to a hundred, never lost his eyesight, but always writ and read without spectacles, and got to horse without help. Until past fourscore he rode to the death of a stag as well as any.

William Dougal Christie, in his edition of Shaftesbury's memoirs (1859), gave a footnote about Hastings and his pudding song—'part of an old catch':

> There lies a pudding in the fire,
> And my part lies therein-a,
> When shall I call in, O!
> Thy good fellows and mine-a?

If, instead of turning north and crossing the A354 to come direct to Sixpenny Handley, you stay in the Cranborne and Wimborne St Giles area, take the B3078 towards Wimborne Minster and turn left at the crossroads where stands the large and lonely Horton Inn. The church of St Wolfrida at Horton was built by someone who knew Vanbrugh's and Hawksmoor's work. Such a delightful piece of Georgian architecture is unexpected in a fairly remote Dorset village, but Eastbury, which was designed by Vanbrugh, is only a few miles to the north. The tower, which is massive, squat and crowned with an almost pyramidal spire, was built in 1722, and the north transept was put up during the next three decades. In the tower of the old church, which was pulled down in 1720, were five bells, of which four were sold to pay for the restoration. The remaining bell is inscribed 'Love God — 1684'. There are two early-fourteenth-century effigies, of Sir Giles de Braose who died in 1305 and his first wife, Beatrice. His is of Purbeck marble and hers of Ham Hill stone, and we can deduce from that what we will. Under the belfry of the old church was an aisle belonging to the Hastings family, and the figures of Sir Giles and his lady were formerly here before the aisle was screened off and used as a vestry. Here, high on the wall and looking down on the surplices, collection-bags, spare light-bulbs and keys, and lit by the sun streaming through the broad and clear glass Georgian window, is the monument to "The Honorable Henry Hastings of Woodland second sonne to George Hastings Earle of Huntingdon. Departed this life the 5th of October 1650 Aetat 99". Above this memorial and a little to the left hangs the massive cylindrical weight of the clock placed in the tower in 1900—a leaden pudding that lies therein-a. The memorial is topped by a helmet bearing a ram's head, and on either side are the heads of cherubs who wear pained expressions and cock their ears to each other as though trying to carry on a conversation above the energetic tocking of the clock above them.

The village of Horton seems to be growing quickly and in a variety of architectural styles, some of which would have set Vanbrugh's wig on end. But above the village stands a ruin which even old Hastings, had he lived for another hundred years, might have found a little eccentric, though useful to the compulsive sportsman.

Horton Tower was built c1750 for Humphrey Sturt of Horton Manor. It was called an Observatory, but it is thought that Sturt was more interested in the movement of the herds of deer in the forest than in that of the stars in the heavens. Built of brick, and hexagonal in shape, it was originally surmounted by a cupola and was 120 feet high, consisting of six storeys, with pointed windows, domes for the turrets and a fireplace half way up. None of the floors remain, and there is no evidence that there was ever a staircase of brick or stone. There was either a wooden stairway or a series of wooden ladders. Now you can stand inside and look up at a hexagon of sky, and if you shout or clap your hands, you are answered by the irritable caws of jackdaws and the clacketing wings of the pigeons who are now the only top-storey observers left.

On the B3078 from Cranborne, about a mile before the Horton Inn, stands a very different sort of ruin in a unique setting. Roofless, but still complete, are a Norman nave and chancel and fourteenth- fifteenth-century tower, of mixed red sandstone, limestone and bands of flint. Around stand a few yews much the worse for age, and the village which the church once served has vanished completely. Knowlton Church is of unknown dedication, but it was built in the centre of a circle a hundred yards in diameter, a Bronze Age henge or sacred place with, on the inside of the rampart, a ditch designed not to keep human invaders out but to prevent the evil spirits confined to the inside from wandering abroad to exert their malignant powers. It is plain (particularly in a remarkable photograph taken for the Committee for Aerial Photography, Cambridge) that there were barrows close to the three henges. Most of them have been lost to the plough and are visible only from the air, but one prodigious mound, twenty feet high, still stands in the middle of a cultivated field to the east, alone and covered with crowded trees like those deer-free islets in Scottish lochs. Worship began here nearly four thousand years ago, and perhaps the church was built in a spirit of 'if you can't beat them, join them'.

There is a strange air about the place, not menacing but of a powerful timelessness or the power of compressed time. One December morning, when the frost lay white and thick as snow, and the light picked out the multi-coloured stones of the tower, I became aware of a strong, sweet smell which I could not immediately place. Incense? Fresh-sawn timber? Crushed cattle-cake? No, it was the scent of summer, of new-mown grass, when the yew branches were hung with needles of ice. But it was not magic. When I walked to the other side of the church, I found freshly cut grass revealed where the sun had melted the rime.

Still going towards Wimborne Minster, there is a turning (and only a good map can show which one) to Witchampton, whose name owes nothing to either witches or magic but more likely to its having been a dairy farm belonging to people in a town— probably Wimborne Minster. Witchampton at one time had a town of its own, the hamlet still marked on the map as 'New-town', a mile to the south. This completely new village within Witchampton parish was built to house the people of Moor Crichel when Humphrey Sturt (son of him who built Horton Tower) inherited Crichel House in 1765, enlarged it to make a Palladian palace and had the park laid out with bosky groves, a winding lake and splendid views in which country people and their dwellings had no place. So the village was moved. Now little remains of Sturt's alternative accommodation, but Crichel House still stands in its park, the most palatial eighteenth-century house in Dorset. But there was much more to Sturt than his state dining-room with a view. He was full of ideas for the advance-ment of agriculture, not only on his own land but on Brownsea Island in Poole Harbour, where he had the heath burned off and the soil fertilized and brought under cultivation.

Witchampton stands on the little River Allen, and the bridge carries a warning of about 1830: "Any person wilfully INJUR-ING any part of this COUNTY BRIDGE will be guilty of FELONY and upon conviction liable to be TRANSPORTED FOR LIFE." Owners and drivers of traction engines are warned on another plaque that "This bridge is insufficient to carry weights beyond the ordinary traffic of the district", and yet another states that "The owners and persons in charge of Locomotive Traction Engines and other ponderous Carriages are warned against using the Bridge for the passage of any such Engine or Carriage." A bridge of sighs for the carriage trade and the Common Market juggernauts.

The street of this secluded and lovely village winds between thatched houses around which a tumble of colours splashes the gardens that slope to the Allen from the wooded hillside.

There was once an abbey here, and there is still an 'Abbey House', mostly Jacobean, near the church of St Mary and St

Cuthberga, which has a light-and-shade exterior of banded dark brown and grey stone and flint. This church was much restored around 1832, but the interior is light and pleasant. A certain John Cole may have seen the Civil War coming, for his epitaph, dated 1638, states philosophically and with a certain air of relief at being out of it all:

> Heaven have my soule, let dust to dust returne;
> There's no rest like that to within the Vrne. . . .

Witchampton has a manor house of stone-dressed flint walls that stands on the bank of the Allen, a tithe barn and, beyond the gigantic wrought-iron gates that guard the drive to Crichel House, a paper-mill that has been in operation for two centuries. Among the warehouses and lorries and fork-lifts, and looking out and along the little river, is a house like a small rectory in a nineteenth-century novel. It is now the mill's office and is neat, blue-painted and somewhat unexpected at the core of this discreet industrial oasis in an agricultural plain.

A trio of Gussage 'saint' villages lie in the open-chalk Gussage valley at the western edge of Cranborne Chase. On the valley side the church of All Saints surprises by its size and age, for, apart from the chancel, which is mid-Victorian restoration, it is early-fourteenth century. In the nave there is a carved 'Easter Sepulchre' over six hundred years old, where, in the Middle Ages, the Blessed Sacrament would be set on Good Friday and a watch kept until dawn on Easter Sunday, and just beyond it is the pierced stone piscina for the washing of the sacramental vessels. An Elizabethan chalice is inscribed "The Cop of Allhollowe Gvvsshedge Parrishe". Close to the church is Gussage House, a compact red-brick Georgian manor house. The inn is named for a soldier of a much later period than either church or house—the Earl Haig.

Gussage St Michael is a mile up the valley, and the road crosses the Ackling Dyke Roman road at a point where it shows up high and clear on its unswerving way. St Michael's has a Norman tower and a late Norman font. Its bells were cast in 1603, the year in which Queen Elizabeth died; one instructs listeners to "Feare God", and another bids "Hope Well".

Two miles north, the Cashmoor Inn is set with consideration

for horses and travellers in a hollow between two hills on the A354 opposite the turning to Gussage St Andrew. About a mile along is a bend, a farm and a very shy signpost to the church. Through the farmyard, and behind and above the farmhouse, is the plain and simple twelfth-century flint chapel of St Andrew which was originally the chapel of the nunnery (where the farmhouse now stands) founded by the Abbess of Shaftesbury who was King Alfred's daughter.

The interior is as simple as the outside, including the Jacobean pulpit, which was new when the church was five hundred years old. Some wall-paintings, found in 1951 under the layers of limewash, depict the Betrayal of Christ, the Scourging, the Crucifixion, the Deposition and the Suicide of Judas. Although they are much damaged, their power and the faith that inspired them remain clear.

From the doorway of the church (the key hangs beside the door with instructions to insert it, Dorset-fashion, upside down), you look down the slope of the farmhouse lawn to the house of sixteenth- to seventeenth-century red brick, formerly Minchington Manor and now Lower Minchington Farm, mature, calm and spacious. Both church and house benefit from the open space between them, which brings each into relief and establishes a unison which railings or a hedge would impair. As you go down the path to the farmyard, look back at the church's little bell-turret with its weather-vane in the form of a fish. St Andrew was a fisherman.

Dorset's wide variety of scenery and architecture in a small area is well shown within a few square miles hereabouts. There is Farnham to the north and Chettle to the west, each within an hour's walk of Gussage St Andrew and each with its own particular style and interest.

Farnham is beech-shaded and has a long street stitched with thatched cottages. Here in 1880 the nineteenth-century archæologist General Pitt Rivers set up a museum in which he displayed the finds from the Romano-British village he had excavated in Cranborne Chase, with meticulous models of the villages, graves, wells and huts which he had uncovered. Do not be misled by out-of-date guidebooks: the museum is no longer open, and most of the exhibits have been taken to Salisbury Museum. Pitt Rivers also laid out a pleasure-park, just over the boundary in Wiltshire, known as 'Larmer Tree Grounds', which in 1899 drew forty thousand visitors. There was a classical temple and houses from northern India set among laurel rides through the forest. He also restored 'King John's Hunting Lodge' at Tollard Royal ('Royal' from King John), a mile to the east of which stood the Larmer Tree under which John was said to gather with his huntsmen. The tree was a wych elm, of which it is said some vestiges still remained in 1894 when an oak was planted to replace it.

Two miles north-west of Tollard Royal is Ashmore, the highest village in Dorset at seven hundred feet above sea-level. To make the most of Ashmore, approach it from the north by Zig-Zag Hill and over Charlton Down and Ashmore Down. Go in winter or in early spring, if possible, when the trees are bare and the sky clear —asking a lot, perhaps, in the way of conditions on what may be a chance visit, but in coming to Ashmore this way, you may catch stupendous views over Wiltshire and Salisbury Plain and to the south and east over Dorset and Hampshire to the Channel and the Isle of Wight. In summer many sensible people stop their cars to gaze on the large round duck-dappled pond, perhaps the 'lake among the ash-trees' because there has probably always been water at this spot just off the Roman road from Badbury Rings to Bath and close to the trackways that preceded it.

Because the village is high and remote and is reached by narrow roads, Ashmore has often been victim of the weather. The wife of an Ashmore carrier (whose father and mother were also carriers for forty years before he took over for the next twenty-five years) wrote:

Often the springs were up very high at Stubhampton. I well remember that in 1910 they were up to the bed of the van, and we had to drive through in a high trap taking orders over the hedges, till we got to Prince's Corner, where the van met us, having been driven round by the Larmer Tree. We were met there on our return by another horse which helped to pull the van through the water. It was not a very pleasant experience to hear the water rushing on in the darkness, and the horses stumbling along. . . . Years ago the big van was loaded up with various things from a pair of bootlaces to barrels of beer. Anything and everything the people wanted, the carriers did their best to bring. On the whole people were very kind-hearted, and often gave them something hot to warm them up on cold winter nights.

But Ashmore has probably never suffered from drought. Even in the long dry summer of 1976 its pond did not dry up. Ashmore inhabitants respond by treating their pond with respect, and at an annual Midsummer merrymaking called 'Filly Loo' (surely something to do with magic and the water, *l'eau*) there is country dancing to the band that plays on a wagon pushed out into the water.

A track leads out of Ashmore from the left-hand side of the pond as you come from the church. This will take the walker through thick woods of beech and conifers across Stubhampton Bottom, lonely country that gives a good idea of what Cranborne Chase was like when it was a forest. There is still the sudden crash of deer through the brush and the startling swish of pheasants getting up from the bracken under your nose. Once I had the feeling of being like a very early inhabitant as I dodged between the trees and padded over the turf while carrying a weaponly-looking flint in one hand. I had been walking the Dorset–Wiltshire border through the Chase by the old tracks—the Ridgeway, the Ox Road and the Shire Rack. In the greenish scrabbled chalk at the entrance to a deserted badger's sett lay what looked like a stone turtle. When I picked it up, I found it had not only feet and tail but a partly-retracted head too. Yet, when I turned it on its side, there was the silhouette of a cormorant. That dual-personality flint had struck several sparks from my imagination. I had to keep it, and, as I was travelling light and without a rucksack, I carried it in my hand like a Stone Age poacher.

In Stubhampton Bottom rises the Tarrant, a chalk stream that gives its name to eight places in its ten-mile course to join the Stour south of Blandford at Spetisbury: Tarrants Gunville, Hinton, Launceston, Monkton, Rawston, Keynston and Crawford. The Tarrant can be followed very closely by road throughout its length, and these quiet and pleasant chalk-stream villages are worth taking slowly. Gunville's church has a lot of Victorian stencilling, and thistles, lilies and ivy crowd in exuberantly on the congregation. Josiah Wedgwood is said to have lived at Gunville Manor at the beginning of the nineteenth century, within easy distance of the china-clay to the south should he wish to inspect the workings on the heaths. Hinton's Easter Sepulchre, bearing the initials of Thomas Weever, rector 1514–36, is a splendid but somewhat startling display of Italian Renaissance influence. Launceston is a tiny churchless hamlet on the way to Monkton where the Tarrant is forded and mostly thatched cottages are gathered about a flint and stone church. At the Thatch Cottage in Monkton is The Workshop Press, where Rena Gardiner prints and publishes the delightful books of lithographs, with her own text, on villages and landscapes of Dorset and of other counties too.

Rawston's church sits in the garden of a farmhouse but is now disused, while at Rushton the small flint church (which has a carving of the Lamb on the interior lintel of the south door, which may be early-twelfth century) and the village seem to sit tightly beneath the down that has an airfield on the top—and much more too if 'development' had its way.

A great house, a mighty yet unintentional folly, stood just south of the hamlet of Stubhampton and the village of Tarrant Gunville. Eastbury House was designed by Sir John Vanbrugh for George Dodington, a Lord of the Admiralty. It took twenty years to build, was finished in 1738 and cost more than £140,000—a great sum of money at that time. George Dodington had died before his house was completed, and the house—still being added to—passed to his nephew and heir, Bubb Dodington, the son of a Weymouth apothecary, who later became Lord Melcombe. In this house, the third largest of Vanbrugh's mansions after Blenheim and Castle Howard, Bubb liked to entertain the literary lions of the day, and his guests included the poets James Thomson and Edward Young and the novelist Henry Fielding. Their host, an overweight dandy decked in lace, embroidery and brocade ". . . was not to be approached but through a suite of apartments and was rarely seated but under painted ceilings and gilt entablatures". When he died, Eastbury passed, under his uncle's will, to Earl Temple, who could neither sell it nor get anyone to live there even if they were paid to do so. After twenty years in the building and thirty years in use, it was battered down and blown up with dynamite until only part of the north wing and its arcade now remain. Of the formal garden, canal, ha-ha, vista and innumerable carefully-sited groves of trees, very little trace now remains beyond a mound here and a bank there. Perhaps the most striking sight is the astonishing pair of fir trees growing out of the masonry on top of an archway.

About two miles to the east of Eastbury is Chettle House, designed by Vanbrugh's pupil Thomas Archer and built by the Bastards of Blandford between 1710 and 1720 for George Chafin who held the post of Ranger of Cranborne Chase. Chettle is much smaller, but it has survived—even the addition of two rounded ends in 1912, which are, in fact, in perfectly matching red brick and stone dressings. Chettle is a small village of variegated architecture, brick, stone, thatch and tiles, all very compact, with church and manor close to it and to each other.

St Mary's Church is actually in the grounds, up against the trees at the edge of the greensward, romantically dark and solemn and primly enclosed by iron railings. It was extensively but thoughtfully restored in 1850, retaining its Perpendicular tower of flint and stone bands. The interior was changed by the Victorians and given that typical 'dim, religious' light; a three-decker Jacobean pulpit was turned into two chairs, now in the chancel, and a new pulpit of Portland stone was brought in, along with a stone font replacing one said to have been designed, along with the earlier and now vanished pews, by Vanbrugh. Among the memorial tablets is one to George Chafin, for whom Chettle House was built, one to Thomas Chafin who commanded a troop of horse at the battle of Sedgemoor where Monmouth was defeated, and one to John West (d.1845), a remarkable rector of Chettle who in middle age became chaplain to the Hudson's Bay Company. During three years in Canada he founded a church and school at the Red River Settlement, on the site of which Winnipeg Cathedral now stands, for the children of both settlers and Indians, and he was the first Englishman to preach to the Eskimos. John West made two further visits to Canada and is commemorated in the calendar of the Anglican Church there. When he returned to Dorset, he founded a school for gipsies at Farnham, and it was this building that later became the Pitt Rivers Museum.

I wanted to have my first sight of Chettle House from a distance, so when I came out of the church, I walked away from it for about a hundred yards and then turned. I was not disappointed. In the sunshine the mellow brick and the Queen Anne proportions made a harmony of taste, calm and elegance. While I was taking it all in, two men passed me on their way towards the house and bade me a very civil "Good Morning". I dislike trespassing, so I apologized and explained that I was loitering with intent to admire. I was immediately invited to look over the house, although permission is usually given only in answer to a written application.

The entrance-hall is two-storeyed, and staircases rise to left and right to join at a balcony where a short flight of steps leads through the spine wall and re-emerges as a balcony to left and right. The large drawing-room at the south end was designed by Blake of Wareham and decorated by the father of Alfred Stevens, the sculptor, who was born at Blandford and who at Chettle contributed the reliefs over the doors in the staircase hall—but this was in the 1840s by which time the house had passed from the Chafin family.

The last of the Chafins was the Reverend William (1731–1818), a sporting parson who gave up hunting at eighty-three. If he carried some of his energy from the field into the pulpit and composed his sermons in the same lively style as he wrote his *Anecdotes and History of Cranbourn Chase*, it is unlikely that his congregation nodded off. But this athletic old man of God was struck by lightning under the dome of his house while writing his book. Perhaps it was a divine reproof for turning from sermons to local history, but fortunately he survived to complete the most fascinating record of the Chase.

Many encounters in the Chase ended in blood and tears. Here is one told by Chafin:

On the night of the 16th of December 1780, a very severe battle was fought between the keepers and deer-stealers on Chettle Common, in Bursey-stool Walk, which was attended with very serious circumstances. A gang of these deer-stealers assembled at Pimperne and were headed by a Serjeant of Dragoons, a native of Pimperne, and then quartered at Blandford, and whose name was Blandford. They came in the night in disguise, armed with deadly offensive weapons called swindgels, resembling flails to thresh corn. They attacked the keepers, who were nearly equal in number but had no weapon but sticks and short hangers. The first blow that was struck was by the leader of the gang, which broke a knee-cap of the stoutest man in the Chase, who was not only disabled from joining in the combat but has been lame ever since. Another keeper received a blow from a swindgel, which broke three ribs and was the cause of his death some time after. The remaining keepers closed in upon their opponents with their hangers, and one of the Dragoon's hands was severed from the arm, just above the wrist, and fell on the ground; the others were also dreadfully cut, and wounded, and obliged to surrender. Blandford's arm was tightly bound with a list garter to prevent its bleeding, and he was carried to the Lodge, where I saw him next day, and his hand in the window. . . . As soon as he was well enough to be removed, he was committed, with his companions, to Dorchester gaol. The hand was buried in Pimperne church-yard, and, as reported, with the honours of war. . . . Several of these offenders were labourers. . . . They were all tried by Sir Richard Perry at the Dorchester assizes, found guilty and condemned to be transported for seven years; but in consideration of their great suffering from their wounds in prison, the humane Judge commuted the punishment to confinement in gaol for an indefinite term. The soldier was not dismissed from His Majesty's service but suffered to retire on half-pay or pension; and set up a shop in London, which he denoted a Game-factor's, and dispersed handbills at all the public passages, in order to get customers, one of which he himself put into my hand in the arch-way leading into Lincoln's Inn Square. I immediately recognized him, as he did me, and he said that if I would deal with him, he would use me well, for he had, in times past, had many hares and pheasants of mine; and had the assurance to ask me if I did not think it a good breeding-season for game. Whether he is living now, I know not; but I know that the person who cut off his hand is alive and well.

There is something enigmatic about that last sentence, as if the Reverend William did not tell the whole story and may have been closer to that fight than he admitted.

Those who habitually engaged in these Chase battles wore a specially padded jerkin and a helmet like a beehive made of closely-plaited straw into which brambles were woven. The five men dressed in this fashion who appear in an engraving as frontispiece to Chafin's 1818 book look like something between Chase samurai and a Dorset team ready for American football. From Chafin's account it is unlikely that men dressed in this way were Rangers supporters.

3

Valley of the Little Dairies

ONE Christmastide, after an unexpected fall of snow, I climbed cautiously up steep and cobbled Gold Hill in Shaftesbury towards the Town Hall and St Peter's Church, turning left at the top along Park Walk and then stopping about twenty yards along to look out on a sight of which I never tire in any season. From this seven-hundred-foot-high greensand escarpment I could see the fields in the plain below, smooth as icing on a wedding cake, traced with the hieroglyphics of dark mud churned up by tractors, cows and the tankers that call daily for their milk. Farmhouses and barns, dairies, machine-sheds and bare trees showed in relief against the snow, but in summer when leaves are thick on the elms and oaks many of the roads and farms are hidden in the green patchwork over which the grazing cattle move in a heat haze rising from the small streams that meander there and water the lush pastures. The air was ice clear on that still December morning, and the encircling hills stood out mauve and slate-grey like miniature mountains.

Hardy wrote in *Tess* of

the beautiful Vale of Blackmore or Blackmoor . . . a vale whose acquaintance is best made by viewing it from the summits of the hills that surround it. . . . This fertile and sheltered tract of country, in which the fields are never brown and the springs never run dry, is bounded on the south by the bold chalk ridge that embraces the prominences of Hambledon Hill, Bulbarrow, Nettlecombe Tout, Dogbury, High Stoy and Bubb Down. The traveller from the coast, who, after plodding northward over calcareous downs and corn-lands, suddenly reaches the verge of one of these escarpments, is surprised and delighted to behold, extended like a map beneath him, a country differing absolutely from that he has passed through. Behind him the hills are open, the sun blazes down upon fields so large as to give an unenclosed character to the landscape, the lanes are white, the hedges low and splashed, the atmosphere colourless. Here, in the valley, the world seems to be constructed upon a smaller and more delicate scale; the fields are mere paddocks, so reduced that from this height their hedgerows appear a network of dark green threads overspreading the pale green of the grass. The atmosphere beneath is languorous and is so tinged with azure that what artists call the middle distance partakes also of that hue, while the horizon beyond is of the deepest ultramarine. Arable lands are few and limited; with but slight exceptions the prospect is a broad, rich mass of grass and trees, mantling minor hills and dales within the major. Such is the Vale of Blackmoor.

Hardy called it 'Valley of the Little Dairies', but when you search for this land of milk and butter on a map, it becomes a shifting Cloud-Cuckoo Land. The position of the Vale is charted as idiosyncratically as those unexplored continents on which medieval cartographers placed fire-breathing flocks and monstrous herdsmen who glared beady-eyed from their never-never shore at spouting whales and puffing cherubs. On some maps Blackmoor lies almost entirely in Somerset, propped on an elbow placed just within Dorset near Stalbridge, but elsewhere it appears almost completely within Dorset boundaries, with a mere shoulder-tip in Somerset. Yet from Shaftesbury and the hills listed by Hardy it is, as he says, "extended like a map", an inescapable geographical reality of a well-watered vale enclosed by hills.

Blackmoor Vale has five towns in or on the edge of it: Blandford, Shaftesbury, Gillingham, Wincanton (in Somerset) and Sherborne, and by using these towns as marker-buoys, the Vale takes on a definite area. On the east it is bounded by Cranborne Chase, so we can take the A350 Blandford–Shaftesbury road as the eastern limit, continued north of Shaftesbury by the county boundary, with the northern limit set by the A303 at the only point where it dips into Dorset, seemingly nervous of crossing directly from Wiltshire into Somerset. Gillingham is the centre and capital of this Dorset enclave north of the A30, and Sherborne is the town of the other and smaller incursion into Somerset which culminates in Sandford Orcas which belonged to Somerset until 1896. The A30 running westwards to Yeovil from Shaftesbury serves as the northern border, with the exception of the two enclaves. The A37 from Yeovil Down to Holywell is a sensible western limit, and the southern edge is the clearly-defined escarpment of the Dorset North Downs, running from west to east: Batcombe Hill, High Stoy, Dogbury Gate, Ridge Hill, Church Hill, Ball Hill, Nettlecombe Tout, Bulbarrow, Woolland Hill, Bell Hill and Hambledon Hill, which is just to the west of the Blandford–Shaftesbury road from which we started.

Four miles north of Blandford on the A350 and just beyond the village of Stourpaine there lies a steep and impressive hill, charged with history and embroidered with flowers. Hod Hill was first fortified in the early Iron Age and further strengthened by ditches and ramparts in the middle and late Iron Ages, much of the material used being taken from quarries on the inside. This multivallate fort (that is, one possessing several ramparts) must have been almost impregnable until the Romans came with engines of war to hurl iron-pointed missiles over the defences before the infantry battered their way in. This was Vespasian's Second Augustan Legion, which thrust its way through Dorset in an AD 43 *Blitzkrieg*, fighting thirty battles, conquering the Durotriges and other native tribes and doubtless putting them to work immediately on road-building and setting up a camp for more than six hundred Roman soldiers on Hod Hill.

A deep chalk valley through which a narrow road runs westwards separates Hod Hill from the larger and higher (622 feet) Hambledon Hill, which was also a many-ramparted British fortress that eventually fell to Vespasian. There was another battle, of a different tempo and temper, in 1645, when a number of Dorset locals banded together as 'the Clubmen' against the depredations of both sides in the Civil War. They attacked first the Royalists and then the Parliamentarians and petitioned both sides to stop the war, then two thousand of them gathered on Hambledon Hill under the command of the rector of Compton Abbas and defied Cromwell himself, who seems to have shown great patience in asking them several times to lay down their arms. When they refused, he routed them with fifty of his dragoons, who, as Cromwell wrote to Fairfax ". . . did some small execution on them, I believe not twelve of them killed but cut very many . . ." and took about three hundred prisoners, locked them in Iwerne Courtney church and harangued them before letting them go home ". . . poor silly creatures . . . they promise to be very dutiful for time to come . . .".

A century later another soldier, Wolfe, put his soldiers through a battle-course here and trained them on Hambledon Hill for the assault on the Heights of Abraham and the taking of Quebec.

Tucked under Hambledon on the north-eastern side is a village with two names and an independent way of standing apart from the highway on its own little looping road. Iwerne Courtney's alias is 'Shroton'—'Sheriff's Town', which is what it was in the Domesday Book. Both names are marked on most maps, but I have heard only visitors to Dorset call it Iwerne Courtney—the Devon Courtenays held land here on the Iwerne stream.

There used to be a great autumn fair at Shroton, and it was one of the main Dorset events of the year, one where old friends and sometimes enemies had their annual meeting among the crowds, the sideshows and the trading. Barnes wrote of "wheedling father for the meäre An' cart, to goo to Shrodon feäir," of how the girls dressed in snow white lace and best frocks and blue-lined bonnets, "while Dick and I did brush our hats An' cwoats, an' cleän ourzelves li' cats". His poem tells of the booths, the barrels and mugs of beer, meat cooking out of doors, the tumblers, tightrope walkers and conjurers and a crowd so dense that a wedge was needed to force a way through.

Shroton Fair has gone, but Shroton remains, a neat, cheerful, prosperous-seeming village with some well-maintained old houses and some well-maintained new ones in the main street and in the road behind that runs parallel to it, a ribbon of gardens between them. Shroton House is at the northern tip of the village and is uncompromisingly early-eighteenth century behind its massive Doric pilasters to the façade. Eighteenth-century too and much larger as well is Ranston House, but here the west front pilasters are fluted Corinthian. The house has been reduced in size from what it was when it was completed in 1758 by the Bastard brothers of Blandford and incorporated a ceiling and other paintings by Andrea Casali who, unlike the Bastards, was down from London.

There is local craftsmanship in the church of St Mary in the massive monument to Sir Thomas Freke which was raised in 1654. It was Freke who had the Gothic alterations and additions made in 1610, and the memorial to him is much too large, touchingly unsophisticated in its carrying out of sophisticated mannerisms such as the golden ears of wheat sprouting from skulls. It is obscured to some extent by the fine oak screen of about the same date which is ornamented with the Freke family's bull's head. The reredos too is local work, terracotta designed by Lady Baker, who apparently also directed the local pottery where it was fired.

Half a mile north of Shroton is the place where General Pitt Rivers, in 1897, started his excavation of Roman buildings and found that the same site had been used at three different times from the early Iron Age to the fourth century AD. Pre-Roman brooches and coins were found, as well as those of Roman times, including coins of the reign of Vespasian, the pacifier of the Dorset highlands immediately to the north.

Iwerne Minster is called just that and has no other *nom de jeune village* and neither a minster nor a Roman villa, although red-brick and half-timbered villas abound. The Iwerne rises under the vicarage, but the air of the village is much less Dorset than that of Shroton downstream. This is due to its geographical position, sheltered by the surrounding hills and the well-ordered and 'model village' appearance which would make it at home within thirty miles of London or in parts of New England. Iwerne Minster was lucky in having belonged to a series of benevolent lords of the manor. Lord Wolverton bought the Iwerne Minster Estate in 1876, converted more than 150 acres into a great park complete with mandatory ornamental lake and had a mighty mansion designed by Alfred Waterhouse and built in 1878. Not only that but "nowhere are the poor more comfortably or healthily housed than in the Wolverton Cottages at Iwerne Minster", stated a contemporary record. In 1908 the Iwerne Estate was bought by J. H. Ismay, and it was he who added the 'model' air, giving the shops hand-painted signs, designing clothes for the village children and building a village hall complete with miniature rifle-range. Then, in 1929, the estate was put up for sale again, and Wolverton's High Victorian mansion is now Clayesmore Public School for Boys. The village itself still has a well-washed, trimmed and groomed look about it, and Ismay's pump still stands beneath the shelter which he had built so that people might gather there and read the latest news of the Great War. But his village hall is now a private house called The Homestead, and I have never heard a rifle-shot fired in either anger or practice there.

The Saxons built a church, or minster, which controlled the surrounding district, but the present church is predominantly Norman with a fourteenth-century stone spire, one of the three in Dorset (the others are at Winterborne Steepleton and Trent).

To the north of Iwerne Minster village stands an early-nine-teenth-century white house with four stone Tuscan columns and a wonderful view to the south-east, which comes naturally to it as it is the West Lodge of Cranborne Chase. Sutton Waldron church nearby was built at the expense of the rector in 1847, a pretty flint church with a dark red stone tower. The pews are imaginatively different in shape from the majority of church benches yet very functional, and one is assailed by colour from the light through the east window and the purples, reds and gold of the wall-decorations—somewhat overpoweringly enthusiastic and high-flown but kept in order by a curly-legged piano which retains a workaday voice and country accent in its plain and comfortable late-middle age.

Fontmell Magna, the next village, has many thatched cottages of flint and brick, and one of them has a clapboard extension that took me by surprise. There are modern houses of brick and stone which will probably weather and blend in with the rest of the village. At a three-way junction there is an enormous tree trunk, the top protected by a covering of lead. Fontmell Brook rises in the greensand of the downs and has been dammed to form a lake in the garden of the converted red-brick millhouse before running under the road to gurgle its way in front of a row of cottages and going on and out into the Vale.

On the western side of Hambledon Hill there are three Okeford villages: Childe or Child Okeford, Shilling Okeford, which is usually called Shillingstone, and Okeford Fitzpaine. Shroton Lines, marked on the map but having little to show, lie on one of the two roads from Shroton and are a reminder that Wolfe's men did their commando training here. There is a track to Hambledon Hill from the T-junction at the Lines. Another track to the left of the

D

road from Iwerne Minster is called 'Sandy Lane' and is a dramatic 'blind' approach up a sunken track. A third path to the top of Hambledon goes from the other, southern, end of Child Okeford.

Apart from pre-history, the Dorset Clubmen and the simulation of the Heights of Abraham, what about Child Okeford as a village? The 'Child' part is either from 'chill' or from some family who lived there. The adding of a final 'e' is an affectation prompted by *Childe Harold* or *Childe Roland*. I found no dark tower but a greensand Perpendicular tower at St Nicholas's Church, the rest of the building being Victorian, flint with bands of stone. Inside, much marble on the walls and a marble pulpit give an over-all effect of green and white, purple and brown. In front of the church is a village cross, restored and turned into a war memorial of great taste and dignity. There are some mellowed and well-porched Georgian houses and an almost hidden pub called 'The Saxon Inn' that has a sign of a warrior in full Saxon battle-gear and enough to put the fear of the heathen into General Wolfe himself.

In addition to having spare names at the ready, a number of Dorset villages have prices on their heads. There is Sixpenny Handley and Shilling Okeford (masquerading as Shillingstone), and Okeford Fitzpaine is called in the vernacular 'Fippenny Ockford', though more frequently just 'Ockford'. It began in the Domesday Book as 'Adford'. By the time of King Stephen it was 'Aukford Alured', and in the reign of Edward IV it had become 'Ockford Phippin'. Hardy called the village 'Oakbury Fitzpiers' in *The Woodlanders*, but it has a history to itself called *Fippenny Ockford and Thereabouts* by Tom Graham, with illustrations by Margery Underhill. Every lane and turning, each legend and story is carefully examined and recounted. A reminder of how much can change in society in one century is the story of the Brown family of this village. Two brothers, Robert and George, aided by a Shillingstone builder and two younger Browns, built a Primitive Methodist Chapel in Okeford and opened it in 1859, when to be 'chapel' was to place oneself under suspicion of being a subversive worker against Church, State and Establishment. One of the brothers, John, was put into the Okeford lock-up in 1864, but his 'crime' cannot have been serious because he was soon released, though in the dank village dungeon he caught cold and two months later was dead of 'inflammation of the lungs' leaving a wife and daughter. The filled-in door to the cell can still be seen in a wall of a house close to the church, mainly Perpendicular with additions and changes of the 1860s, which stands on a rise, facing the eighteenth-century rectory. Grouped around closely are cottages on a raised footway, the village stores and post office which was once a coaching-inn, and the stone base of a fifteenth-century cross. Okeford is as compact and traditional an English village as it is possible to find, but it is at the same time a very lived-in place.

If you take the route up the hill by Sandy Lane, which I mentioned earlier, be sure to go to Merridge, a bluff above a chalk-pit, because from the Stickle Path (*sticcle* or *sticol* = steep), which is a kind of corniche, you can see over most of the Vale.

Shillingstone straggles along the Blandford–Sherborne road. The 'Shilling' probably comes from the twelfth-century lords of the manor, the Eskellings, and the 'Okefords' were just that—fords in what used to be Blackmoor Vale's oak forest. Shillingstone was even easier to reach until a few years back because beside the Stour the railway ran on its meandering way from Poole up to Bristol. Even allowing for the nostalgia for things past and lost, I remember the delight of that journey as I do that other vanished line from Maiden Newton to West Bay. Now Dorset, like the rest of the United Kingdom, bears the herringbone scars of railway transport duels fought and lost.

This long main-road village of mostly modern houses holds the remains of an ancient village cross which have been turned very effectively into a war memorial. In the Great War Shillingstone sent more volunteers in proportion to its size than any other village in the Kingdom, and George V acknowledged that "His Majesty is gratified to learn how splendidly the people of Shillingstone have responded to the call to the Colours." The Norman church, with 1888 arcade and north aisle, 1902 roof-decoration and Purbeck marble Norman font, has in the belfry the Shillingstone Slab, on which a face is incised between the whirling rays of the sun and a new moon, one representing Christ and the other the Virgin Mary, a bringing-together in a dramatic and disturbing simplicity out of the stone of a combination of fundamental beliefs. The pulpit, on the other hand, is a record of fundamental human gratitude. It is of Jacobean carved oak and was presented by William Keene of Bread Street, London, who fled to Shillingstone from the Plague, was not turned away and lived to return to the Great Wen but did not forget Shillingstone and Holy Rood's congregation.

There used to be dancing round the maypole in the village, but no heathen behaviour was tolerated in the belfry, where the bell-ringers were warned:

> Praise the Lord with lowd symbols, if
> You curs or sware in the time of
> ringing You shall pay threepence
> There is no musick play'd or sung
> is like good bell if well rung.
> Put off your hat, coat and spurs
> and see you make no brawls or
> if you chance to curs or sware harde
> Be sure you shall pay sixpence here
> or if you chance to break a stay
> 18 pence you shall pay
> or if you ring with spurs or belt
> We will have sixpence or your pelt
> 1767

Shillingstone has always taken chalk from the hills for burning in the preparation of lime and also for treating acid soil on the farms. The white scars of the chalk-workings are some hundreds of feet high and give, so to speak, an inside look at the downland. Another traditional work was the gathering of moss to be sent to Covent Garden. There are also two craft-centres producing high-standard objects: Cecil Colyer at Orchardene, Blandford Road, undertakes commissions for furniture, wood-turnery and church and domestic silver, and Pilgrim's craftsmen sell hand-made solid wood furniture made on the spot, and they have a first-class display in their showroom and shop. I once examined in their yard a green and black spindle-backed gig made to specification for a customer in Germany. The finish was superb, and the pleasure of running my hands along the delicately turned shafts recalled horse-drawn vehicles of my childhood.

On its way from Sturminster Newton the River Stour makes a loop northwards and is joined by Chivrick's Brook, Manston Brook and smaller streams that all make a contribution to an area that is well-watered and sometimes flooded. Two miles on, the A357 on the way to Sturminster Newton brings you to a crossways where the left-hand turn goes back to Okeford Fitzpaine and the right-hand narrow lane, marked "Liable to Flooding" and flanked by water-meadows, leads to Hammoon, a hamlet built on Stour silt, very easy to miss and, when the Stour is in flood, an unapproachable island.

Hammoon takes its name from the Saxon word for a dwelling followed by that of the Mohun family. Hutchins in his *History of Dorset* wrote: "In Domesday Book William de Moion held it. He came to England with the Conqueror, with a retinue of forty-seven knights of note. For this great service he obtained eleven manors in this county; also the castle of Dunster, co. Somerset, and fifty-five other manors in that county and Devon with a great number of knights' fees."

For many years I had intended to visit Hammoon, and eventually got there for the first time on an October afternoon. It had been raining for most of two days, but suddenly the sky had cleared, and the sun, sliding away over the Vale towards Sherborne, sent peach-coloured shafts of light that reflected in the pools of water lying in the meadows.

As the guide to the church says, "St Paul's does not seem at first sight to be a church of very much interest. Looking from the road towards the West end of the church, the building shows little sign of its real age, but on closer inspection its real antiquity is quickly discovered." I have been there many times since that first visit, when I soon realized the stupidity of trying to take in by fading twilight a church begun in the mid-thirteenth century. It was, I discovered when I returned in daytime, the bizarre addition in 1885 of a little belfry that would look more at home on a Home Counties stable that had put me off. But there have been later changes which are improvements, and most of all there is an early-fifteenth-century West Country reredos, discovered in 1946 in a dealer's yard outside London, which was bought for the church by a local benefactor. It is of Ham Hill stone and depicts the Crucifixion and three Apostles.

A few steps from the church towards a farmyard is Hammoon Manor, compact and solid stone under the warm security of thick thatch that wraps itself around the dormers. A Purbeck limestone porch of classical proportions and a modest grandeur was added *c*1600 to the house, which is mostly of a century earlier. The Tuscan columns, mullioned Tudor windows, thatched roof and great sycamore that stands in front of this manor-become-farmhouse contribute to Hammoon's title to be one of Dorset's most pleasing houses.

About two miles south-west of Hammoon the Stour is put through a watery marshalling-yard of hatches, ponds, rolling-bay, high bridges and much massive iron machinery to bring the river under the control of Fiddleford Mill, built in the late-fourteenth century and now being restored by the Department of the Environment, *née* the Ministry of Works. On the mill house there is a black-letter inscription dated 1566 (now picked out so that it can be read):

> He thatt wyll have here any thynge don
> Let him com fryndly he shal be welcom
> A frynd to the owner and enemy to no man
> Pass all here frely to com when they can
> For the tale of trothe I do alway professe
> Myller be true disgrace not thy vest
> If falsehod appere the fault shal be thine
> And of sharpe ponishment think me not unkind
> Therefore be true yt shall the behove
> To please God chiefly that liveth above

And the name 'Fiddleford'? In 1244 there was recorded 'Fitel Ford', and Fitel was most likely someone who lived or worked there and guarded the ford. The mill has been worked for five generations by the Rose family. Barley has been ground for cattle food in the 1970s by Job Rose whose great-grandfather was the miller of whom Barnes wrote:

> John Bloom he were a jolly soul
> A grinder o' the best o' meal,
> Bezide a river that did roll
> Vrom week to week, to push his wheel,
> His flour were all-a-made o' wheat,
> An' fit for bread that volk mid eat.

Barnes might have added something about what "volk mid drink" because in the eighteenth century the outbuildings of the mill were used to store contraband brought from the coast on the backs of horses linked together in tens or dozens.

I have seen night-riders come to Fiddleford after the sun has set. Some of them bring strong spirits with them, and they certainly need them as they sit on their canvas stools, watching Stour and floats for hours on end, quieter than smugglers, with only the flare of a match or a gentle cough to show where they wait. I have also seen similarly dogged anglers there on bitter winter days of rimed silence. But summer at Fiddleford is loud and merry with the splashing and laughter of bathers.

There is not much of Fiddleford village, but what there is pleases the eye: a small collection of houses, many of them thatched, and a general air of leafy hedginess and well-dug gardens. It would seem that there was never a church, and those who wished to attend divine service used to walk over to Sturminster Newton, where, until 1827, there was a Fiddleford aisle in St Mary's Church that had a separate entrance.

A short mile westwards on the A357 the Stour is crossed by the bridge that connects Stour Minster and New Town. Sturminster Newton Bridge, of six arches, was built early in the sixteenth century and widened three hundred years later. The cutwaters were built out from the original ones and vary in both size and angle; on the upstream central one there is a date which, seen from the road, is upside down. If you walk along the bridge and look over the coping, this apparently perverse mason's joke makes sense because you look down and can read that the stone was set there in 1820.

A few hundred yards upstream, a short lane leads from the right of the A357 down to Sturminster Mill. There has certainly been a mill here since the early Middle Ages but the present building of stone and brick with a roof of tiles and stone, was built in the seventeenth century. Until 1904 there was a giant waterwheel which was then replaced by an under-shot turbine. Later still, steel hammer-stones and a crushing-mill were installed, and not only Dorset corn but Indian maize and Russian barley have been ground here. Now the mill is often silent except for the cats who live below and the pigeons in the dovecote above, or when John Holmes, the burly miller, who wears an Australian 'digger' hat, is grinding his own or his neighbours' corn. Local history, past and present, is grist to his mill too, as I have found in conversation with him.

Newton is a village in its own right, with a pub and cottages and houses of the seventeenth to nineteenth centuries set mostly behind front gardens and an amazing variety of porches but some are set directly on the main road at the bottom of Glue Hill, the T-junction where the road from Hazelbury Bryan joins the A357. At the top of that hill is the Cattle Breeding Centre and unit for freezing the semen from the bulls tethered in the next field, seemingly docile and complacent donors of their beefy attributes to the whole world.

On Monday mornings a stream of lorries crosses the bridge into Sturminster, for Monday is Stur Market Day, and beast after bewildered beast is driven and prodded into the ring, surrounded on three sides by tiered wooden benches, for its future to be decided at the next lull in the Gregorian chant of the auctioneer, to which there is a counterpoint of pig squeals in the neighbouring sheds. Farm implements, cheese, garden sheds, fertilizer, the RSPCA, bedding-plants, creosote, wellingtons—everything that makes up a market in a country town is in evidence on a Monday in this capital of the Vale.

To the north of the A357 the ground rises in a bluff, and opposite the bridge stood an unfortified fourteenth-century manor house which became known as 'the Castle'. Little remains of it but a few ruins of buttresses and a blocked doorway, but most of what there is is hidden by brambles and nettles. It was given to Catherine Parr, Henry VIII's sixth and last wife, at the Dissolution of the Monasteries in 1539 until which time it had been under the rule of Glastonbury Abbey. The hill is still called 'the Castle Grounds', and in 1921 in this natural open-air theatre scenes from Thomas Hardy's novels were performed in Dorset tones by Dorset players who were accompanied by the Frampton String Band. Hardy was there and took tea with the cast at Riverside, the house in which he had lived in 1876-8, the first two years of his marriage—'the Sturminster idyll'.

Hardy named this castle-that-never-was 'Stourcastle' in *Tess*, and three miles to the north is Marnhull, the 'Marlott' where she was born. Sounds here are different from those in Sturminster Newton: the motor lawnmower rather than the cattle-truck and tractor, hi-fi through open windows instead of the auctioneer's amplifier in a tin shed.

Marnhull is scattered yet has managed to keep itself within a meeting-place of several roads without being bisected and bothered by any of them. There are good reasons for its comparative isolation, standing as it does on a limestone ridge above the clays of the Stour, which is its boundary on the west as Chivrick's Brook is on the east; a third stream, Key Brook, lies at the north-east. It is from the local limestone, similar to Bath stone, that the greater part of the village is built, including the church of St Gregory whose fine fifteenth-century tower is a landmark and the finest in the Vale. Perpendicular and Victorian, there is a single Norman pier in the north arcade, a fifteenth-century nave roof and alabaster effigies of a man and his two wives, perhaps the twice-married John Carent of Silton who died in 1478.

Just beyond the west wall of the churchyard is Senior's Farm, a solid rectangular building of about 1500 that has withstood much tampering in later centuries, and close to it is the ancient base of a great barn.

In 1892 the Great Down Quarries, from whose stone so many Marnhull houses are built, yielded up a lead coffin and many other Romano-British relics. Nash Court, the old manor of Marnhull, another Dorset house given to Catherine Parr by Henry VIII, has been widely altered, including the insertion of eighteenth-century windows on the ground floor.

There is some over-Hardyfication in Marnhull. A house once known as 'Barton' is now called 'Tess's Cottage', and there is a 'Pure Drop Bar' in the Crown Inn, a part-thatch pub pleasant in its own right. But Marnhull is a village to walk around and inspect carefully, in both architecture and atmosphere are most rewarding. And it is worth looking at nearby hamlets such as Todber, which seems to have been deserted when the quarries of yellow Marnhull stone were no longer worked. It has a church that looks Saxon but is not yet a hundred years old—though there are pieces of medieval masonry in the tower, and a cross in the churchyard is made up partly of Anglo-Saxon pieces.

A memorial to Marnhull that you will see only if you are fortunate to find it in a library is *The Marn'll Book*, comprised of material collected by the Marnhull Women's Institute which won first prize in 1931 as the best village history in a county competition. It was edited by Mrs Brocklebank of Nash Court and her daughter, was published in 1940 and was used as the basis for the book planned by the Marnhull Festival of Britain Committee in 1952. This Festival of Britain edition, edited by E. H. Roscoe, was printed by the Blackmore Press of Gillingham, the principal town of the northern part of the Vale.

Gillingham (the initial 'g' is hard) today reflects growth during the railway age, and the predominant colour is the bright pink of its brick. It is a town of light industries, with a brewery looking like a cathedral, a former silk-mill, a small and excellent museum, an early-nineteenth-century lock-up and five bridges over the Stour and its tributaries, the Shreen Water and the Lodden. The Stour rises four miles north of Gillingham at Stourhead, over in Wiltshire, which is now National Trust property. It is just south of here that Dorset, Wiltshire and Somerset meet near Zeals, which is in Wiltshire and Bourton, bisected by the A303, still in Dorset, semi-industrialized and drawing to its milk-processing plant the Vale's largest export.

Between Gillingham and Bourton are two villages of similar name but completely different character and appearance.

Milton-on-Stour is predominantly of the nineteenth century. The church of SS Simon and Jude is one of the five Dorset churches designed by Slater and Carpenter. It has a thin, perforated spire, and the whole effect is one of good Victorian design (it was built in 1868) but somewhat un-Dorset. Across the road is a severe house of a decade or so earlier, Milton Lodge, now turned into a country club. The nearby mill on the Stour, Purns Mill, was painted by Constable in 1824.

Less than two miles distant but centuries away in feeling is Silton, divided by the Stour, which here is a narrow stream, and built at the meeting-place of Kimmeridge clay and Corallian limestone, which gives a landscape more broken than southwards in the Stour valley. The little knolls here are at the rim of both the Blackmoor Vale and north Dorset.

Leaving the main road on the way to Silton, there is a modernized house on the left which takes the eye. It has three dormers, is altogether very pretty and is called 'Spindleberry Cottage'. Further up the road on the right the raw brick council cottages are less attractive. The church of St Nicholas, late Norman and fifteenth century, was built on one of these knolls with prudent foresight. I have never seen the Stour here as much more than a narrow, willow-bordered stream rolling slowly between oak and ash-stippled meadows, but when it has flooded after torrential rain, the results have been dire. In June 1917 a thunderstorm was followed by half a day's continuous rain on the Penselwood ridge where the river rises; Stourhead lake broke its banks, and water rose to the eaves of Milton and Silton but did not reach St Nicholas.

This small church is packed with interest. The arcade is thirteenth century; the wagon roof is sixteenth century and was well-restored and painted in 1869, and the chancel roof is a well-executed Victorian replica of the nave roof. In fact, the extensive restoration was carried out with great taste, but I think that the stencilling by Clayton and Bell of 1869–70 makes the interior of the church look wall-papered.

The 1692 monument by John Nost of Tring to Sir Hugh Wyndham, Justice of the Common Pleas, who died in 1684, is almost overwhelming. There stands the noble judge flanked by two kneeling female mourners who bear skull and hourglass and represent his first two wives. Sir Hugh used to sit in a field beyond the churchyard wall under a giant oak which is still there, and I have sat under it and understand why he did so. A couple of fields away there was the ring and rattle of a chain harrow and the burr of the tractor that drew it, and close at hand a redpoll trilled. The good judge may not have heard the former, but I am prepared to believe that he may well have heard a redpoll there—until some ornithologist produces evidence that it is unlikely.

Going south-west by whichever of the many small roads appeals to you, out of the 'Gillingham enclave' but still at the northern limit of Dorset, is Stalbridge, a small town that has both had and lost a lot. Here the Earl of Cork built a great house, Stalbridge Park, in 1638, and here he entertained Charles I and put his seventh son, Robert Boyle, to study under the Rector. Whether or not the parson was responsible for arousing his pupil's interest in scientific matters, it was this Robert Boyle who became the mathematician and chemist. He inherited the house in 1643 and lived there for several years. It was demolished in 1822, and nothing remains but a pair of eighteenth-century gate-piers surmounted by lions which can be seen just past the church. They are set in the wall that ran for five miles around the park and of which great stretches remain, the craftsmanship of the long-dead masons still living in the lichened stone.

Four miles south and east towards Sturminster Newton on the A357 is Lydlinch, where the Caundle Brook joins the Lydden on the way to the Stour. Here a steel bridge built in 1943 stands beside the eighteenth-century bridge at a spot called 'Two Fords,' a name that commemorates what was there before either bridge. This is actually in Bagber, and it was at Rush-Hay, beyond Bagber Common, an open space decorated with brambles, willow herb and gypsies, that William Barnes was born on 22nd February 1801. This saintly teacher, linguist and poet left school at thirteen, studied and wrote with prodigious energy and intellectual application, took holy orders when he was over sixty and is remembered now chiefly for his *Poems in the Dorset Dialect*. It was of the landscape and people of the Blackmoor Vale that he wrote. One of his best-known poems is 'Lydlinch Bells':

> Vor Lydlinch bells be good vor sound,
> An' liked by all the näighbours round.

The bells are still there, rehung in 1959 in the thirteenth century tower which was largely rebuilt in Tudor times. Four pieces of fifteenth-century glass depicting angels have been set in a window above the pulpit, and the font was carved in the twelfth century from a solid block of stone. A tomb outside the porch contains the remains of a woman known only as 'The Lady of Lydlinch', whose heart is said to be in an urn in the church at West Parley on the Hampshire border. The lack of detailed history is intriguing, and I wonder that it did not inspire Thomas Hardy to write a novel around it. Among horse-chestnut trees at the end of an avenue of pollarded willows, Lydlinch church of St Thomas à Beckett (yes, in the church it is spelt with two ts) keeps an eye on the time with three sundials and a clock.

The Caundle Brook gives its name to four villages—Purse Caundle to the north on the Somerset border, Stourton Caundle a couple of miles to the south of Purse, Bishop's Caundle and Caundle Marsh, the last two on the A3030 road to Sherborne.

That ubiquitous hunting king, John, gave Purse Caundle manor house and land to a man who tended his hounds taken sick or injured when hunting in Blackmoor Forest. The present manor house is fifteenth century, and a narrow oriel window of that date looks out on the village street. The roof to the hall is original, and the house, sometimes open to the public, should be visited if possible. So should the church, which is Perpendicular but has been much tampered with. There is some medieval glass and a mid-sixteenth-century alms-chest. Nicholas Highmore, the seventeenth-century anatomist, was the son of a Purse Caundle rector. Turning from body to spirit, the manor has echoed to ghostly plainsong and the baying of hounds—King John's canine lame and halt on sick parade?

At Stourton Caundle was a fortified house belonging to the Stourton family, but nothing of it remains except Manor Farm Chapel, of which the chancel is destroyed but the Early English nave remains. The chapel is three hundred yards south-west of the church of St Peter, whose thirteenth-century chancel shelters an alabaster effigy of Agnes, wife of the fourth Lord Stourton, recumbent upon a tomb-chest since the late fifteenth century. The village, like the other Caundle villages, is neat and well-preserved with good thatch and mellow stone cottages.

To the south, on the other bank of the Caundle Brook, is Bishop's Caundle. There are no records of King John and his huntsmen that I know of, but there is a mounting-block beside the pub door. This Caundle village stands squarely on the A3030 and has made the most of a small hillock from which the fifteenth-century square brown stone church tower rises above the road. There are stone cottages and a large farmhouse and many contemporary houses as well, some of which are light-coloured and pinpoint Bishop's Caundle when one looks across from Bulbarrow and Ball Hill, both of which, as well as the Shaftesbury Hills, can be seen from the village street.

The medieval Manor Farm at Caundle Marsh is next to a church of 1857, small, low and a good example of how pleasant some mid-Victorian churches can be—nor does it seem to be in angry exile in the farmyard where it stands.

Close by, in the parish of Folke, is the beautiful unspoilt rubble-stone house called 'Font le Roi', of the fifteenth and seventeenth centuries. Folke has two other manors, medieval and rebuilt in the seventeenth century—Folke Manor and West Hall, but both of these, unlike Font le Roi, have been restored more recently. For good measure in this small area the church of St Lawrence is well-preserved 1628 Gothic and has miraculously retained its Jacobean oaken benches, screens and Communion rail.

Folke is not easy to find, and when you have found it, you must come out the same way, although it is less than a mile across the fields to Long Burton (irritatingly often now spelled 'Longburton' on road signs, which to me changes its pronunciation in line with Warburton), and coming from the south it seems like entering another country. One half-expects a red-and-white barrier to fall and a uniformed guard to ask for passports at the two buildings facing each other across the road like Customs posts, but they were built for improvement of the soul and not for inspection of worldly goods. On the right is a Methodist chapel built in Early English style by Thomas Farrell of Sherborne in 1878, and opposite is a slightly neglected-looking Temperance Hall, also Gothic in style, built by Hayward of Long Burton in 1907. Close by is a wooden sign pointing to the footpath to Cancer Drove.

Long Burton is long indeed, straggling along the main road, with some seventeenth-century houses and cottages and much modern infilling in a variety of styles. St James's Church has a sturdy thirteenth-century tower, a chancel and nave of the fifteenth century and a north aisle of 1873. A small chapel north of the chancel contains ornate seventeenth-century tombs of the Winston and FitzJames families. There are five life-size effigies, knights in armour, their ladies wearing ruffs—all bright in steely grey, scarlet and gold; but there was not enough room for Sir John FitzJames, who died in 1625, and his wife, so their memorial is a scatter of stone bones and skulls. Christian they may have been, but they were not after all tested by lions in the arena. The sculptor was thoughtful enough to provide a stone pick and spade for decent disposal of the remains at the Last Trump. The second monument is to members of the Winston family who died at the beginning of the seventeenth century. A daughter of one of them, Sarah, married John Churchill from the neighbouring parish of Glanvilles Wootton, and they became grandparents to the first Duke of Marlborough and ancestors of Sir Winston Churchill.

The turret clock dates from the 1670s, but early this century it was removed from the tower and now stands in the north-east chapel. It was cleaned and restored, with many new parts made, by A. L. James, a Sherborne scholar, in 1972. It is a fascinating piece of mechanism, and in the church there is a detailed leaflet about it.

Passing south between the Scylla and Charybdis of Methodism and Temperance in just over a mile is Holnest, easy to miss because there is no village nucleus, and the road is straight and busy enough to claim all one's attention. Along the right of the road a high wall runs for some distance, and just over a small bridge it is broken by a pair of gates. They are unlikely to be missed because they are brutally massive and made of black iron, more like a traitor's gate than the entrance to a rudimentary and grassy pathway leading to Holnest church. The reason for these astonishing gates was an immense mausoleum that used to stand in the churchyard. I remember it as a neo-Byzantine monstrosity in this deserted churchyard where the church was collapsing into ruin. Now the churchyard has been cleared, the mausoleum removed and the church restored and re-opened.

A few yards south of the church is Dunn's Farm, a mellow house of 1610 which, like another old house on the other side of the road, always puts me in mind of wallflowers because of the gold and pink texture of the stone. Several times I had prowled around St Mary's Church and found the door locked, and once, when the snow was melting and the snowdrops opening in the lemon rays of a tentative sun, I found a hole in the churchyard: either a fallen-in grave or a field-drain was below because there was a great subterranean gurgling. On another visit I went to Dunn's Farm, and the farmer's wife told me that the key to the church was in their letter-box on the new farm gate.

Mostly fourteenth to fifteenth century, with a chancel of 1855, the church is cheerfully exciting and conveys the feeling that it really has been brought back to life again. The glass is clear, the interior uncluttered, the proportions somewhat haphazard, some of the walls still run with water, and there is a piano in a box pew and a restored organ blocking off the end of the short south aisle. The church has heart and warmth and light, a twelfth-century font and a seventeenth-century pulpit that has been robbed of its sounding-board. But the church has received as well: "The fifteenth-century bells were given by Miss Marjorie Ouvry, Easter 1975." The Georgian box-pews have been painted cream, but the panelling around the walls has been spared. Over each pew is a half-hoop of iron with sockets in each for three candles.

A few miles to the north lies Sherborne, which has no place in this book about villages. It is the loveliest town in Dorset, yellow ochre stone, a cathedral town in feeling although it ceased to be one in 1075. Sherborne demands a lot of time to itself, not only for the Abbey, the almshouses, the schools, the remains of the medieval castle and the 'new' one built by Sir Walter Ralegh, but for just walking in and behind the streets and discovering hidden lanes and courts.

Sherborne Castles are in the parish of Castleton, in the eastern corner of which is the 1533 old church of Oborne—the new one, of 1862, functions further along the valley. So the old church is not only out of its own parish but perched on the lip of Dorset and on the very edge of the A30. The present chancel was built in 1533 for use as a chapel of ease served by the monks of Sherborne, a mere six years before the Dissolution of the Monasteries in 1539 by Henry VIII, whose royal arms, ironically, survive in the church over the east window.

The barrel roof and moulded wall-plates of the sixteenth century remain. The Communion table, altar rails and pulpit are early-seventeenth-century rustic work, and there is a coffin-rest with the date 1790 picked out in nails. Some tiles of the fourteenth and fifteenth centuries have been reset on the west wall, and the fifteenth-century Ham stone font was originally in the now vanished church of North Wootton. The church was transferred to the Redundant Churches Fund in 1975, and further restoration has been made to the bell-cote and roof.

For fifty-seven years, from 1693 to 1750, John Shuttleworth was the incumbent. At the age of fifty-seven a parishioner, "Mr Robert Goadby, late of Sherborne, Printer, departed this life, August 11th 1778 . . .". South of the present churchyard lies Goadby's tomb, forced apart and destroyed by an elm tree; the inscription on it has succumbed to neglect and age but has been recorded:

> Death is a Path that Must be Trod
> If Man would ever Come to God.

Ashmore, Dorset's highest village

Knowlton church

Horton Tower

Fiddleford Mill

The River Stour and
Sturminster Newton Mill

Cranborne Manor House

Chettle House

The Pitt Rivers Museum at Farnham, originally a school for gipsy children

Hammoon Manor

Milton Abbas

Iwerne
Minster

Rampisham – the post office beyond the ford

Rampisham – the Tiger at the crossroads

The Fir-Tree aspires to the Sky and is clothed with Everlasting Verdure; Emblem of the Good, and that everlasting Life which God will bestow on Them. Since Death is the Gate to Life, the Grave should be Crowned with Flowers.

In his notes on Old St Cuthbert's Church, Kenneth Smith comments: "The fir-tree and perennial flowers planted on Mr Goadby's grave have long vanished: even the elm is dead. The weekly paper Mr Goadby published, the *Sherborne Mercury*, was the ancestor of the modern *Western Gazette*—which flourishes."

Also just in Dorset by a nanny-goat's whisker, but having been for most of its existence in Somerset, Goathill is more like a village in Wales or Norway. It is surrounded by woods, and here rises the stream that feeds the lake in the grounds of Sherborne Castle. Formerly a mill worked at Goathill, and there were more cottages, more cornfields and fewer trees.

The lane to Goathill is exceptionally narrow, and I stopped to let a large sand-coloured dog trot by towards Milborne Port. In the church I read some typewritten notes by Alexandra M. Hannam on the history of the village, which end: ". . . Of course, Goathill has its ghosts. One, a little old lady wearing a poke bonnet and shawl, and carrying a basket on her arm, is to be seen on the road below the Lodge. Another, a dog, which comes down the hill and goes on to Milborne Port." On my way back I looked out at bends for little old ladies—not one in sight, but I passed the same dog again, this time nearer to Milborne Port.

Ladies in poke bonnets and peripatetic dogs are commonplace at Sandford Orcas Manor, where the supernatural was, in the 1970s, a local industry. Sandford Orcas—the 'Orcas' is derived from the Norman family of Orescuilz—is a village Tudor in appearance, golden Ham Hill stone in colour, with a manor and church dating from the late-fifteenth and early-sixteenth centuries, and very little changed. There is more the feeling of Somerset than of Dorset here, but, as I said earlier, Sandford Orcas was in Somerset until a county border change in 1896.

Among the monuments in the south chapel of the church is one to William Knoyle, who died in 1607, unusual in that—as in Sir Hugh Wyndham's memorial at Silton—his two wives are shown, but in this instance the first is depicted with four dead children and the second with living children kneeling around her. Their husband is portrayed in armour. The thirteenth-century font is shaped like a marsh marigold, fluted and very simple. Despite some rich Victorian restoration, the church remains resolutely Perpendicular.

Alongside the church stands the manor gatehouse, through which one must pass and then turn about right and right again to come face to face with the front of the house, impressive with two irregular bays and mullioned windows. The manor was then open to the public, so I walked down the path, between two hip-bath-sized tropical seashells serving as flower bowls on the terrace, and rang the bell at the side of the gabled two-storeyed porch.

I assured the middle-aged cheerful woman who had opened the door that my boots were less muddy than they looked and held only rubber hobnails, but she was already busy calling to someone who emerged through a doorway as onto a stage, a portly, flushed elderly man with bright shrewd eyes and a deaf-aid, his green jacket arrived at that stage of decrepitude that has taken on the manner of a sturdy tweed cobweb and draws dogs, cats, mice and moths for miles around. I have worn jackets like that, held together by ancient brambles and trampish pride.

"Which are y' interested in? The house or the ghosts? They go together, mind you."

Well, they certainly did at Sandford Orcas Manor, but the then tenant who showed me round claimed twenty-two ghosts in all, ranging from a nice old lady with a red shawl to a seven-foot-tall former ravisher of virgin maidservants who now brings the smell of decaying flesh with him. The way of all flesh, presumably. The ghosts were unco-operative when a television team called to investigate.

There is a real feeling of Tudor and Jacobean living in that house as one goes through the panelled rooms with their draught-excluding porched doorways, sees the priest's hiding-place made by the Roman Catholic Knoyles who once lived there, and looks through the mullioned windows that contain some sixteenth-century armorial glass. The house has been closed to the public since 1978, when the tenant left and the owner, Sir Christopher Medlycott, undertook a programme of repairs and alterations.

Trent, a few miles away, was also in Somerset until 1896 and has a ghost of its own at Trent Barrow, where there was a deep pit called 'Bottomless Pit' into which it is said a coach, horses, driver and passengers plunged and disappeared. Since then, and naturally on dark and stormy nights, the sound of galloping horses and cries for help have been heard.

Twice Trent provided a safe hiding-place for a fugitive wanted more than any priest was—King Charles II. In flight after the defeat at Worcester in early September 1651, Charles was hidden by Sir Francis Wyndham in "an old well-contrived secret place" in his manor house. Charles left to take ship to France from Charmouth, but the plans went agley, and he found his way back to Trent through Bridport and Broadwindsor by a route thick with Parliamentarians. In all he spent nearly three weeks at Trent before making his way to Salisbury and eventually to Shoreham and refuge in Europe.

Visiting Trent is a leisurely delight, because the village has no centre, and you have to spend time finding each fresh building in stone that ranges from light champagne through amber to russet and grey, and all of the fifteenth, sixteenth and seventeenth centuries. By the church is the Chantry built in the reign of Henry VI, just over the road from it the Dairy Farm and south-west of the church Church Farm, both farmhouses built in the fifteenth century. The Rectory dates from the same time, but the front is mid-eighteenth-century classical. And blending perfectly with all this medieval stone are Turner's Almshouses, Tudor buildings grouped around a central courtyard with a Perpendicular pump—all built with taste and skill in 1848.

In the centre of this group of buildings is the church of St Andrew, one of the very few Dorset churches with a spire. In the early 1840s much renovation was carried out by the Reverend William Henry Turner, mostly at his own expense. He was handsome and cultured and married a rich heiress, Mary Lance—known in the West Country as 'The Golden Lance'. The Turners built the almshouses and the school, and brought in Flemish and German stained glass, now in the east window, and also the early seventeenth-century Dutch pulpit. The fifteenth-century benchends were retained and added to in faithful copies—even if Turner did introduce his own arms into them. Some of the Victorian stained glass, as so often, is too much of a good thing, and so are some exuberant nineteenth-century tiles and decorated plaster, but their impact is lessened by the beauty of the fifteenth-century rood-screen, the three fourteenth-century effigies, the elegant 1715 tablet to Sir Francis Wyndham—and the recumbent 1875 effigy of William Turner himself, his hands folded on the Bible. The lower part and steps of the fifteenth-century cross in the churchyard were topped off in faithful harmony in 1924.

In 1962, the year after his retirement, a former Archbishop of Canterbury, Lord Fisher of Lambeth, lived at Trent Rectory and often officiated here and at Nether and Over Compton as curate. When he died, he was buried, at his wish, in the churchyard. Trent, which hid a king, is thus also resting-place for a former Primate of the Church of England. Enough to discourage any Puritan ghost from wandering abroad.

At Over Compton, a short distance along a minor road, the patron attended personally to the restoration of St Michael's Church, in style Perpendicular with a west tower rich in Somerset tracery. A north chapel was built in 1776, but in 1821 the patron, Robert Goodden, acted as his own architect and had it changed to Perpendicular style. There is a lively white marble statue of him in the church and many memorials to other members of the Goodden family.

The church stands across the drive from Compton House, built in the 1840s in Tudor style and still in the hands of the Goodden family. Mr Richard Goodden's Worldwide Butterflies and Lullingstone Silk Farm are there, and the public is admitted to both every day between 10 a.m. and 5 p.m.

Yetminster grew from the local stone, and little has come since to spoil this largish village whose buildings were constructed mostly between the end of the sixteenth and the middle of the eighteenth centuries. Gable Court, with its mullioned windows, was built around 1600; St Andrew's Church has a thirteenth-century chancel, and the rest is mid-fifteenth-century, with large, clear glass windows, the original roofs and their paintings and some of the original early sixteenth-century seating at the back of the nave. Gravestone philosophy in the churchyard:

Here lies the body of William, son of William Taunton and Jane his wife. He died 13th Feb. Ano Dno 1691, aged ten weeks:

Our life is nothing but a winter's day
Some only break their fast, and soe away;
Others stay dinner, and depart full fed;
The deeper age but sups and goes to bed
He most in debt, that fingers out the day,
I die betimes and have the less to pay.

From Yetminster one can go south along the valley of the Wriggle by way of Hell Corner, but just to the east is the village of Leigh which, pronounced 'Lie', completes a Bunyanesque route. South of Leigh, which spreads itself over a large area, is—or was—a Miz Maze. It is now very difficult to pick out anything much of the turf-cut labyrinth on banks raised in prehistoric times, probably as a site for rituals of life, death and fertility. What remains now is a raised round earth platform surrounded by a hexagonal bank. It is said that this 'Troytown' was a meeting-place on holidays and, according to an early-seventeenth-century record, the young men of the village used to re-cut the paths annually. It was also said to be the meeting-place of witches. In a paper presented to the Dorset Field Club in 1879, William Barnes wrote: "Many years ago I was told by a man of this neighbourhood that a corner of Leigh Common was called 'Witches' Corner'; and long after that a friend gave me some old depositions on witchcraft . . . one of the witches' sisterhood said that they sometimes met in Leigh Common." The last witch burned in England is said to have been arrested here and executed in Dorchester at Maumbury Rings in the seventeenth century. But there are solid reminders of Christian faith in Leigh, in its village cross on a fifteenth-century shaft and a much-restored fifteenth-century church of warm brown stone.

Yet go as far as Hell Corner and to the village of Melbury Bubb, where the church of St Mary is framed by the wood of Bubb Down behind. The font is pre-Conquest, hollowed out of the shaft of a column and intricately carved. But *why* was the bowl hollowed out of the wrong end so that the carvings of lion and wolf, horse and stag, all wound around with tendrils, are upside down? What was at work here, and why was it necessary to indicate in a church notice that "all cruelty shall cease through the influence of Christ"?

Two miles south of Hell Corner, at Batcombe, we are right

against the southern rim of the lowlands: the chalk of the central Dorset highlands begins abruptly here, with Batcombe Down, at the foot of which is set the village, not much more than a hamlet. The church of St Mary is so under the hill that a member of the local Minterne family, supposed to be in league with the Devil and known as 'Cunger' or 'Conjuror' Minterne, set his horse to jump over the church from East Hill. In doing so he knocked one of the pinnacles off the church tower. It was replaced in 1906, but it is harder to find the date of John Minterne's steeplechasing. Creature of the Dark One or not, he asked to be buried half in and half out of the church, and it could be that the curiously short tomb just beyond the porch on the left is the part of his tomb that projected from the transept before the church was re-built.

There is a Saxon inscription on a buttress, and inside the church is a round Norman font. One of the bells, long cracked, was cast at Leigh in 1592. In October 1973 all the bells were stolen but were recovered at Ringwood a few days later.

Although there seems to have been something always going on in Batcombe, it is one of the most remote and quietest villages in Dorset, reached by narrow, steep lanes. Just above it the Wriggle rises and starts on its northward course to join the Yeo. And beside the road that runs from Holywell to Minterne Magna, from which there are magnificent views over the farms and tree-dotted plain below, there stands a small monolith known as 'the Cross in Hand', although now neither cross nor hand can be distinguished on it. Nor is its history known. Hardy wrote of it in his poem 'The Lost Pyx', and in *Tess* he made Tess swear on it not to tempt Alec d'Urberville again:

He stepped up to the pillar.
"This was once a Holy Cross. Relics are not in my creed; but I fear you at moments—far more than you need fear me at present; and to lessen my fear, put your hand upon that stone hand, and swear that you will never tempt me—by your charms or ways."
"Good God—how can you ask me what is no unnecessary! All that is furthest from my thought!"
"Yes—but swear it."
Tess, half frightened, gave way to his importunity; placed her hand upon the stone and swore.

At Newlands Farm I learned two things that I had not known before: one was that the farmhouse was built in 1622 (unless the gate only is of that date), and the other was told me by Mrs Davis at her back door as the geese were picking around among the February ice-puddles, giving me a glare and a hiss as a matter of form:

"They are well over ten years old," she said. "Geese are the oldest living creature you'll find on a farm if there isn't a donkey. If they're not in the oven when they're young, they just stay on."

Hilfield is the next village eastward from Batcombe and has its back to the chalk escarpment that hereabouts has a mountainy and European air about it, due mostly to the plantations of conifers and birches on the slopes and the calvary near the Friary of St Francis. On the day I photographed it, I opened *The Times* a few hours later and found a photograph of it there.

St Nicholas, Hilfield, is one of the smallest parish churches in England, fifteenth century but much restored in 1848 after it had fallen into disrepair. The bench-ends are said to come from Cerne Abbas. Each one is different, many of them unusually spirited. In the 'Flight into Egypt', for example, there is a most expressive donkey; in another the Risen Christ carries a spade, and David as harpist conveys serious application to his music. They are thought to be Flemish, and dates have been hazarded ranging from the fifteenth to the nineteenth century. Both the seating and the pulpit are made up from sixteenth-century panelling.

Hermitage, just north and more into the Vale, is a collection of farms and cottages named after a former hermitage connected with the Augustinians but abandoned in the fifteenth century. The approach is down a winding lane from Hilfield, and the thatched cottages, the farmhouse near the church and the church itself that seems to sit on the farmhouse lawn, are all very self-contained and sheltered by High Stoy Hill to the south. Much of the church at Hermitage was rebuilt with materials from an earlier church and in a style of about a century earlier than its date of 1799. It is spacious and light, with a barrel roof and clear glass, and has the only bellcote I have ever seen that has a stone ball on top. Hermitage is secluded, watered and leafy and yet only about three miles from the dramatic bareness of Batcombe.

Walking once at evening roughly along the line of the ancient

Great Ridgeway, I was drawn to look yet again into Hilfield church. When I got there, the sun had just set, leaving a carmine stain in the sky as I looked to the west from the slope of the churchyard, bare but for a few leaning gravestones and two tall firs. Church Farm is a little way along on the other side of the road, and I did not want to cause anyone there to think I was burgling the church, so I examined the bench-ends by flashlight and was baffled yet again as to when they were carved. When the church was restored, or some time since, wooden parquet flooring was laid, and I was tempted to lie down and spend the night in that calm place under the gaze of the wooden eyes. But I left and climbed to cross the ridge at Gore Hill and paused at the Cross in Hand, feeling its uncommunicative shape in the dark. The flashlight revealed nothing but turned the lichen into splashes of copper.

Buckland Newton, on the very edge of the Vale, is disposed on hillocks and hollows. Entering from the east, off the B314 at a crossroads, you pass an ordinary red-brick school on the left and some modern houses on the right and start up a hill towards trees. The next house on the left used to be the vicarage and is now called Buckland Newton Place, a largish early-Georgian house behind a brick wall alongside which runs a high terraced walk leading to the churchyard. The first impression of Holy Rood is of a dismal church, but it is not the fault of the church but of those who rendered the exterior with cement, dark brown and patchy now and giving the Perpendicular square tower the look of a Foreign Legion fort—very sad, because it is a lovely church, mostly fifteenth century with a thirteenth-century chancel with widely-spaced lancets. The interior too has been badly served by having at some time been given a shortbread-coloured wash. But the graceful arcades and large windows, and the early sixteenth-century seating, give a feeling of space and dignity. High above the south door there is a carved slate figure, said to be Saxon, which was dug up in the vicarage garden. There is also a medieval alms-box on a pedestal, the whole carved from a single piece of oak, and a brass plate of 1624 to Thomas Barnes, ancestor of the poet.

It is not the church, which is masked by trees, that commands Buckland Newton but the Manor standing opposite, half way up a wooded slope, a seventeenth-century twin-gabled house remodelled at the beginning of the nineteenth century. Standing outside very early one morning, I was invited in for a cup of coffee and saw the interior, which has retained the proportions of the earlier house more than has the exterior, which is stucco and used to be the colour of a ginger biscuit until it weathered to a more attractive and lighter shade.

Crossing the B314 along a narrow and somewhat deserted road through typical Vale lush meadows, rich fields, stout oaks and elms, with over to the south the line of the wooded escarpment, one passes a farm here and there and Brockhampton Green and Westfields, which can scarcely be called villages because there is so little of them. Turn right at the junction after Westfields— that is to say, not to Sturminster Newton, and you come to another fork. Take the one to the right where the signpost states melodiously "Folly, Plush and Piddletrenthide". You are now in Mappowder—the 'May Powder' named by John Claridge in 1793 as the southern limit of the Blackmoor Vale (Old English *mapuldor*=maple tree).

Walk slowly through the village street and savour a Dorset village that has changed and developed very little over the centuries, apart from some council houses built on another road leading off the street. Where the functions of buildings have changed, the present occupants have preserved the fabric almost intact and the former use, for example, 'The Old Pound' and 'The Old School House'. Mappowder once had a pub but has one no longer, and the post office was a general shop too until just recently. So although it is a village without pub or shop, it has no air of decay. Next to the post office there is the entrance to a farm, and there is another farmhouse and yard at the end of the street just before the church of SS Peter and Paul. In the lodge beside the church the novelist T. F. Powys, brother of the writers J. C. and Llewelyn, lived the last years of his life, and he lies in the churchyard.

The church is a well-restored (1868) Perpendicular with large clear glass windows letting in the light that gives the interior a joyous spaciousness. In the south wall is a miniature effigy of a crusader, about eighteen inches in length, which may commemorate a heart burial. Mappowder Court, hidden a quarter-mile south-east of the village, is not the original great mansion of the Coker family—that was demolished in the mid-eighteenth century, but the house one sees now, announced by the old big gate-piers, is a seventeenth-century stone farmhouse of three bays with many stout outbuildings that add to its solid rural self-possessed air.

Talking of heart burial I find that I almost left out Blackmoor Vale's best-known legend of an unmarked grave, simply because it is already so well-known. While hunting, King Henry III spared the life of a white hart and decreed that nobody should take its life, but it was slain by Sir Thomas de la Lynde, and the King was so enraged that he imprisoned de la Lynde and laid a tax called 'White Hart Silver' on the Vale, thus giving it its other name of 'Vale of the White Hart'. Kingstag, on the B3143, four miles north of Buckland Newton, is said to be the spot where the beast was slain. In the church of St Mary at Glanvilles Wootton (or sometimes 'Wootton Glanville'), a parish linked with Buckland Newton and Holnest, a weather-vane on the tower recalls the legend, and encaustic tiles in the chantry, some of them copies made at the restoration in 1875–6, tell the story of the white hart.

The real heart of the Blackmoor Vale is close to Barnes's Lydlinch, in the fields watered by the Lydden and the Caundle Brook on their way to the Stour, by the Divelish (Devil's Brook) that flows with such undiabolical singing under Fifehead Neville packhorse bridge. In Fifehead church's west wall is a black marble tablet referring to a piece of land bordering the Divelish: "In Memory of Roger Goodfellow who died in ye Year 1730 and left ye Yearly rent of his Meadow call'd North Close to ye Second Poor of this Parish for ever." A notice says that a fiddler used to play at services, and in the churchyard an enormous tomb or mausoleum to the Brune family stands solidly square. Surrounded by six-foot-high black iron railings, the tomb has been partly roofed over with lead. There are gigantic yews in the churchyard, and the manor house backs on to the church end, but the front of the house is on the other side, and an extension built on at the other end made at one time another house called The Spinney.

There is not much change anywhere in the Vale, not sudden and dramatic change at any rate. To me the very centre of the Blackmoor Vale is the junction of four roads called Barnes Cross. Here stands the oldest pillarbox in everyday use in Britain, made by John N. Butt & Co of Gloucester between 1853 and 1856; it is hexagonal and has a vertical slot for letters. If the Vale does not revolve around it, a great deal of Blackmoor news and history has passed through it.

4

Up Along the Central Highlands:
1, Eastern

BLANDFORD is a difficult place to leave. It is such a pleasing small town, with much Georgian elegance (result of rebuilding after the great fire of 1731 which was even worse than those of 1570, 1579, 1677 and 1713), a broad market place and the noble church of St Peter and St Paul built in 1733–9 by the Bastard brothers. At the church end of the market place stands John Bastard's 1760 pump and fire-monument, a tabernacle of Portland stone, with two Doric pillars and a triangular pediment, the whole of it a minor triumph of classical harmony. There is a lead relief of a phoenix, and part of the inscription thanks "DIVINE MERCY that has since raised this Town, like the PHOENIX from its Ashes, to it's present beautiful and flourishing State".

I hear the local news in Colliers the butchers who write on their window such observations as "We split hares" and "We have brains". Down in the yards I buy old country tools and odds and ends I think I need, and in the Dorset Bookshop there is always something new or second-hand which I cannot resist. Blandford is good for dawdling and wandering around. Apart from the many fine Georgian houses, you will find, for instance, after going through the narrow Plocks, the pre-Fire 'Old House'. Dating from 1661, at first glance it does not seem to be as old as that. It was built for a German-born physician, Dr Sagittary, and its cut and moulded brickwork has the look of having risen from an inspiration alien to that which conceived the other buildings in The Close.

Built in 1682 of brick, and standing well up the hill on the way to Salisbury, are the Ryves Almshouses, set in a U-plan and described on the face as the 'Gerontocomium'—a word that some present-day civil servant, with that profession's gluttony for ponderous euphemism, might revive.

But back at the other, western, end of Blandford, lie green meadows, the Stour and the stone bridge of 1783 and 1812 that crosses it, and on the other side the choice of three roads by which to leave Blandford, or four if you count the private road to Bryanston School. This western bank of the Stour is steep, wooded and named 'The Cliff'. At the northern end of the Cliff, where a wood called 'The Hanging' almost meets it at right angles, and standing within a loop of the Stour, is Bryanston School. The house was built during the 1890s for Viscount Portman and became a public school in 1927.

The second turning to the right beyond the bridge is a public road leading to the hamlet of Bryanston, which stands at the edge of the parkland and is protected first by beechwoods and beyond them by the hills to the north and west: thatched cottages, carefully-tended gardens and the feeling of a Big House nearby. The original mansion was further down the hill and was demolished in 1890. The Old Church of 1745 is topped by a cupola, and light from the north and east is filtered through Venetian windows onto the many Portman memorial-tablets and the Georgian Communion-rail and pulpit. This small, graceful church was the Portman Chapel. The second church, of 1895–8, is stone, much larger and with a fine tower. Near the two churches are mid-eighteenth-century stables and outbuildings of red brick and greensand ashlar.

The second road of the fork, leading to Winterborne Stickland, leads up a steep hill, between high banks and then out to open downland and a dead straight west-bound road for a couple of miles. From the top of the hill not much is seen of Blandford in the summer but the square brick chimney of the brewery rising above the green billows of the treetops, Hall and Woodhouse's temple, from which rises the Christmas-pudding tang of the malt that goes into Dorset's renowned Badger beers. At night, eastward and high above Blandford, there is the startling vision of the cluster of red lights that tops the high masts beyond Blandford Camp.

Across fields to the south of the Winterborne road lie plantations, and to the north woods come to the edge of the road and, after a ninety-degree turn to the right, the conifers of Broadley Wood. Here pheasants strut like hens, and, in early morning and late evening, badgers, like animated advertisements for Blandford ales, lumber white-streaked and round-bottomed into the tall grass of the hedgerow. Another right-angle turn, to the left, leads past Normandy Farm to Winterborne Stickland, one of nine villages along the course of the Winterborne River—'the bourne that runs [or runs deeper] in the winter' which joins the Stour at Sturminster Marshall.

Just north of Bryanston lie France Farms, and early one dry morning, just as the hay had been cut, I walked in a general westerly direction beyond the northern border of Bryanston Park and the other side of The Hanging along high deserted country, about four hundred feet above sea-level, beech-green and hay-gold at that time. Following a track towards some large buildings, I found myself at Normandy Farm. One day I intend to find out why France and Normandy Farms are so called. Winterborne Stickland once belonged to the canons of Coutances in Normandy, but France Farm was originally called 'Nutford Lockey', although Hutchins states that by 1587 it was known by the name of France as well.

Winterborne Stickland derives the second part of its name from the Old English *sticol*, or steep, and has outskirts of bungalows and modern houses so that one has the impression of coming into a small town. The village has a true and unmistakable centre with a pair of lime trees and the base of an old cross. The nearby church, begun in the thirteenth century, is of flint with a banded stone and flint tower. A sixteenth-century wagon-roof in the chancel has been restored, and the roof timbers of the nave wagon-roof are painted bright yellow and blue with red and other coloured bosses. In the Skinner Chapel, now the vestry, is an immense table-tomb with a black marble top in which the Skinner arms are incorporated; it is a memorial to Thomas Skinner of Quarlestone who died in 1756. On the wall of the vestry hangs a black board lettered in gold: "Charity Winterborne Stickland 1769. Mrs Barbara Skinner by will gave £200 South Sea Stock to be distributed to the poor of this parish in Bread. Interest £7 2. 6."

On the north wall of the chancel, directly to the left of the altar, is a strange black marble column that stands on a bracket and has running round it a Latin inscription that begins: *Statua Sepulchri*' and is in memory of Rachel Sutton who died in 1653. Here is a translation:

Statue of the tomb of Rachel. Beneath this marble rest the bones of the pious and generous lady Rachel, most faithful and loving and beloved wife of William Sutton STD, who of a seven days fever as though by a refining fire that she might be the purer to occupy a place in Heaven for her husband willingly and at length submitted to the Divine Will and straightway hastened from here to Heaven September 12 1653, aged 35. She sent before her William, a little four-year-old, her first-born October 30 1645 and Barbara last of the family daughter of 19 days March 17 1652 their mothers ashes enfolding them in the same urn. . . .

The brick and flint vicarage was begun in 1685; a wing was added in 1768 and further additions in the nineteenth century. Interspersed with modern houses are thatched and cob cottages and a very good inn, also thatched, called 'The Crown'. Beyond the bungalows on the southward-bound road is Quarlestone Farm, whence Thomas Skinner was brought to his resting-place beneath the black marble. Parts of the house date from the early-fifteenth century, but the front and the side visible from the road have been rendered, and one must go into the farmyard and round to the back to see the walls of banded stone and flint as they were originally. The farmhouse looks rather forlorn and deserted now that it is divorced from its buildings and the farm. The name comes from the family of William Quarel, first mentioned here in 1232, and most likely it went to the family at the time of the Conqueror.

Winterborne Houghton, a mile due west of Stickland, is a hamlet of modest houses, many of them thatched and some of brick, and a mid-Victorian church. There is also an abandoned (or it was the last time I saw it) trout-farm that had been set on the chalk stream that rises on the hill above Houghton and from which, given the right weather, there are some of the finest views in Dorset: Wiltshire and Win Green to the north-east, and to the coast as far as Poole to the south-east. I have had both views but never at the same time, mist or cloud intervening in one quarter or the other. There is a remote and mountainy feeling on these downs, bare for centuries but now in many places planted with beech. The people of this village used to be called 'Houghton Owls' from the story of a villager lost in the woods at night who called for help and was answered by owls that he took for humans. Was this the story that Thomas Hardy recalled when he described Joseph Poorgrass lost in Yalbury Wood in *Far From the Madding Crowd*?

Going back to Stickland and turning north up the Winterborne valley, there is Turnworth where Thomas Hardy left his mark as designer of the capitals and possibly of the bearded head corbels in the church by G. R. Crickmay, who took over its restoration on the death of John Hicks in 1869. Robert Gittings, in *Young Thomas Hardy*, tells how

> . . . The whole of the old and ruinous church, except the tower, was to be demolished, and a new church built with the addition of a north aisle. The faculty for this was published on 7th May 1869, and on 13th May work started under Hardy's supervision, the specification having already been drawn up by Crickmay, with what appears to be Hardy's revisions. Demolition finished, the new foundation-stone was laid on 19th June. The interior building was to be of Corsham Down stone, and considerable freedom was left for the embellishment of the capitals and corbels. Hardy's designs for the capitals are delicate traceries of birds, fruits and flowers in the French Early Gothic style, which he had probably learned from the work of William Burges. Even more striking, though less successful, are the bearded heads serving as corbels. Furthest west, there is a particularly pert and lifelike owl, which is almost certainly Hardy's individual design. It resembles the small, witty animal drawings, also based on the work of Burges, which appear in Hardy's own architectural notebook, and in which an owl is actually included. This delightful interior shows that Hardy, in church architecture at least, had brought considerable skill from his experiences in Blomfield's office. This commission also added to his knowledge of the great houses of the district; he later took Turnworth House as the model for Hintock House in *The Woodlanders*.

Is the owl in Turnworth church a sly Houghton Owl from the next village and Hardy's private joke? And was he reminded of it when, twenty-four years later, he read the lessons there on a summer day in 1893 when his friend Thomas Perkins, formerly headmaster of Shaftesbury Grammar School, had just been appointed rector? One of the squire's daughters had 'a vivid recollection of Hardy, bearded and rather small, with the steam rising gently from his bald brow after riding from Dorchester'. Dorchester is seventeen up-and-down miles away, the roads were not macadamed, and Hardy was fifty-three and rode there on a bicycle.

Hardy said that Turnworth "stood in a hole, but the hole is full of beauty". It is true, for it faces south, is sheltered by Bell Hill and Shillingstone Hill and is all wooded downs and hollows bright with primroses and violets in spring, and gorse, heather and honeysuckle in summer. Here is another Cliff, a steep chalk down protecting Turnworth from the east wind, and to the north are Turnworth Down and Ringmoor, where there is a well-preserved Roman settlement on the site of a prehistoric one. Turnworth is the most northern village to lie right up against the eastern edge of the line of the central or north Dorset Downs. A walk—or a choice of several walks—of about two miles brings us startlingly and dramatically to the steep edge of the downs beyond which the Vale of Blackmoor stretches; green pasture, white farms, black and white cows and bluish air, peaceful and totally unlike the bare high hills. To get the real feeling of this great contrast which Dorset offers within a relatively small area walk over the top and look at Belchalwell which has nothing to do with *sauce béchamel* but names the place where there is a cold well on the side of a hill. There is a church with a Norman doorway and an Elizabethan pulpit. It is down off the highlands, while Belchalwell Street, consisting of a farm, a chapel and some cottages, lies on the lower slope of Bell Hill.

Ibberton is another village that backs into this long hill or continuous line of hills, looking westward across Blackmoor, with Bell and Woolland Hills and Bulbarrow rearing high over it. A small place of cottages built on various levels, it has a manor house with two dates on it, 1666 and 1686, a delightfully trim and compact house, almost a mini-manor. Having come down a

F

one-in-five gradient from the road along Bell Hill, you have to climb again to get to the church, fifty steps bordered by ferns and foxglove and nettles and mossy stones. A fifteenth-century church dedicated to St Eustace, a rare dedication, was starting to fall down the hill at the beginning of this century before being restored and shored, and it still has a somewhat precarious air about it when seen from some angles, with outward-leaning walls. There are some fragments of fifteenth-century stained glass and two fine Elizabethan pieces in the chancel windows. There used to be a chained *Book of Homilies* dated 1673 and, to quote Ralph Wightman's *Portrait of Dorset*, "open for the casual visitor to see". I enjoyed climbing up the steps past Stachy's Spring, looking out over the Vale and then going into the church to look at the homilies again. But some visitor, anything but casual, stole that rare and ancient book.

Woolland, the next village and a mile south-west, is totally different from hill-town Ibberton and lies in its own green deep porringer surrounded by Victoriana. The manor is eighteenth century but was 'done over', and there are iron railings and laurel hedges and diamond-paned windows, a church of 1857 by Gilbert Scott, a great yew in the churchyard and next to it a partly Elizabethan rectory; beyond church and rectory can be glimpsed the lake. It all has a Romantick and wistfully deserted air despite brisk activity in the nearby brick stables. The church is a Victorian delight, built of parti-coloured stones in thirteenth-century style, with a polygonal bell-turret topped by a spire. In the windows are panes of black, white and pink glass; there is a tiled floor, and a superb Victorian touch is a beautifully-carved stone robin's nest to the right of the east window where a live robin had nested when the church was being built.

A still-climbing mile due south brings us to the top of Bulbarrow, 902 feet above sea-level and the second highest point in Dorset, because at the other end of the Central Highlands Pilsdon Pen is a giantkin more at 909 feet. In the large parking-place at the summit where four roads meet, there is a circular orientation dial presented and erected by the AA which was hacked out of commission by vandals in 1976. (They have also torn off most of the signpost arms on and around Bulbarrow and in many other places in Dorset.) The dial has been replaced, and this will give an idea of what can be seen or imagined on a clear day:

18 miles NNW	Stourhead
12 miles NE	Shaftesbury
13 miles ENE	Cranborne Chase
15 miles NNW	Wincanton
27 miles NNW	Glastonbury Tor
11 miles NNW	Sherborne
13 miles NNW	Yeovil
43 miles NWW	The Quantocks
40 miles NWW	The Blackdown Hills

Less than a mile due west and to the left of the road to Stoke Wake there is a tumble of green hills and mounds, with trees ahead and beyond and, giving a Breton air to the landscape, a great wooden cross on a summit. Rawlsbury Camp is the second highest Iron Age camp in Dorset, the highest being Pilsdon Pen, and it encloses four acres. The cross was set there in 1966, and in that pre-Christian setting I find it intrusive and menacing.

Repeating yet again the point about the wide scenic variety of Dorset, and returning to Bulbarrow as a centre, there is the steep drop to Woolland and Ibberton and thence to the Blackmoor Vale. Walk along to Rawlsbury Camp for the view over the Vale to the right and the tumbled downs, topped by that cross, to the left; take the road towards Blandford from the car-park and the view-finder, and immediately open downland has vanished and a great beechwood begins beyond a stone wall where there is a sign, "Delcombe Woodlands". Look over the wall and you will see the woods plunging down to a hollow with open fields. The Blandford road runs alongside the top of this wood, and down in that hollow are Delcombe Manor, Delcombe Dairy and the pastures of Delcombe Bottom. Fork right at the sign to Milton Abbas, and soon there are trees on both sides of the road, until a sudden and surprising estate of council houses come into sight just before a turn to the right leads in a straight and narrow line to Milton Abbas.

The Monastery and Collegiate Church of Milton for Secular Canons was founded in AD 938 by King Athelstan, grandson of Alfred the Great. In 964 the Monastery was converted into an Abbey with forty Benedictine monks. Struck by lightning in 1309, the Abbey Church was almost completely burned. Rebuilding started on the present Abbey Church and went on nearly to the time of the Dissolution in 1539, when the Abbey buildings were granted to Sir John Tregonwell by Henry VIII. Two restorations were carried out, one in 1789 by James Wyatt and the second in 1865 by Sir Gilbert Scott, at the request and expense of Baron Hambro.

The first and lasting impression of the Abbey is of light and height—white limestone columns and Ham stone, the height accentuated by the absence of a nave because the Dissolution overtook the rebuilding before a nave had been started. At the Dissolution the reredos, which was coloured, lost its twenty-six figures, and what we see now are plaster and were restored by Wyatt in 1789. Designed to hang in front of the reredos but now, on the north wall of the chancel, after being restored about twenty years ago, is the Hanging Tabernacle, which is of oak, nine feet high and in four sections.

There is a grey marble tomb to that first Sir John Tregonwell who died in 1565. A marble tablet to a John Tregonwell Esquire, who died in 1680, states that he gave his books to the use of the Abbey Church, ". . . as a thankful acknowledgement of God's wonderful mercy in his preservation when he fell from the roof of this church". When he was five, John had been taken up the tower by a nurse, and, as he leaned over the edge to pluck a rose, he fell, but his nankeen petticoats acted as a parachute, and the terrified nurse on arrival at the ground found Master John, cheated of his rose, contentedly picking daisies instead from the grass on which he had landed.

In the north transept is a white marble monument, designed by Robert Adam and carved by Agostino Carlini, to the memory of Lady Milton, who died in 1775. Beside her on the tomb-chest reclines her husband, propped on one elbow, elegantly attired, bewigged, wearing a sword and gazing reflectively at his late spouse. I find it intrinsically comic. Not that there was anything remotely funny about Lord Milton, who changed both history and geography in and around Milton Abbas.

He began life as Joseph Damer, a rich local man who married a daughter of the Earl of Dorset. In 1752 he bought the Milton estate, was created Lord Milton the following year, had the monastic buildings (with the exception of the abbot's hall) pulled down in 1769 and employed Sir William Chambers to construct a house for him on the site. This was raised between 1771 and 1774, built around a courtyard, Gothic and imposing had it been standing alone on the level lawns instead of having the Abbey Church towering over it. Chambers himself was aware of that and chafed at his employer's demands in the design of what Chambers called "this vast ugly house in Dorset". He resigned in 1774, and James Wyatt took over, while 'Capability' Brown laid out the surroundings. Today the house is a public school for boys, and the best time to visit both abbey and house is during school holidays.

Over one hundred turf steps climb from the green floor, on which stand abbey and school, to reach in the woods St Catherine's Chapel, high up on the side of the valley and directly in line with the church.

A Saxon chapel here was rebuilt by the Normans, and over its main door is an inscription carved about AD 1200: "INDULGEN-CIA H'SCI.LOCI C ET (XXDIES)", meaning, "the indulgence of this holy place is 120 days", that is, a visit to the shrine got one into heaven 120 days earlier after death.

About the beginning of the nineteenth century a ceiling was added, the chancel was converted into a bedroom, the nave into a living-room; a kitchen grate and chimney were added, and the chapel became a labourer's cottage. Later it was used as a carpenter's workshop, and then as a lumber store. In 1901 it was cleaned out, and the windows were repaired, and on St Catherine's Night, 25th November 1901, prayers were offered that the chapel might be treated as the holy place of the inscription. Restored by Everard Hambro, then owner of Milton estate, it is now owned by the Salisbury Diocese, and services are conducted there regularly.

Not content with his new house built from the stones of the old monastic buildings and the church next door stripped of heaven-knows-what medieval decoration and treasures that had escaped the greedy hands of Henry VIII, Lord Milton—who clambered even higher to become Earl of Dorchester—looked at the little town of Middleton, 'the middle town of Dorset', that was spread around his great new house, and decided to get rid of it. About a hundred houses, a grammar school, the George Inn, the market cross, 'the King's Arms' and 'the Red Lion', shops and a brewery, were all demolished. Milton bought what he could, waited for leases to run out and in one case flooded the sitting tenant out of his house. But the tenant in this case was a solicitor, who brought a successful action against his landlord. When Milton was leaving for London just afterwards, he heard the church bells ringing to celebrate Guy Fawkes Day and thinking it was local joy at his defeat in court, ordered that the bells be taken out of the tower and sold.

Milton employed 'Capability' Brown to design a model village, out of his sight and hearing, in the heart-shaped valley over the hill, to rehouse the people he had dispossessed but who were still needed by him to run his estate. A lake was made where the town had been, and he used a Bill to move the school to Dorchester. The first time he brought it, Parliament threw it out, but the second time it was passed, and the school and the boys he said had stolen his fruit and eggs were sent to school in Blandford.

It is only just two hundred years since this single-minded and wilful man moved a town and its population, both living and dead, in order to have his house and grounds to himself. The bones of the dead, when they came to the surface, were broken up and scattered, as were the headstones that had marked what had been thought to be their last resting-places.

So there stands Milton Abbas village, a long street with twenty identical houses on each side, lawns in front of them and gardens behind them on the sides of the combe. Each house, designed for two families, was built of Dorset cob and thatched. They used to be painted yellow, but almost all are now white, and in the spaces between each pair are rowan trees where there used to be horse-chestnuts. I remember arriving in Milton Abbas in the dusk one May evening in 1941, and the street was full of the scent of the flowers that seemed to hover luminously overhead. In 1953 the trees were found to be unsafe and were felled, and the rowans were planted to take their place.

Lord Milton planned a church for his displaced population. It was started in 1774 and consecrated in 1786 by the Bishop of Bristol. It is of mauvish grey ashlar, late Georgian Gothic, very much in place in that neat and precisely-planned village street, but it was added to overmuch in 1888 by some of those Victorians who could never leave a church alone.

The story of what happened to Milton Abbas is unique, and what resulted from it is unique too. The village is fastidiously preserved and cared for. Dale Cottage survives from the old town of Middleton, and the almshouses opposite the church were built in 1674 in the old town and were transferred here complete when the town was demolished in 1779.

If you have visited the Abbey first and come into the village from around the lake, look out for the sign of the Brewery Farm Museum outside the first building on the right in the street. With the new village a brewery was built in 1775. In 1848 Robert Fookes took it over, and it was run by his family until it closed in 1950. In 1970 Mr C. H. R. Fookes, great-grandson of the original Robert, opened a museum of brewing, farming and rural life exhibits in what had been the brewhouse. It is open every day of the year, and available inside is an *Illustrated Guide to Milton Abbas* by C. H. R. Fookes, which everyone should buy before moving further up the ordered street to explore the village. The museum itself is a treasure-house of tools, old photographs, cooking-utensils, early sewing-machines dug up in gardens, bakers' handcarts, milk-floats and cream-separators. You can wander around for as long as you like without ever being bothered, and Mr Fookes welcomes rural relics to add to his collection. If no-one is there, you are invited to leave a message in the Visitors' Book. Whenever I am in Milton Abbas, I call in for another look and to savour such oddities as a Heath Robinsonian apple-peeler which, the notice points out, would seem to have the disadvantage of reducing all apples to the same size.

Dewlish is south of the high land proper and lies on the west bank of the Devil's Brook. High up on the chalk hillside above it, some sand, very rare around here, was found in 1814 where a mouse had scrabbled it out of its hole. When excavations were made to see how much sand was there, the remains were found of two prehistoric elephants or mammoths among some fossilized willows from around a million years BC. Two of the tusks are now in the museum at Dorchester. A Roman villa was built at Dewlish, and a tessellated pavement was discovered there in 1740. A house was built in 1702 on the site of the villa, a house beautiful in its simplicity and changing in material and colour as you walk round it, from grey and yellow stone to dark red brick. In the middle of the eighteenth century it was bought by the Michels, a military family extensively commemorated in the little church, including an enormous monument to Field-Marshal Sir John Michel, who died in 1886. The stone and flint church is approached through a short avenue of yews, and there is a fine view, particularly in the autumn, from the bottom of the churchyard to the wooded hillside beyond the valley. The manor, Dewlish House, is about half a mile to the south-west, but the house next to the church, Manor House Farm, of about 1630, might easily be taken for the manor house itself. In fact, for some time I thought it was.

The road to Cheselbourne is clearly marked from Dewlish, but as it is a straggling village with four roads running into it and out of it, it is difficult to know when you are there. There are flint and thatched cottages and some modern houses, and at a bend, nudging its back into a green bank, there is a black wooden house with a white verandah that looks as if it had been lifted from some Indian hill-station. The centre of widespread Cheselbourne was probably the remains of the cross in the churchyard. Part of the shaft remains with the base and steps. The church is thirteenth- to fourteenth-century, with a good tower, well-gargoyled and pinnacled and battlemented in yellow stone that shows up against the grey of the flint below. There is an epitaph here for a rector who died in 1684:

> Here lies all that was mortal
> of the Reverend divine Mr Richard Basket—
> once the ornament and delight of
> St Mary Magdalen College in Oxford
> at last the exemplary Rector of this
> church and parish—whose pious soul took
> her flight hence to heaven
> upon the 24th of February 1684.

> In the same grave lies interred
> Mrs Urith Basket, the most worthy wife
> of such an excellent husband
> who being full of good works and days
> departed this life the 27th September
> An Domini 1707 at 85.

I like the way the wording implies that Cheselbourne was a fine step up from Oxford and also the touching compliment to the good Urith. Cheselbourne put all excellence into their two Baskets.

Village maidens, dressed in white, used to walk through the fields on Palm Sunday in the ceremony of 'Treading in the Wheat', probably pre-Christian in origin and perhaps connected with the long mound just to the north of Cheselbourne which has two large boulders near it. Two legends about this place, which is called 'Giant's Grave', were set down in *Notes and Queries* in 1866. One was that the stones move when they hear cocks crowing in Cheselbourne, and the other is that two giants met to see who could throw a stone the further over the valley of Hanging Hill (now marked on the map as 'Henning Hill'). The loser died of vexation and was buried on the spot—hence the name.

The pagan grave is in much better state than the Christian church at Lyscombe, two miles north of Cheselbourne. A narrow road rides over the crests of the downs to Piddletrenthide through magnificent and deserted country. On the right of the road is Lyscombe Farm, lying at the opening to the hollow in the hills called 'Lyscombe Bottom'. A tiny stream begins somewhere around here and chortles over a stony bed on its way south towards Puddletown to join the Piddle. As the hills begin to rise from this flat floor of the combe, there stand the remains of a chapel of about AD 1200, a chancel arch and east lancet and sturdy Norman columns. The nave was later used as a bakehouse and then became a farm worker's cottage—the evidence of that domestic conversion is the rusty iron grate hanging out half way up the remaining wall. In 1957 a Dutch barn was built over these ruins, but nothing more seems to have been done since. The last time I was there, nettles, ivy and jackdaws were in command of the shattered chapel and what used to be the priest's house beside it. It was the joyful murmur of the nearby stream that brought to mind what that isolated place must have been like. A garden, a goat, a cow, a pig and some hens and, as the chapel was not a hermit's cell, a bell called to some congregation—the farm people obviously, but from how far around did others come? Were there more people living in that high valley and on the hilltops around than now? Almost certainly, since the farms were smaller than in the present century.

Readers who are at any time close to Cheselbourne should make the small effort to walk to Lyscombe Farm and its chapel. (This area can be thoroughly explored only on foot because there are so few roads.)

On the east side of Henning or Hanging Hill and Giant's Grave, at the junction of the Devil's Brook and the stream called 'Mash Water' is Bingham's Melcombe or Melcombe Bingham (whichever form I use, I always find that the person to whom I am speaking uses the other), a house in the Bingham family for six hundred years until the end of the nineteenth century. But the parish is called 'Melcombe Horsey', taking its name from the owners of the other medieval manor close by. Yet the parish church of St Andrew, fourteenth- and fifteenth-century, of flint with a chunky stone tower, lies in Bingham grounds close to the manor. Although Bingham's Melcombe is not open to the public, the drive to the house, entered between stone piers topped by the Bingham eagles, is a public road to the church as well. Sir Richard Bingham was present in 1571 at the battle of Lepanto against the Turks where Cervantes also fought. The house was built from 1500 onwards and has never been spoiled by that kind of improvements and additions that gets out of hand to take a house beyond its natural proportions, so that it is a perfect example of a small medieval manor house, of pale ashlar and golden Ham Hill stone. There is a large sixteenth-century limestone gatehouse, and the gardens, which have preserved their original plan, lie within warm brick walls that hold at one corner a semi-circular summerhouse dated 1748.

Higher Melcombe, also of the mid-sixteenth century, is of banded stone and flint but, unlike Bingham's Melcombe, has been considerably altered at various periods. At the end of the eighteenth century it was divided into two floors and used as a brewhouse and laundry. The large chapel, added in 1633 by Sir Thomas Freke in an earlier style, has been preserved and restored.

This is a book about villages, but villages stand where they do for good reasons, such as available water, well-drained soil and so on. The Dorsetshire Gap, a break in the line of chalk hills that runs east-west across the county, is no village and is the most isolated spot in the centre of this roadless area bounded by the roads between Cheselbourne–Piddletrenthide–Mappowder–Ansty Cross. Lyscombe Bottom, immediately south-west of the Gap, can be seen clearly from the northern side of Blackmoor Vale, accentuated by one of the highest peaks of this part of the range, Nettlecombe Tout, standing next to it. One way to reach the Gap is to take a footpath going east off the Folly-Mappowder road and leading around the edge of Nettlecombe Hill, which is crowned by the banks and gullies of a hill fort. Ancient trackways, some holding to the chalk ridges and others keeping to the bottoms of the narrow ravines, meet at a point where a signpost proclaims "Dorsetshire Gap". At the foot of the post there is usually a biscuit-tin containing an exercise-book and a pencil for visitors to record their names. They have done so for several years, and among the many local children and young walkers in rambling-clubs there are names of people from the USA, Europe and the Commonwealth and details by some of the contributors of plants found there. There is a very varied landscape visible from the hills here: bare downs over towards Bulbarrow; steep wooded slopes and combes to the south; the woods of Melcombe Park to the north, and all around the chopped-up look of the Gap itself, difficult to estimate where man has taken advantage of the contours and then excavated or built up or whether it remains as the distant ice carved it out.

Coming down on the western side of Nettlecombe Hill brings one to Folly, more gladly in the past when one of the two houses that now make up the hamlet was the Fox Inn, now retired from its sparse trade in that lonely place to become a private house named 'The Old Fox'. The footpath carries on past the Fox and up Ball Hill and Church Hill and on to Buckland Newton, over to Little Minterne Hill, Dogbury Gate, Mount Sylva or High Stoy and Batcombe Hill, of which I have written earlier. Walking these paths, I find I am drawn on and on, either because the weight of the traffic of the past keeps the feet moving or because one has the same feeling as prehistoric man had when on the heights, a sense of not being quite as much at ease down in those tree-filled and muddy hollows as up here where the way ahead is clearer. Any section of this old trackway allows the traveller to keep an eye on as much of the lower lands as possible. Closer to the present day, someone had the idea of keeping an eye on the game too, because on the top of Church Hill, in the middle of a plantation of young beech trees, a twenty-foot-high platform, reached by a metal ladder, has been built against a Scots pine. There are two other pines and two yews forming a high and shady grove. Allen Hiscock, who farms Armswell, which stretches its pastures on both sides of the Folly–Mappowder road and reaches to the top of this hill, told me that the owner of the adjoining farm, a Mr Saunders, loved to sit beneath these trees. When he died, his ashes were spread there as he had requested. Allen also told me that because the pine branches present the shape of clock hands when seen from the valley roads, their silhouette is called 'Twelve-o'-Clock Tree'.

Two woods, that adjoin Watcombe Wood are known as 'Bloody Tent' and 'Little Elias', and from the ridge there is a view across the green bowl of Watcombe Bottom to an Italianate grouping of a small church with a bell turret framed by yews, cypress and cedar. In front of the church is a small white object, mystifying and unidentifiable at that distance. I will come to that later.

Down in the Piddle valley, and just past the village shops and Piddletrenthide Manor, there is a steep, sharp turn to the right where a signpost used to state "Plush, Folly and Mappowder", but since the Fox closed, "Folly" has been painted out as though the spot ceased to exist, like a dried-out oasis, once the beer ran out. At the top of East Hill the road runs beside the tall beeches of Redlands Coppice, matched, across a narrow valley, by those of Tokenhills Coppice. At a dip and a turn there is a bridge over a narrow stream, scarcely more than a culvert, where stands a square block with a pot on top. It looks like the bake-oven of some long-vanished cottage but was the hydraulic ram in an earlier water-supply system whose ingenious workings were explained to me by Geoffrey Seed, fighter-pilot turned Water Board Rivers Officer in Lancashire.

Past this bend a grassy down rises to the right above the road, and in late spring it gleams gold with cowslips. At right-angles to the road on the right, where the down flattens out into a pasture, a half-dozen sycamores give a Corot-like outline. Just beyond here outbuildings and old cottages lie behind Plush Lower Farm, a

red-brick and no-nonsense sort of house where at one time in-
geniously constructed wrought-iron spindly birds and mammals
stood here and there on a hummocky lawn.

'The Brace of Pheasants' is the only pub between 'The
Poachers' at Piddletrenthide and 'The Antelope' at Hazelbury
Bryan—and that must be close on eight miles. It has been a pub
on and off, and I can recall a time when it was not, but that was
when 'The Fox' at Folly was still open, and so was 'The Nag's
Head' at Mappowder, which betrays its former station by the
horse's head knocker on the front door and the electric light overhead. There is a palm-tree in the back garden, which, I was told
by Mrs Harvey, who was 'The Nag's' landlady and still lives
there, has grown from a cutting she took from an earlier palm
some fifty years ago. Originally, 'The Pheasants', a long white
thatched house with a wrought-iron cock pheasant on the wall
and a brace of stuffed pheasants in a glass case over the door,
was a pair of cottages and the village forge. It was preserved so
that its character was not changed. There were good bar meals and
a first-class restaurant until the whole pub was gutted by fire in
March 1979. The cock-pheasant plaque survived, and the pub was
rebuilt and thatched as before.

Beyond 'The Pheasants' and its car-park are stone cottages,
and then the road comes to an end at the Regency manor which
stands, tree-hidden, on a slight knoll. Plush's sheltered position
below surrounding hills inspired Keith Andrew to start his inter-
nationally-known orchid-growing enterprise here.

To carry on towards the north, the road makes a Z-bend and
climbs the hill between steep chalky banks out of which project
the roots of the beeches whose branches meet overhead. On the
left at the top of the hill and just beyond the trees is the church
of St John the Baptist—much less Italianate than it appears from
the top of the downs. It was designed by Benjamin Ferrey and
built in 1848. The windows are Perpendicular, and the nave has
a hammerbeam roof. The church is bare, with an air of being poor
but proud, more Franciscan friar than rich abbot. The font is
round and Norman and I suspect that it was lost for a while and
came out of semi-retirement only recently. Another font, whose
place it took, has been put out to grass and stands on the turf in
front of the church door which faces the pastures and the downs

beyond. It is this font that can be seen as a white dot from the hilltop ridge track and through fieldglasses seems to be a piscina or a bird bath.

When I said there was no pub for eight miles, I meant in a direct line going towards Sturminster Newton from Piddletrenthide, because there is the excellent 'Fox' at Ansty, just north of Melcombe Bingham, and beyond that a straggling settlement called 'Hartfoot Lane' on which I shall, yet again, quote Ralph Wightman:

> . . . there is another village straggling along through a very narrow gap between the ridges and yet not a parish. Dorset has got over this difficulty by referring to this settlement as Hartfoot Lane. Actually part of it is in Melcombe Bingham and part in the even more distant parish of Hilton. To make things even more complicated, the names Higher and Lower Ansty come into it. This must be near the geographical centre of Dorset. Hartfoot may be the correct name but 'Arfurd' is nearer the local pronunciation. . . . Every 'yokel' story is fathered on Arfurd Lane. It was here that a cottager rushed to get the pig out of the sty to stand with front hooves on the wall, and to share the march past of the band on the Friendly Society Feast Day.

Wightman remembers that, when he was a youth, it was a place of incredibly old people and that it was at 'The Fox' that he played his first game of shove-halfpenny. 'The Fox' is lively and cheerful, set back from the road, with tables and chairs under the trees, a choice of food inside and a lot of outside green light-bulbs which, when seen at night from the ridgeway on Nordon Hill, draw the traveller down by their mesmeric twinkle.

I have taken some time over this eastern end of the central highlands and have dodged all over the place, but a look at the map will show that this is unavoidable because of the lack of roads and the difficulty of getting in anything like a straight line from A to B.

I shall leave out the valleys of the Piddle and the Cerne until later chapters and take a giant's stride six miles westwards.

5

Up Along the Central Highlands: 2, Western

THE next village is also on a stream, the Sydling Water that gives its name to Sydling St Nicholas and Up Sydling and which flows down to Grimstone to join the Frome. The road to Cerne Abbas rises sharply from Piddletrenthide to a wide and open plateau. During the last war some Land Army girls lived in a hut up there, and I remember one of them telling me that when it was misty, it was like being on a mountain top. The land drops on the north side to Kiddle's Bottom and on the south to King's Grove Bottom. There is a copse and a triangle of open ground and heaps of granite chips for use in icy weather at this point where the road joins the Old Sherborne Road at about seven hundred feet. I often saw a large truck standing on that exposed triangle, and I wondered why the 'Battle Hymn of the Republic' always came into my mind. One day I realized why—the name on the side of the lorry was 'John Body' and into my mind had floated the line "John Body's lorry stands a-mouldering in the rain."

Beyond the Old Sherborne Road the minor road crosses open pasture, from which can be seen Hardy's monument and the Dorset South Downs along the coast. Then the road plunges down a steep tree-lined hill into Cerne Abbas where, at the end of Long Street, the New Sherborne Road is crossed and once more the road climbs steeply to over seven hundred feet. Just beyond the crest and to the right of the road is a wood in which I found a stone inscribed "Win Col 1913" and I wondered about Win Col's identity. Dog? Horse? Unlucky beater? A gypsy woman waiting for Thomas Hardy to invent her tragic life? George Millar, the writer, who lives at Sydling Court and farms a thousand acres around here, told me that the wood was planted by Winchester College in 1913. Henry VIII gave the Sydling Valley and part of the Piddle Valley to Winchester in exchange for the freehold of part of Hampton Court site, and Win Col own most of the top Sydling lands to this day.

On the crest of Hog Hill, not far above the Win Col plantation and its runic record, there is the old Furzey Down trackway, now just a footpath and sometimes not always that, that follows the ridge between the River Cerne and the Sydling Water and passes close to the Cross in Hand stone on Batcombe Down.

A fast-running stream crosses the road from Cerne Abbas at a ford called Three Guinea Bridge. This is the Sydling and the left fork at the edge of the ford leads to Sydling St Nicholas and runs beside the stream whose bank has been reinforced by a shoulder-to-shoulder regiment of pawn-like concrete cylinders topped with iron handles. A few hundred yards along, the road is joined by another and in the V of the junction and on the edge of the stream is the Congregational Chapel, the date 1834 above the door. The front has been cement-rendered, but the tall and pretty round-headed windows on either side of the doorway are untouched and original. To the right of the iron gateway to the church path there is a black noticeboard almost hidden by the spreading hawthorn of the hedge. It states that the Sydling Congregational Church was founded in 1775, Service Sunday 3 p.m., Women's Meeting at 3 p.m. on alternate Thursdays.

At the back of the chapel and built as part of it is a kind of pastor's earth, as opposed to a priest's hole, furnished with an earth-closet alongside. Were these overnight quarters for visiting preachers or designed to provide a quick brew-up and light relief for members of the congregation who had far to travel? In the little burial-ground the graves have subsided into the turf, and in early spring the ground is bright with primroses and white violets.

The interior is dignified simplicity with a gallery at one end, supported by pillars, pine pews and a very plain pulpit set on a raised

Sydling St Nicholas

Sydling St Nicholas: the shaft of the village cross stands at the end of the white lines, with East House beyond it

Evershot

Whitchurch Canonicorum

Pilsdon Manor

Broadwindsor

Fishpond — the march of power

Evershot – detail of brass to William Grey (d.1524)
Leigh – village cross

Whitchurch Canonicorum: the shrine of St Wite

Wynford Eagle church with (inset) 'The Honour of the Eagle'
perched on the porch gable of Wynford Eagle Manor (1630)

St George, Reforne, Portland

Thatching at Turner's Puddle (above) . . .

. . . and at Burton Bradstock

Portland – old Lower Light

platform. The floor, part wood and part slate, has been broken up in one place. If it is going to be lived in, I hope it will be soon, because each time I pass I notice yet more broken window panes.

Sydling St Nicholas is in a valley high on the downs, miles from a town, surrounded by hills, loud with the bubbling of water, compact and full of the feeling of what villages used to be when they were units in which people lived and worked together over a long time. It probably also had its share of local chauvinism, family feuds and assorted rustic violence which exist together with isolation. Before the Romans came, the Celts kept to the hilltops above the marshy valley of the lower Sydling. The Saxons settled here in the seventh and eighth centuries, and land was given in AD 933 to the Benedictine monks at Milton Abbey. The abbot provided the church with a priest who drew tithes and paid a pension of thirty shillings to the Abbey.

Because the stream divides into three when passing through Sydling, many of the cottages, stone and flint, brick and flint or cob, some thatched, are reached by little bridges. At the southern end of the village there is a battered golden Ham Hill stone cross and a chestnut tree, planted in 1911, where High Street and East Street meet and where Church Lane, narrow and overhung by trees, leads to St Nicholas. At this meeting-place of roads the St Nicholas Fair used to be held on 6th December.

Going up High Street from this point, one is unprepared for a surprising trio of houses. The first one after Church Lane is the Old Vicarage, which has grown up around an early Tudor house, added to and 'improved' in 1640. The vicar of that time had his initials, R.T. (Ralph Taylour), and the date cut into the stone over the doorway. A yew tree said to be over eight hundred years old grows in the garden and looks every year of its age. The house joined to the Old Vicarage was the bakery and has mullioned windows and a date-stone of 1733. Beyond it is East House, a red-brick Georgian house with a Venetian window in the centre of the front and a great central chimneystack towering above it. Leading to the front door is a short flight of semi-circular shallow steps of brick. It is a house that seems to have strayed into this village street of stone buildings from a cathedral close in a county town.

Further up the street on the left is a working smithy and not an Olde Smithie teashoppe or a shop selling plastic lucky horse-

G

shoes. In between clanging away on a set of shoes for a pony—
"Don't pick up that one, it's hot"—Dick Newman told me that his
father took over in 1918 and that his grandfather worked there
at the beginning of this century; before him the smith was a man
called Rogers. It is still a place of filings, clamps and vices, square-
headed nails, sparks and red-hot iron and hissing steam and information about the past and present of Sydling. Over the smithy
door is a small iron figure of a naval officer of Nelson's time,
Captain Hardy perhaps?

There were two inns in Sydling, the philosophically-named 'Hit
and Miss' at the end of East Street, now a private house, and 'The
Greyhound' in the High Street, still going strong. At the back of
'The Greyhound' you are close to water again in Diamond Lane
and, obviously, beside water in Waterside Lane. The sawmill to
the south of the village was built on the stream but now uses
electricity from the mains. Downstream too is John Barnard's trout
farm where he nets a brace for me while I wait.

With all this water around (and, in one flood in 1889 after a
thunderstorm, a man was swept away and drowned: ". . . the
body of Tom Churchill . . . found about a mile from where it was
drowned, and removed to the Greyhound Inn, Sydling, to await
an inquest"), it is not surprising that the church of St Nicholas
was built in the fifteenth century on a rise. But it seems that even
there the foundation was none too solid because the columns of
the south aisle settled, and two solid external buttresses were
built to support the south wall which, in order not to weaken it
further, has a very small south door in it and no porch.

Nearly all the glass went during the Civil War, but a few pieces
remain in the heads of some windows. Light, open, airy, free of
restorers' excesses and with a splendidly practical fireplace in the
porch to warm Parish Council meetings in the past, there is a
noble wagon-roof in the nave to gaze at during long sermons. The
font is said to have been adzed from an early Roman capital, and
an octagonal font-bowl stands on its side close by, another under-
study like the one at Plush. Two oak chests are seventeenth
century, and a third, with a slot in the top, is early thirteenth
century. There are box-pews, and in the squint to the right of the
chancel arch there is a stone corbel which came to light in 1961.
In the form of a man's head, it is open-mouthed and shows a

robust tongue, more good-humoured in expression than a comedy mask.

For 150 years a Smith family lived at The Court, the manor house beside the church. Twenty-six Smiths lie beneath the floor of the chancel, and there are memorials to many Smiths on the wall. One, to Elizabeth, Lady Smith, is a standing monument but in the form of a three-dimensional tablet. Set in a pointed arch, at the top there is the figure of a mourning woman and, below, her husband, Sir John Smith, rising from the tomb. Late-eighteenth century and worked in marble, the hands and feet are delicately carved, but the hand at the end of the extended arm has been broken, and Sir John's gesture has been reduced to an unfortunate two-fingered salute.

Should you wish to see Sydling from the hills around, there is a choice of bridleway or footpath to Breakheart Hill from Church Lane, but, before going, visit the great Tithe Barn to the left of the churchyard. The walls are flint with stone buttresses, and the roof, now of corrugated iron, is supported by oaken beams and pillars making a three-aisled interior. One of the beams was said to be marked with the initials LVW for Lady Ursula Walsingham, wife of Elizabeth I's MI5 chief, and the date 1590. I have never seen it, and Treves, writing in 1906, says that he too "searched in vain". George Millar tells me that some of the older locals believe that the beam may have been removed at the same time as the thatch earlier this century. But the clock in the church, made in 1593, is still there. It strikes the hours but has no face, and it bears the initials ETC, those of the smith who made it, and the marks of his hand-forging are there too.

The manor is called 'The Court' because it was here that the Court Leet met to deal with local offenders. In 1582 Sir Philip Sidney, poet and soldier, signed the surrender of the lease of the Manor. He married the daughter of Elizabeth's Secretary of State, as Walsingham was correctly styled. Shortly after, Sidney's mother-in-law, that same Ursula of the elusive initials, took on the tenancy.

Beyond the High Street and forking left at the Congregational Chapel, the road from Cerne Abbas is soon reached again, opposite the lane to Up Sydling. Turning left, the road climbs to the top of the downs again. On the right are the mounds and hummocks of one of the biggest Iron Age villages known in southern England. The outlines of its fields, corrals and outworks can be seen still running down under the turf of Hare's Hill to the south and in the bottom below and on Breakheart Hill beyond. The ground here is some of the flintiest in England, and in Iron Age days the flints were collected and made into the walls whose outline still shows through the turf.

A signpost names another Folly. Fork right, cross the A37 from Dorchester to Yeovil—and cross with care because the long straight stretch makes a Stirling Moss of many a driver. The way lies between two Bottoms, Charity Bottom and Lankham Bottom, and there are more Celtic fields on the left. Then take the first turning to the left, and you are in Cattistock—a village on a hair-pin bend: "elbow-streeted Cattstock", Barnes called and pronounced it. Here is another village that gives the impression of being all of a piece, a self-contained place but in a totally different way from Sydling. To quote Treves again:

> Cattistock is a cheery townlet, with a very noble church, rebuilt by Sir Gilbert Scott in 1857. . . . Its glory in the minds of the villagers would seem to depend upon its carillon of thirty-five bells and the enormous size of its clock. This was the first carillon introduced into England and owes its existence to the generosity of the Rev. H. Keith Barnes, rector from 1863 to 1875, who defrayed the cost of over £2,000.

People used to come to Cattistock or gather on the surrounding hills to hear this Louvain-cast carillon, says Marie Langford, who lived in the village as a child and long afterwards, and who wrote an affectionate pen-portrait of it. But on 15th September 1940 a mysterious fire damaged the tower, melted the bells and destroyed that enormous clock which, on old photographs, seemed to spread its face across the entire side of the tower. After the fire the tower was taken down; the blocks of stone were meticulously numbered, and it was rebuilt in its former style. Treves did not mention that the best parts of the church are the work of Gilbert Scott's gifted son George. Newman and Pevsner state that "What survives of before the nineteenth century is negligible, but for the mid- to late-nineteenth century, this is the masterpiece among Dorset churches." The hundred-foot-high slender stone tower with its long vertical belfry windows is seen at its best from the foot of the slope on which the church stands. William Morris's 1882 window, six angels in white and red robes against a dark blue background, is in the south aisle. George Gilbert Scott's baptistery is in the tower, separated from the nave by a stone screen. The only hints of Victorian excess are in the dark red and purple wall-decoration here and the astounding twenty-foot-high elaborate font-cover.

Whatever the season, whether gold with daffodils or wall-flowers, white with snow or glistening with rain, Cattistock in its hollow in the hills has always a warm calm about it. But life was hard in Victorian times for the poor. Marie Langford found in the School Record Book, for example, this entry: "John Tucker left school for field work. A pity, as he was making good improvement. He is not ten years of age." But that was only a century ago, whereas the Cattistock Hunt dates from the mid-eighteenth century when a hunting parson established a pack at Cattistock Lodge and called it 'The True Blue', a name to bring to the boil the blood of Anti-Blood-Sports demonstrators.

About a mile and a half north of Cattistock is Chantmarle, a house of Ham Hill ashlar with the date 1612 and the word 'Emmanuel' engraved on the keystone of the porch doorway to ensure that God was there forever. Sir John Strode, who had this house built on the site of a medieval one, left a detailed record of the construction, complete with the names of the architect and the masons employed. In the nineteenth century it was a farmhouse, and the end wings were demolished and later redesigned by Inigo Thomas in 1910 and extended in 1919 by St John Hornby, who printed his Ashendene Press books here. At that time the garden was laid out in terraces with yews, beeches and ponds. Chantmarle is now a Police Training College but may be visited on receipt of written application to do so.

The most enjoyable way to catch the full surprise of Rampisham is to approach it from the Maiden Newton–Crewkerne road, that lonely highway that is so open and bleak when it rains or when the mist comes down but is all blue air and larks and hawks and chalky treelessness when the sun shines. The side road drops into a narrow chalk valley where beeches hide the centre of a large and somewhat straggling village. The centre, such as it is, holds a Jacobean manor, an agreeable creeper-covered pub that is no brewer's predator but is nevertheless called 'The Tiger's Head' and is placed at a point where four roads do not so much run as stagger together. There is no gaudy sign, and you could easily miss it, but that would be a mistake because it is as pleasant inside as it is out, and there are some interesting old local photographs in the bar.

Further down the slope is a shallow ford and just beyond it a thatched Post Office. The church of St Michael and All Saints stands on a wooded knoll above the village. It was rebuilt in 1845-7 and 1859, the Perpendicular tower retained complete with its ancient bells and many gargoyles infinitely more alarming than any tiger's head. If you squeeze by the lectern and then nearly stand on your head, you will find a fine brass, nineteen inches long, of a man and his wife, Thomas and Isabell Dygenys, whose faces are startlingly lifelike. Their clothes, engraved in great detail, are displayed like a fashion-plate of the time. Thomas wears a long, belted, fur-trimmed gown and round-toed shoes, and his hair is long. Isabell has a head-dress and also a fur-trimmed gown with an ornamented girdle hanging to the ground.

"Here lyeth Thomas Dygenys and Isabell his wyfe which was gud benefactors to thys churche which Thomas desesed the VIII day of June and the seyd Isabell desesed the VI daye of Marche in the yere of Our Lord a thousand CCCCCXXIII."

In the churchyard is the massive base of a stone cross carved with many figures and the date 1516. It is very weathered, and imagination has to help the eyes to make out the stoning of St Stephen, the martyrdoms of Thomas à Becket and St Edmund, and St Peter, a pillar with a cock perched on top, fools, monks and two men in armour. The figures are easier to see when it has been raining and the stone is still wet.

Rampisham is pronounced 'Ransom', and there is a story that the choir went visiting another village but on arrival there they heard the choir which they were going to sing with or against giving out "The year of jubilee has come, Return ye ransomed sinners home": without firing a note, the mortified Ransomed Choir turned about and returned home.

Less than two miles to the north-east of Rampisham is Evershot, the second highest village in Dorset, after Ashmore, and about seven hundred feet above sea-level. It stands in a hollow of the hills and is sheltered by beeches. This district of greensand and chalk is a watershed from which the Yeo flows north into Somerset and eventually to the Bristol Channel, and the Frome starts on its way diagonally across Dorset to Poole Harbour. During the nineteenth-century railway boom, Evershot was given a station by the Great Western Railway, nearly two miles away at Holywell. It almost did not get there at all because for a while the engineers believed that the necessary tunnel could not be cut through the greensand. Evershot is a large village which, despite the closeness of the railway, did not quite become a town and lose its attractiveness as a village. The stone houses have stone or slate roofs, and Melbury Gate to Lord Ilchester's Melbury estate has on its piers two lions of about 1690 that look like cream-fed Burmese cats. The village street has a raised walk and many of the houses were given bow windows in the nineteenth century. The Acorn Inn has a porch flanked by two pillars and a room built over it. The tower and arcades of St Osmund's Church are Perpendicular, but what one sees now is mostly the work of R. H. Shout who had two bouts of restoration work there, in 1852–3 and again in 1864. William Grey, rector, who died in 1524, has a brass that originally lay in the chancel floor but has been saved from erosion by feet by being moved to the north wall of the chancel, $18\frac{1}{2}$ inches high, it shows the priest in pre-Reformation (i.e. Roman Catholic) vestments and holding a chalice and wafer between his raised hands. Two miracles must have preserved this brass, from anti-Romish wreckers at the time of the Reformation and again from the Puritans. The poet George Crabbe was rector here from 1783 to 1787, and apparently the appointment to the living gave him just enough money to enable him to marry.

In Evershot at Christmastide there used to be performances of the mumming play of St George and the Turkish Knight which was also played in other parts of Dorset. I have never seen it at Evershot or anywhere else in Dorset, but perhaps it has been or could be revived. I had forgotten about its earlier performance here but was reminded as I watched the Moreška on the Dalmatian island of Korčula. This is a dance that represents the struggles between Christians and Turks or, in the Yugoslav version, between Moors and Turks, a Black King or Knight versus a Red King. They are all versions on a Crusade theme, and the name has the obvious common root—Moorish, Morris, Moreška etc.

There is a narrow pathway going up beside and behind the church to St John's Spring, one of the springs starting off the Frome. I looked for it in high summer, and it was rather difficult to find among the tall nettles, willow-herb, elder and brambles.

Melbury Park is immediately north of Evershot, six hundred acres thickly covered with oaks, chestnuts and limes, with five lakes, two farms, a deer park and Melbury House standing on a narrow ridge of cornbrash limestone. It was built for Sir Giles Strangways in the 1540s, and John Leland, writing at the time it was being raised, spoke of the house for "Mr Strangeguayse . . . with a loftie and fresch tower". Much of the Tudor house remains, but much again has been taken over by the seventeenth- and nineteenth-century additions. It is still dominated by the lofty hexagonal tower, glazed on five sides as a prospect-tower for viewing the park and the deer.

Sir Giles Strangways did not live long to enjoy his house and the view from the tower, for he died in 1547; he is represented in alabaster in the church, where there is a second fine alabaster effigy, of William Bruning, who died in 1467. House and church together are known as 'Melbury Sampford', and at the northern end of the park is the village of Melbury Osmund (or Osmond), which is a calendarsmith's dream of thatched cottages that lie on a southward-facing slope running down to a stream and a ford. Some of the cottages date from the seventeenth century and the church of St Osmund—named after the Bishop of Salisbury who completed the cathedral there in 1092—has a Perpendicular tower that was given a Georgian facelift in 1745 when the nave was rebuilt. Another and ruthless 'restoration' in 1888 toned down or threw out the Georgian and brought in the Gothick with a Victorian vengeance. It now has little left of interest but a stone carving which seems to baffle everyone. It may come from an Anglo-Saxon cross and represents a strange beast wrapped around in foliage. Abraham's ram in a thicket has been suggested, and the figure has been likened to a frog. It baffles me too, so I believe it to depict man in a maze.

The end of Melbury Osmund village is called, somewhat grandly, 'Town's End', yet it is appropriate because the gates into Melbury

Park that stand there opened to a completely different concept and way of life from the village's.

The most unforgettable view I had of the park and of Melbury House was when I was driving south from Yeovil along the A37, which, as I have said already, holds mostly to the high ridges of the downs. It was late one April afternoon, and the trees of the park were lightly touched with green, and there was a sudden half-hour flurry of snow. Down on the right of the road the tower windows of the house glinted and shimmered in the bubble of sunshine, and everything around was picked out in snow, stippled with green and traced in black branches.

Like the rivers that rise on this ridge, the principal roads run roughly north to south, and the only one going westwards hereabouts is that from Evershot which climbs to Toller Down Gate to join the A356. Toller Down Gate is now nothing but a crossroads at about eight hundred feet above sea-level. A semaphore was set up here during the scare that Bonaparte might invade England, and a field is still called 'Telegraph Field'. But it was probably not such a deserted place as it is now because from the time of Charles II until the beginning of this century a fair used to be held here, and a Fair House where food was prepared and sold stood there.

Turning right along the A356 and taking the first or second road to the right, one comes to Corscombe on the north-east slope of the downs. The village spreads across and down the slope, into hollows and along sunken lanes. High above the village is St Mary's Church, Perpendicular in origin and discreetly done over in 1875–7. A mile to the south is Benville Manor, a seventeenth-century house with a noble symmetrical front of the nineteenth-century added to it.

Corscombe Court to the north-east dates from the thirteenth and fourteenth centuries, when it was a grange of Sherborne Abbey. It lies within an L-shaped moat and has a great fifteenth-century barn with a gabled stone porch. At Corscombe lived Thomas Hollis who bought the manor in 1741. He was a passionate democrat whose principles went far beyond the limits set themselves by his fellow Whigs. Hollis's family had made gifts to John Harvard's University in the American colonies in 1690, and Hollis often sent over books and money. Where, since the days of Sherborne Abbey ownership, local fields had been known as 'Monks of Sherborne',

'Abbot's Orchard', 'Bishop of Salisbury' and so forth, Hollis named his fields 'Republic', 'Revolution', 'Toleration', 'Boston' and 'Geneva'. He abstained from milk as well as from alcohol, ate no butter, spices, sugar or salt. I do not know that he was vegetarian, and his dietetic preferences may have been determined by some prescient concern about cholesterol. He certainly said that he hoped to be spared a long final illness and asked to be buried in one of his own democratic fields and that nothing should mark his grave. On 1st January 1774 'Good Mr Hollis' fell dead in a field while talking with some of his workmen. They buried him ten feet deep where he lay and ploughed the field so that no trace of the spot remained, just as he had wished. That was fifteen years before the French Revolution whose early aims he would surely have supported as enthusiastically as he would have deplored the later excesses.

Not named for revolution is Red Post, an ordinary Dorset County Council signpost at the meeting-place of the parishes of Corscombe, Chelborough and Rampisham—ordinary except that it is painted scarlet, its colour and name having been given after some soldiers were killed here during the Civil War. They still haunt the spot, of course.

Mosterton is on the south-facing slope of the Highlands, looking towards Beaminster Downs and Horn Hill and sitting on the A3066 that comes up from Beaminster and Bridport. There is a Tweedledee and Tweedledum brace of villages here—Mosterton in Dorset and less than three miles to the north Misterton in Somerset. Mosterton is a village with an air of attending to its own business, but it is difficult to know precisely what that business is. There used to be a cloth-mill that got its power from the River Axe which rises in the hills two miles away and runs under the road here. The cloth-mill went away, but the church came closer. Formerly at Chapel Court a half-mile away, a new church was built in the village and was dismissed in one guide-book as "built in 1832 on a new site and is of no interest". In fact, it is a plain and pleasant church with a wide nave and a west gallery on columns. The east window, designed by Geoffrey Robinson and made by Joseph Bell of Bristol, portrays Christ Triumphant above a Ford tractor, an International Harvester and a Webb single-seeder drill. The colouring is brilliant, with a lot of red, and the window very effective. It was dedicated by the Archdeacon of Salisbury in July 1975.

A few years ago the Admiral Hood Inn was badly damaged by fire but was carefully restored and thatched and is as shipshape as its name merits—it is run accordingly.

On my writing-table is a green ashtray decorated with the Cerne Giant, and on most mornings I take my do-it-myself muesli or porridge from a bowl thrown by David Eeles in his Mosterton pottery. I first went there years ago and have gone back many times for replacements, gifts for friends or just the pleasure of going. David is a big, golden-bearded Viking of a man, and I assumed that his name was of Scandinavian, Saxon or Dutch origin. One day I asked his mother how the name is pronounced—'Alies', 'E-less', 'Ales'?

"No, Eels, like the fish," said Mrs Eeles, "and David is off fishing in Ireland with his son."

The house, judging from its shape and the general lay-out of the outbuildings, was probably a pub at some time.

At Whetley Cross, a mile south of Mosterton, the A3066 turns sharp left for Beaminster, and the B3164, sharp right, goes south-west to Broadwindsor. One spring day I came into Broadwindsor and heard the bells being rung in the fifteenth-century tower of the church of St John the Baptist. Three of the six bells were cast at least a hundred years before the Reformation, and in his notes on the church the vicar, the Reverend Robert Vincent, says that, "The ringing team is equally noteworthy, Ted Case having begun ringing in 1919 and served forty years at tower captain. The members of the Crabb family can provide a complete team on occasions." There is tradition and continuity! The church stands on a terrace as though conducting the village, which of course it did. From the sixteenth-century pulpit, and sometimes, when the congregation was very big, from the church steps, sermons were preached by Thomas Fuller, author of *The History of the Holy Warre* and *The Worthies of England*. Fuller held the living from 1634 to 1650 when he was replaced by a local Puritan parson, John Pinney, described by one of his contemporaries as "much a gentleman, a considerable scholar, an eloquent charming preacher". At the Restoration of the Monarchy in 1660 the living was returned to Thomas Fuller, but that magnanimous man both liked and admired John Pinney, who was also popular with the people of Broadwindsor, so Fuller let him continue to preach his eloquent sermons from the foliage-decorated pulpit. But higher authority exerted its vengeful will and ejected Pinney in 1662, the year after Fuller's death, and the unfortunate Pinney, who, as is shown later, was not exactly destitute, became a wandering preacher.

There is a lot of *plus ça change* in all this, and, as recounted above, the newly-restored Charles II had been in Broadwindsor in person less than a decade earlier when he spent the night of 23–24th September 1651 there after that tumultuous day when, it is said, he had narrowly escaped capture at the George Inn in Bridport (now Beach's, the chemist's shop), left Bridport by Lee Lane (where a stone commemorating the flight is let into the bank on the corner of the lane and the Dorchester road) and gone on to Broadwindsor, where he stayed at the Castle Inn, which was burned down in 1856.

When the Roundheads headed for Dorchester from Bridport in pursuit, as they thought, of Charles, who had eluded them by nipping smartly north instead, it was not long before they realized that they were on a false trail and decided that he had sought refuge at Pilsdon Manor with Sir Hugh Wyndham, of known Royalist sentiment and uncle to the Colonel Wyndham who hid Charles twice at Trent. The soldiers burst into Wyndham's house and declared that one of the young ladies present was Charles in disguise. At that time, of course, he was not the Merry Monarch, bewigged and sporting a hairline moustache, but a youth of barely twenty-one. When the girl proved or was proven to be neither male nor royal, old Wyndham, Lady Wyndham, their daughters and servants were held under guard in the hall while every room, closet and loft was searched, probably with the angry roughness to be expected of baffled pursuers. "At length, being convinced of their gross and rude mistake, they desisted from offering any further violence to that family."

Pilsdon Manor, of yellow-grey stone and mullioned windows in a long unbroken façade, has changed little since that time except that it is no longer inhabited by Wyndhams. Since late 1958 it has been the home of a religious community based on that which Nicholas Ferrar set up at Little Gidding in 1625. The community

. . . lives a life of simplicity cast within the framework of the ordered worship of the Anglican Liturgy . . . and attempts to offer unconditional friendship to all who come, however defeated and broken and near the end of their tether they may be, and accepts people as they are. . . . The educated learn not to feel superior to the uneducated, and the man who works with his hands feels on the same level as the man who works with his head, and the colour of one's skin matters not at all.

Those who stay there for spiritual comfort and help in coping with the outside world when they return to it take part in the farming and gardening, cooking and cleaning, and the general running of a large manor house and grounds. Behind the house is a great grass quadrangle and round it a range of outbuildings and former stables which have been made into living-quarters. There is nothing monastic or institutionalized anywhere, either in the house or around it, and those who come with weariness or despair come to a place of serenity and gladness. The sheltered setting adds to this feeling, of course. On a bitter December day the wind howling over Pilsdon did not get down to the garden that was still bright with yellow, white and red roses.

A wrought-iron gate leads from the gardens to the church of St Mary, twice restored in the nineteenth century but retaining some Perpendicular features, a bell-turret with spire of 1875 and with the windows renewed in clear glass apart from an unfortunate brown and yellow window of 1918 that casts a light all too dim and religious and which has the look of a window of about half a century earlier and not a very good one at that. The manor, the church, a farm and some cottages stand in the northern edge of the Marshwood Vale where the Char rises. Sheltered from the north wind by Pilsdon Pen and the downs to the north, in early spring the turf in front of the house and church is covered with daffodils.

Pilsdon Pen is a mile to the north, bare but for furze—Dorset 'vuzz' or 'vuzzen'. At 909 feet, it is the highest hill in the county, with Bulbarrow at the other extremity of the Central Heights its close rival. Less than two miles to the east is Lewesdon Hill, 894 feet but more rounded and tree-covered. Sailors who saw them from Lyme Bay used to call them 'the Cow and Calf' (unless that is the invention of romantic landsmen), and there is an old Dorset saying, "As much akin as Lewson Hill to Pilson Pen". I believe that to be subtler than it sounds because the two hills are so unlike. Could it be in the sense of 'chalk and cheese'?

The Iron Age fort on the top of the Pen was still occupied when the Romans arrived, and it was captured by Vespasian's Second Augustan Legion in AD 43. One of the finest views in Dorset may be had from here (weather permitting, of course)— all west Dorset, the sea, Golden Cap, along the coast eastwards to the Fleet, Chesil Beach and Portland, westwards across Lyme Bay to the Devon coast and north to Somerset.

Lewesdon Hill is National Trust property, and there is a sign-post, carrying the National Trust sign, pointing to the footpath to the hill. This is close to the crossroads called 'Four Ashes' where one of the many roads radiating from Shave Cross, and in this case leading to Stoke Abbot, crosses the B3162 from Bridport to Broadwindsor. The path leads up through beechwoods dotted with pines to an undulating plateau covered with bracken and brambles. At every season of the year this is a rewarding and stimulating walk.

Bettiscombe, a mile to the west of Pilsdon and lying under the south-western side of the Pen, has a manor house, a church, a farm and cottages. It is hidden away in the folds of the hills like a sachet of lavender in a linen-closet. The church of St Stephen was almost rebuilt, except for the Perpendicular tower, in 1862, the architect being John Hicks, to whom Thomas Hardy had been apprenticed six years before when he was sixteen. The church is plain, well designed but unremarkable, pleasant, quiet and calm inside and out.

The manor, which is a few hundred yards from the church, was built of brick at the end of the seventeenth century and was later changed somewhat, the windows of about 1800 being particularly noticeable. It was built for that same John Pinney who had been vicar of Broadwindsor during the Cromwellian years. Presumably he had done something other than preach during the thirty-odd years that had gone by. The Pinney family was old-established in Dorset and had been engaged in lace-making, and their money probably came from that. But John Pinney did not live out the rest of his life in peace. When the Duke of Monmouth landed at Lyme Regis on 11th June 1685, Pinney's son Azariah joined him, was captured and later sentenced to be transported to the West Indies as a slave. His family's position and money helped him in his plight, and he worked in the Caribbean as a freeman and became a plantation-owner and made his fortune. His son became Chief Justice of Nevis in the Leeward Islands but returned to Bettiscombe around 1800. A legend grew up around a skull in Bettiscombe House that it was that of a faithful old black slave bought by Pinney in 1765 and named Bettiscombe—that is, the master brought the skull home to the place after which the skull's owner had been named. Further legends became attached to it, such as the screaming of the skull if moved, that death would visit the house were the skull moved and so on. Rodney Legg, in *A Guide to Dorset Ghosts*, quotes the findings of a professor of Human and Comparative Anatomy, Royal College of Surgeons, who wrote in 1963 that it was the skull of a female aged between twenty-five and thirty years, a normal European skull and not negroid. Legg adds that it was probably dug from some barrow on a west Dorset hill. So much for another much-embroidered legend.

Monmouth's Rebellion comes up again and again in so much to do with Dorset people and Dorset history. In passing, having spoken of Azariah Pinney supporting Monmouth, it is worth pointing out that although it was workmen mostly who were hanged or transported in the vicious retribution that followed, it was not a Peasants' Revolt. With young Pinney and other West Country gentlemen on Monmouth's side was a young man called Daniel Foe, about twenty-five, with considerable experience of the London hosiery trade, who fought for the Duke at Sedgemoor. Forty years later the young man had not only become an old man but was now Daniel Defoe, a notorious writer and pamphleteer, much-travelled, frequently arrested and bankrupt and sometimes in hiding. The first volume of Defoe's *Tour through the whole island of Great Britain* was published in 1724, and in it he wrote of "Lime, the town particularly made famous by the landing of the Duke of Monmouth, and his unfortunate troop, in the time of King James II, of which I need say nothing, the history of it being so recent in the memory of so many living." Pope's 'worthy man my Foe'!

A mile from Bettiscombe is Racedown, also a Pinney house that was built during the last quarter of the eighteenth century,

with three broad bays and three storeys below a parapet, in red
brick. It stands high on the ridge that rises to Pilsdon. William
and Dorothy Wordsworth lived here in 1795-7, and Coleridge
often came over to visit them from Nether Stowey until he per-
suaded them to live closer to him—they moved to Alfoxton in
Somerset on 14th July 1797, the eighth anniversary of the outbreak
of the French Revolution in which Wordsworth had put so much
faith and which by now had cast him into disillusion and depres-
sion.

"Know then that I am going to live in Dorsetshire," Dorothy
had written to her friend Jane Marshall in September 1795,
". . . The house belongs to a Mr Pinney, a very rich merchant of
Bristol. . . . It is a very good house and in a pleasant situa-
tion. . . ." Dorothy was then twenty-four and William twenty-five.
They were short of money, and there was a somewhat confused arrangement regarding lending or leasing the house which
involved the Wordsworths taking into their care a small mother-
less boy, Basil Montagu, and some prospect of instructing a few
fee-paying pupils. It did not work out as they had expected, but
Dorothy took great pleasure in having a house of her own, although

> We were a whole month without servant, but now we have got one
> of the nicest girls I ever saw; she suits us exactly. . . . We wash
> once a month. I hire a woman, to whom I give ninepence for one
> day to wash, on the next we have got the clothes dried and on
> the third have finished ironing. It is the only time in which I have
> anything to do in the house, but then I am very active and very
> busy as you will suppose. I have been making Basil coloured frocks,
> shirts, slips, etc. and have had a good deal of employment in re-
> pairing his clothes and putting my brother's into order. We walk
> about two hours every morning—we have many very pleasant walks
> about us and what is a great advantage, the roads are of a sandy
> kind and are almost always dry. We can see the sea 150 or 200
> yards from the door. . . . We have hills which, seen from a distance
> almost take the character of mountains, some cultivated nearly to
> their summits, others in their wild state covered with furze and
> broom. These delight me the most as they remind me of our native
> wilds. . . . If you want to find our situation out, look in your maps
> for Crewkerne, Chard, Axminster, Bridport and Lime; we are nearly
> equi-distant from all those places.

The country around has changed very little from when Dorothy measured their walks with a 'perambulator' and watched for Coleridge to come loping over from Nether Stowey to read his poems aloud and listen to Wordsworth reading his. This period of less than two years at Racedown, which until 1790 had been called 'Pilsmarsh Lodge', was for Dorothy "dearest to my recollection upon the whole surface of the Island".

Thorncombe is on the border with Devon, in which it was included until 1842. The narrow road from the east crosses the Synder Brook, which runs north and into the Axe, by Lower Synderford Farm and a cottage called 'Saint Francis'. There is a strong sense and style of Devon here, with gushing streams, houses on steep hillsides and, at the same time, something of the feeling of being in the suburb of a country town. A vicar of Thorncombe fathered, in 1824 and 1827, two boys who grew up to be the Admirals Lord Hood and Lord Bridport.

A magnificent life-size brass of Sir Thomas Brook and his wife Joan, of 1437, was transferred intact from the floor at the east end of the nave of the old church to the top of a low tomb in the north chancel aisle of the present 1868 church. Sir Thomas is not in armour, which is rare for that date, but wears a wide-sleeved and fur-trimmed gown, with very pointed shoes on his feet, which lie on a hound. His wife is dressed in a long gown with a cloak over it, her hair in a mitred coiffure held by a jewelled net, and at her feet is a tiny lap-dog.

Forde Abbey was transferred from Devon to Dorset at the same time as Thorncombe, and it stands on the Dorset bank of the Axe, which waters nearly twenty acres of gardens and feeds its lakes. The Abbey began as a Cistercian House in 1148 and was much added to by Thomas Chard who became Abbot in 1521 and built himself a great hall and a porch that is a tower in itself. He also built himself extensive private quarters and then started work on the cloisters. Ironically, it was Chard's fate to be the last abbot, and it was he who had to surrender the Abbey to Henry VIII on 8th March 1539. It passed through the hands of several families as a private house and was fortunate in being bought in 1649 by Edmund Prideaux, a Devonshire man and Cromwell's Attorney-General. His ownership protected it from the 'slighting' that would almost certainly have been its fate. Prideaux em-

H

ployed Inigo Jones to plan the additions and changes he wanted made. Jones died before the work was completed in 1660, by which time Prideaux too had died. He was succeeded by his son, who entertained Monmouth on his first and peaceful journey through the West Country in 1680, five years before he landed at Lyme, when Prideaux was arrested as an accessory to the rebellion, committed to the Tower of London and kept there until he had paid a ransom of £15,000 to Judge Jeffreys.

Forde Abbey is open to the public on certain days of the year during the summer and on specific days in other seasons. It is as well to check that the house is open before going there, because, apart from the architectural grandeur of the exterior and the sumptuous interior, there are displayed in Inigo Jones's great saloon, at the top of a grand staircase with richly carved panels of foliage designs, the Mortlake Tapestries of the Raphael cartoons in the Victorian and Albert Museum.

A straight minor road leads south-west to Birdsmoor Gate, a crossroads just south of Racedown. A little to the north of here the Blackwater rises and after less than a mile flows west to the Axe and forms the border with Devon. To the south is a hill-ringed vale of which William Crowe wrote in 1786:

> There woods, there blooming orchards, there are seen
> Herds ranging, or at rest beneath the shade
> Of some wide-branching oak; there goodly fields
> Of corn, and verdant pasture, whence the kine
> Returning with their milky treasure home
> Store the rich dairy; such fair plenty fills
> The pleasant vale of Marshwood. . . .

6

In and Around the Marshwood Vale

EVEN by Dorset standards the Marshwood Vale has a fine collection of euphonious names, including Bluntshay, Cutty Stubbs, Shave Cross, Volehouse Farm, Whitchurch Canonicorum, Plenty House, Gummershaye Farm, Pomice Farm, Duckpool and Fishpond. To find the western frame of the Vale it is best to start from Birdsmoorgate, just south of Racedown, where the Wordsworths lived in brief contentment and where four roads meet, coming from Broadwindsor, Crewkerne, Forde Abbey, Axminster and Lyme Regis. And to what do these roads lead at Birdsmoorgate? To a place set high in the country, with trees on the road that climbs north-west, wonderful views in three other directions and a strategically stationed pub called 'The Rose and Crown'—a friendly inn this, which, being at the crossroads, gets news from all directions. One bitter and blustery day, when the cold found out corners of me that a breakfast should have filled six hours earlier, I sat before the wood fire to a plate of faggot, potatoes and peas and listened to a discussion of the chances of Bridport's football team, the Bees, in Saturday's game, the price of Russian timber, how a jack-knifed lorry became inarticulated on black ice in a Somerset village, and the details of a forthcoming traction-engine rally.

One mile south of Birdsmoorgate the B3165 reaches the edge of Devon and for nearly five miles runs along the border. Where the frontier is actually joined lies the village of Marshwood, sharing the Vale's name although perched on the very rim. Of the 'castle' here, a twelfth-century manor house, nothing remains but a few ivy-covered stumps of what may have been the walls of a chapel. The village is a straggle of unremarkable houses about the church of St Mary, which stands in a bleak and commanding position, the school tucked in protectively close to it, just off the road.

The tower is 1841, the rest of the church rebuilt in 1884 of flint and brown stone. Above the door in the tower are two good heads, one of a square-bearded man and the other of a woman with Medusa-like locks. The door is of Cambridge blue matchboarding, opened by a well-polished small brass knob that keeps company with a Yale lock. Inside the church the effect of clear airiness is pleasant. It is devoid of all ornament, not a single memorial tablet, and an almost Lutheran calm. The nave and chancel are undivided, and the lancets along the south arcade let in the light of the Vale's wide sky to the south. The roof is steep-pitched, well-slated and heavy-eaved, planned to withstand the sou'westerlies. If it had to be thatched, however, Joy and Harold Poynton, the Marshwood thatchers, would do it—the only husband and wife thatching team I know of in Dorset.

The view from the churchyard is over the whole of the Marshwood Vale, the sea seen through a gap in the hills and to the west the Devon landscape, beech and bracken and black patches where fire has struck in summer. The floor of the valley is scattered with white or pale stone farms and black-and-white Friesian cattle, with the lavender hills as background. On a day in late November I felt the bite of the sou'westerly from Lyme Bay that bustled the red roses blooming on a sturdy bush by a grave: Crowe's two seasons momentarily fused into one.

The little school, built in 1842, that faces the west door of the church, is attractive in its grey stone and architectural unobtrusiveness. It is a functional building, with a quiet style of its own, too early in time for the Victorians to get there and raise a highly-decorated establishment for the improvement of the minds of the children of the labouring class, the design matching in spirit the interminable Scripture classes, prayer-clasped hands and small bowed heads to which the chanting of multiplication tables came as a relief as sweet as madrigals.

Across the main road the view into Devon shows a land less low-lying and regular than Dorset's Marshwood Vale. Just over the border to the south-west is Lambert's Castle, an Iron Age fort which has never been excavated and now belongs to the National Trust. At the southern extremity of the same spur of high land and a mile inside Dorset is Coney's Castle, a univallate Iron Age fort, also unexcavated, apart from the gravel-workings. It is thought to have been Egbert's camp when he fought the Danes in AD 833.

Coney's Castle, Lambert's Castle, Pilsdon Pen and Lewesdon Hill are the hills that dominate the Vale from the north and north-west. The Vale is drained by the River Char which rises on Pilsdon Pen and is joined by another stream from Lewesdon and a dozen more rivulets during its journey of about eight miles to the sea at Charmouth.

Between Lambert's Castle and Coney's Castle on a south-western flank of the high ground is a small hamlet called Fishpond, with a church that looked like a little mountain chapel when I first walked through the village and as snow covered the hills around and the sun was low in a steely blue sky. Built in 1854, it has undergone changes since I first saw it in the bitter early months of 1963. A fine slate floor was laid in the chancel end in that year, and some new, very clear window glass in an abstract design was put in in 1967. Towering over this simple and peaceful little church is a gigantic pylon, whose proximity arouses all manner of reflections and makes one wonder if the invaluable and inevitable march of 'energy' could not have made a slight detour at this point to avoid the effect of bullying brutality.

Monkton Wyld is another village that sits on the western rim of the Vale I have seen it described as recalling the remoter parts of Surrey and, again, as being on a wooded hillside of 'Nordic gloom'. There is certainly none of the hard and remote and self-sufficient feeling of the villages on the high ridges; houses of varying kinds and in many different architectural styles are hidden behind discreet hedges, and there is perhaps a hint of laurel and rhododendron among the ubiquitous beeches. The former rectory, built around 1848, is now a school, a pleasing piece of Early Victorian Gothic with a number of modern additions by R. C. Carpenter. Carpenter was also responsible for the church of St Andrew, built in 1848–9 in Decorated style of flint (certainly not found in the Marshwood Vale), whose central tower has a spire.

Those early Victorians really let themselves go in the interior. There is a fine oak and painted screen with well-made brass gates of good workmanship studded with glass spheres like the cats' eyes from the middle of a road—a bit Byzantine for a small country church. The Communion-rail is decorated with brass bracelets studded with more marbles, this time from gingerbeer bottles, and the brass is turned on itself like the end of a shepherd's crook. There are gigantic brass candlesticks and so much brass throughout this church that Carpenter must have had a reliable full-time cleaner in mind.

There are five good Victorian windows at Monkton Wyld, original and striking portraits of the apostles looking for once like men who worked and walked, sailed and caught fish.

About half a mile from the A35, which makes the Devon–Dorset border here, is a small stone and thatched house called Elsdon's Farm. In 1902 a plaque was set in the wall to state that Charles II stayed in the house on 22nd September 1651. In his scamperings around West Dorset, weighed down by the price on his head, Charles was not only lucky to keep it on his shoulders but fortunate in always finding a pillow on which to lay it at night.

Wootton Fitzpaine and Catherston Leweston are the only two villages in this far western corner of Dorset which are not on the coast, like Lyme Regis and Charmouth. The blue clay of the floor of the Vale was always a waterlogged problem that inhibited the forming of villages, but there was also a difficulty facing settlers on the coast here. Where the clay occurs on the seaboard, it has been easily eroded by the sea, and other soils slip off it on the cliffs. That is how it became a fossil-hunter's paradise, and it was on this part of the coast that Mary Anning, starting out at twelve years old in 1811, liberated from the rock that thirty-foot-long fish-lizard, the ichthyosaurus, which is now in the Natural History Museum in Kensington.

There is not much of Wootton Fitzpaine, but Charmouth is encroaching fast on what there is, bungalows marching towards stone cottages, and Catherston Leweston is now almost a continuation of Charmouth, though very much a village in its own right. It has a manor house that was carefully constructed in Tudor style in 1887 of warm cider-coloured stone, and a church of 1858 that is built of polygonal pieces of blue lias, carefully cut and running through shades of light grey and fawn, giving it a shimmering texture.

The village that can claim to be the capital of the Vale of Marshwood is Whitechurch or Whitchurch Canonicorum. It is the capital but not the centre, which is undoubtedly Shave Cross: in this part of Dorset it is said that, if you ask the way in Marshwood Vale, the directions always begin with "Go to Shave Cross and . . .".

The second part of Whitchurch Canonicorum's name comes from the time when it was divided between the Canons of Salisbury and Wells. King Alfred left the village to his son Ethelward, and William the Conqueror gave the living to his chaplain, Guntard.

There is more to the whiteness in the first part of the name than the white stone of the interior of the church of St Candida and St Cross. Candida is otherwise 'St Wite' or 'Wita', but little is known about her. It has been suggested that she was St Blanche of Brittany or a Saxon woman killed during a Danish raid. Her shrine, in the Early English north transept, is thirteenth century, a plain stone chest with a Purbeck marble top. There are three oval holes in the front of the tomb, through which diseased limbs could be thrust into the interior by pilgrims; articles of clothing belonging to those too sick to come in person were also put there to lie under the bones of the saint. And St Wite's bones are there —or at least some of the bones and teeth of a small woman of about forty years of age. They were found in a lead casket during repairs to the inner stone coffin in 1900. The lid of the casket was inscribed *"Hic Reqiesct Reliqie Sce Wite"* ("Here lie the remains of St Wite"). It is one of the few churches in England to possess the relics of its own saint. Although so little is known about the saint, her feast day is celebrated on 3rd October. There is St Candida's Well at Morcombelake, and the wild periwinkles on Stonebarrow Hill over towards the sea are called 'St Candida's eyes'.

But there is much more to St Wite than her bones and traditions. Her church is very much alive, and I recall a Palm Sunday parade through the village when a group of children led a furry donkey called 'Melba' who carried her thirteen years with agile dignity as she preceded the bishop.

For the first time in this book the coast of Dorset is reached, one of the most beautiful coastlines in England, over seventy miles long and vaunting Golden Gap, 619 feet, the highest point on the South Coast. On the border with Devon is Lyme Regis, enfranchized by Edward I in 1279 and thus one of the oldest boroughs in England. Lyme Regis is a proud and lovely town with a long and often turbulent history. It was never a village.

Charmouth, three miles to the east, is principally a long street set in the valley of the Char between the hills, of Regency elegance and bow-windowed poise shared with Lyme Regis. It is half a mile from the sea and from that "sweet retired bay, beached by dark cliffs, where fragments of low rock amongst the sands make it the happiest spot for watching the flow of the tide; for sitting in unwearied contemplation", so dear to Jane Austen. But that sweet retired bay has seen violence too. In 833 the Danes came in thirty-five ships and carried out fierce raiding and forced hard fighting, in which they drove Egbert and his men inland. They left the coast alone for seven years, and when they came back, in 840, it was defended by King Ethelwulf; once more the Danes were forced to sail away.

It was here that Charles II came and waited for the Lyme Regis skipper, Stephen Limbry, to carry him off safely to France. When Limbry's wife got wind of the dangerous mission he had undertaken, she prevented him (some say she locked him in a room) from keeping his appointment. Charles, travelling as servant 'William Jackson' to an eloping couple, played by Lord Wilmot and Juliana Coningsby, stayed at the 'Queen's Arms'. Suspicions were aroused when an ostler noticed that the horses were shod 'Worcester fashion', and the parson, Bartholomew Wesley or Westley (great-great-grandfather of John Wesley), is reputed to have said to the landlady at 'The Queen's Arms': "How now, Margaret . . . Charles Stuart lay at your house last night and kissed you as he went so that now you cannot be but a maid of honour,"—to which Margaret answered, "If I believed it was the king, as you say it was, I would think the better of my lips all the days of my life."

The parson went to the magistrate, and the magistrate dallied. The ostler went to the military at Lyme Regis, and they did not dally, but by now Charles had got away to Bridport and was on his way to Trent for the second time.

'The Queen's Arms', now with an early-nineteenth-century front, was originally a medieval building that got its name from Catherine of Aragon staying there in 1501; some years ago her badge in plaster was discovered at the back of the house. She was apparently not in as much of a hurry as Charles was in the next century.

The old road from Charmouth to Morcombelake used to run to the south of the present A35, nearer to the sea and along the flank of Stonebarrow Hill which is now National Trust land. Travelling in the opposite direction, in 1716, John Gay wrote:

> Through Bridport's stony lanes our route we take
> And the proud steep descend to Morcomb's Lake.

Not so steep as Hutchins found Charmouth Down a few years later when he was "surprised at the Descent of ye Hill, a steeper than which I never travelled down. It is ye Plinlimon of Dorsetshire."

John Gay was wrong in splitting the village's name into two components but right in omitting the first 'e' which has so often intruded. There is no lake here, and the elements of the name are *mor* ('barren land, swampy ground'), *cumb* ('valley') and *lacu* ('stream'), all from Old English. It is sometimes spelled in two words in guide-books, and there are stories of summer visitors with hopeful-faced children asking if boats can be hired on the lake, and where is the lake? More often than not, it is not mentioned at all in guide-books because it is primarily a discreet and mostly hidden settlement for those who have retired from the wage-earning battlefield to nurse their scars in houses built along a web of little lanes on the southward-facing slopes of Hardown Hill.

On the other side of the village is Chardown Hill. Hardown and Chardown used to be known together as 'Gollops'—presumably following the name of the landowner, as does Colmer's Hill at Symondsbury further eastward along the coast. But whatever the names of these hills, the lanes between and around them were on the old smugglers' routes, and Morcombelake's Five Bells Inn, burned down and vanished now, had a deep hole under a window-seat for hiding the contraband spirits. But even if the spirits have gone—the pub is there and open at certain times in case of dire need, there is the pure water of St Candida's Well which is said to be a certain cure for sore eyes, and, furthermore, 'Dorset knobs', Morcombelake's special version of the staff of life, which are spherical and about the size of table-tennis balls. On the seaward side of the main road is Moores' famous pink-washed bakery, where Dorset knobs have been made since Samuel Moores established his business here in 1880.

The present owner is Keith Moores, great-grandson of Samuel, who now bakes some half-dozen kinds of biscuits, including Dorset shortbread and Dorset Easter Biscuits, as well as the famous knobs, which he bakes during the slacker season at the beginning of the year. This restriction is because they have to be baked three times, which takes ten hours and is uneconomical. Although the most modern Swedish ovens are used now in place of the old steam ovens, the knobs retain their original distinctive consistency and flavour which Thomas Hardy used to enjoy with Blue Vinny cheese and a glass of burgundy.

The bakery is open to visitors Monday–Friday, and there is a shop where knobs and biscuits and a variety of craft-products may be bought.

Two miles east of Morcombelake is Chideock, divided in two by the A35 that forms its main street. In the Domesday Book it was spelled 'Cidihoc', and it has been given in many ways since but however it is spelled, it is pronounced 'Chiddick'.

Chideock lies in a hollow of the downs and has its own little stream called 'Wynreford', 'Winniford' and on some maps 'the Chid'—obviously a back-formation from the name of the village. It rises on Hardown Hill and after running due east for almost a mile turns due south through North Chideock, past the manor and the site of the castle, to find its way to the shingle shore at Seatown.

Chideock is filled with well-built and well-maintained cob and sandstone cottages, some of them thatched. There is colour everywhere in the wash on the house walls and in the gardens, which seem to have something in flower throughout the year. The Castle Inn was rebuilt after a fire at the end of the last century—it is curious how many pubs were burned down in this part of the world; perhaps it was because their flash-point had been lowered by having been soaked in so much French brandy through

the centuries that they took fire readily at the flare of a match,
like Christmas puddings. But 'The George' never caught alight
and stands there as much as it did when it was built at the end
of the seventeenth century. The Clock House Hotel is an old house
with a new licence, and Chideock House Hotel goes back to
Elizabethan times and has a priest's hole. This was always staunch
Roman Catholic country, and it was in the main hall of this house
that the Chideock Martyrs were tried. Up Ruins Lane, to the
north of the village, stood Chideock Castle, built by Sir John de
Chideock at the end of the fourteenth century. Taken and re-
taken during the Civil War, it was eventually 'slighted' by the
Cromwellians, and nothing now remains but the traces of a moat
and, standing on a mound, a later great wooden cross to the
memory of the four martyrs who perished in the reign of Elizabeth and a fifth who was killed in 1642.

Religious wars and religious faith marked Chideock heavily.
Ruins Lane, leading to the Catholic martyrs' memorial, is also
called 'Meeting House Lane', but the little Methodist Chapel that
gave it its second name is closed now. And close by is a Roman
Catholic church, dedicated to Our Lady of the Martyrs and St
Ignatius, built in 1870–72 in a Romanesque yet highly original
style by the local landowner Charles Weld to his own designs.
The Welds were a Catholic family who came to Chideock in
1802, succeeding generations of Roman Catholic Arundells, and
they built Chideock Manor in 1810. There are paintings by Charles
Weld in the church, and he also carved the capitals and a Crucifixion in the wall of the Weld mausoleum and was responsible
for the paintings in the mortuary chapel in the Catholic burial-
ground next to the Church of England graveyard.

Church of England St Giles is basically of the fifteenth century,
restored in 1888 by Crickmay, who also built the chancel. In the
Arundell Chapel, close to the organ, is a black marble tomb with
an early-sixteenth-century effigy of a knight in plate armour who
is said to be either Sir John Chideock or Sir John Arundell.

A narrow road runs from the A35 to Seatown, less than a mile
away. Here the Wynreford makes a small pool before losing itself
in the shingle. There are a few cottages and a pub, 'The Anchor',
that now stands uncomfortably close to the cliffs which, in my
time, have carried away a succession of storage-buildings and

holiday huts. It was at Seatown that a Whit Monday Fair was held where furmity used to be eaten. Many people now must know of furmity through the television dramatization of Thomas Hardy's novel *The Mayor of Casterbridge*: it is a kind of *muesli* composed of wheat, raisins and currants, sweetened with sugar and, as Michael Henchard discovered when he got drunk on it and sold his wife, often laced with smuggled 'speerits'. *Dorset Up Along and Down Along* records that at Seatown on a Whit Monday "an old woman living in the cottage next the inn dispensed it at a ha'penny a plate." And Mrs Goodenough in Hardy's novel: "Just a thought o' rum in it?—smuggled, you know—say two penn'orth—'twill make it slip down like cordial!"

West Bay is the port of Bridport, for long a separate place. The harbour here is entirely artificial, first made in 1740–44, reconstructed in 1824 and repaired at frequent intervals ever since. It is, in fact, a harbour built not on a bay but at the estuary of the small River Brit between a break in the cliffs, yet it is still mainly a mere indentation on the open stretch of coast of Lyme Bay. The harbour has been here for a long time: Joan of Navarre arrived here in 1403 on her way to marry Henry IV. Nearly five centuries later the railway came here too, from Bridport and Maiden Newton, but the track has been torn up now.

West Bay in winter is much as it has always been—the thatched 'Bridport Arms' on the quay, 'The George' on the green, the little harbour-basin almost dry when the tide is out, the surprising terrace of five tall houses with a tile-hung mansard roof at three levels. This was built about 1885 by E. S. Prior but looks as if it had been towed over from a Norman or Breton port. In point of fact, because of the French look this building gives to West Bay, it was chosen as a training-area during the preparations for the Dieppe Raid in 1942.

Through the year my visits to West Bay are just after the sun comes up over Portland way, buying fish from my old friend Des Gape and discussing the West Dorset news—such as the recurring question of shortfall sewage from Bridport, how 'Johnny Frenchman' has lifted too many lobsters too close in, how Peter Northover's spick and span newly refitted boat got her anchor chain caught in the harbour so that she could not rise with the tide and stayed on the bottom to be flooded along with all Peter's stores and fishing gear. But during the summer West Bay puts on the air of being a holiday resort, which it is not in its bones, despite the 'attractions', new car-parks, holiday villas and directions to toilets. West Bay as a 'resort' is as incongruous as an old fisherman on whose head someone has stuck a carnival cap.

Ropemaking has been Bridport's principal industry since the thirteenth century, and the Bridport rope used by the hangman was called a 'Bridport dagger'. The town is full of interesting buildings: the fourteenth- or fifteenth-century Chantry in South Street, the Friends' Meeting House of 1697, the Wesleyan Chapel of 1838 in South Street and the Unitarian Chapel of 1794 that lies at the end of its garden off East Street and Downe Hall of 1789 in its little park on rising land in the north of the town.

Going westwards out of Bridport a conical hill topped with half a dozen pine trees fills the horizon at the end of West Street. It is such a sudden and amazing hill, too large to be man-made and yet in that landscape like something strayed from a Chinese painting. It is called 'Colmer's Hill', after the owner of the land about it. Having been intrigued by its shape and position for many years, I eventually set out to climb to the top. It was a windy day in February with a crust of ice on the deep, cow-trodden mud in the gateways at the foot of the hill and a dusting of snow on the frost-browned grass of the upper slopes. A rickety wire fence enclosed the trees on the summit, and, as I bent to get underneath it, two things struck me simultaneously: first, that the magnificent view of Lyme Bay had been blotted out by heavy snow borne on a gale-force wind, and, secondly, that in the centre of the skeletal copse there was a dark column that seemed to move among the snowflakes.

I abandoned looking beyond the edge of the hill, which was like looking out of an aeroplane window in thick cloud, and went to investigate the partially-moving shadow. I found this to be composed in equal parts of a concrete triangulation-point and a duffel coat containing a human being. As I came close, the duffel coat turned around, and out of its hood and above a blue scarf were two eyes, tear-rimmed and looking out of a jet black face. To me the view was not essential, but he was a student surveyor and had been trying to get a fix on Thorncombe Beacon when the view of the coast turned to an instant blizzard in the face.

Symondsbury, set between Colmer's Hill and another rounded hill, gives the feeling of being geographically well-protected as well as having been thoroughly cared for through the centuries by the local landowners. Most of the buildings are of golden stone, some thatched and some stone-roofed. 'The Ilchester Arms' remains obviously the development from the original sixteenth-century building. It too is of stone and very sturdily thatched. As far back as I can recall, it has been run by members of the same family, and it is the kind of inn where there is good rough cider and pink and blue pint-pots for the regulars, and where a drink is drawn on an order given by a raised eyebrow.

The fourteenth- to fifteenth-century church has a barrel-roof made by the shipwrights of West Bay. It was plastered over for many years but brought to light again in 1920, when it was cleaned and renovated by Symondsbury carpenters. The whole village worked to renovate the church, giving time and material and expert workmanship free. The choir and clergy stalls, for instance, were carved with beasts, birds, fishes and flowers by parishioners. The roof is of slate, but had it been of thatch, it would certainly have been renovated by the Thomas family, renowned Symondsbury thatchers. The story of Symondsbury church is given in a little book by Mary Johnson who also illustrated it and donated the proceeds to church funds. It can be bought in the church.

The Manor House is seventeenth century but much restored, and the Old Rectory dates from about 1730 and had two wings added in the early-nineteenth century. With its verandah and the trellis supports and the trees that crowd the garden, it has an air of having once been in a Regency novel or at least of having been the home of someone who wrote them. As far as I know, there are no literary connections, but the Wordsworths, I feel, would have liked it and the proximity of Colmer's Hill.

Raymond's Charity School, opposite the church, was built in yellow stone in 1868. The Victorian designers really let rip, and the result is certainly a spirited one.

At Salway Ash a farmer raises Dorset sheep, and the *Bridport News* once published a photograph in March of a pair of lambs being held by the farmer's daughter, just home from school and called, musically but unDorsetlike, Tinkle de Greef. At Broadoak is C. J. Creed's printing-press which undertakes all kinds of work, including John Eastwood's local guide-books. Mr Creed showed me round his compact and well-laid-out press, where three Gutenbergs were humming and clacking away beside the narrow lane.

The Brit rises near Beaminster and flows through Bridport to the sea at West Bay. The A3066 road runs to the east of it to Beaminster, and the only village actually on the main road and mid-way between Bridport and Beaminster is Melplash.

A family called More or Moor lived at Melplash Court, an early-seventeenth-century house (which has since been gabled, added to and restored). One James More was killed during the Wars of the Roses on the road to Slape, a nearby farm and manor, and a Sir James More was Sheriff of Dorset during the reign of Henry VIII and is said on one occasion to have ordered the doors of Dorchester Prison to be thrown open (he was either drunk or mad at the time) and let out all the sheep-stealers, robbers, brigands and assassins held there. This brought down trouble from Henry VIII, and he was only saved by Lord Paulet. Hutchins recorded, but produced no evidence for, his story, that ". . . he was obliged to solicit a pardon by means of William, Lord Paulet [afterwards Marquess of Winchester], on condition he should marry one of his daughters and co-heiresses to Paulet's second son, Lord Thomas of Corsington, Somerset." Melplash Court was part of this daughter's inheritance, and it then passed to the Paulet family, who rebuilt the house at the beginning of the seventeenth century. A circular pigeon-house of that time survives to the west of the house.

Early in the nineteenth century the vicar of Netherbury and Melplash was a Dr Bandinel. His son, James Bandinel, was Senior Translator to the Foreign Office, and he paid for a new church to be built at Melplash in memory of his father. It was designed by Benjamin Ferrey in the Norman style, with a high square crossing tower and in cruciform shape. Everything was carried out impeccably, including zigzag ornament, with only the hammer-beam roof a departure from the true Norman. Netherbury, less than two miles to the north, is a collection of stone houses built on both sides of the Brit off to the west of the Bridport–Beaminster road. There used to be mills along this valley, which processed flax for the Bridport nets and 'daggers'. At the bottom of the village is the bridge over the Brit, a bridge with a style of its own, having three totally dissimilar arches. The east span is the largest and is circular and serves the millrace; the centre one is a Gothic arch, and the west span is the smallest of the three and circular. The bridge was built in the seventeenth century, and the white-painted railings are supported from the original projecting coping stones.

Flax for the Bridport net and rope trade was grown all along the Brit Valley, and its cultivation brought about an ornithological comment by William Chafin in his *Cranbourn Chase* of 1818:

> Although Falconry had such a despotic sway for many ages, yet it was obliged to submit to Time, the destroyer of all things, and is now entirely neglected and gone by; and I question whether there is one reclaimed foreign hawk in the Western part of the kingdom; but, I believe, there may be a few English hawks annually trained in the neighbourhood of Bridport, in Dorsetshire, for the taking of Land-rails in the hemp and flax fields near that town, in which in some seasons they are plentiful.

Neither flax nor land-rail is plentiful now along the valley.

Parnham, close to Beaminster, was for three hundred years the seat of the Strode family. A Tudor house, it was altered in the eighteenth century, and again in 1810 by Nash. The south front we see today is entirely Nash. For some twenty years Parnham belonged to the National Association for Mental Health and was open on certain days in the summer to the public. Since 1976 it has been the John Makepeace School for Craftsmen in Wood—ten young students live and work there. When early in June 1978, Parnham was visited by the Duke of Edinburgh, it was decided to mark this visit by a Job-Creation Scheme project, which was to be the landscaping of the southern end of the house, providing work for young men who were unemployed.

The house, grounds and school are open to the public, and there could not be a better centre than Parnham, a house with a long history going back to about AD 1400 for the creation and display of work in wood of the very highest craftsmanship. Two scholarships are being offered, each worth £1,000, one for a graduate from a British school of art and the other for a student who has been born, is living or has been educated in Dorset. You

Cerne Abbas, looking up Abbey Street to Abbey Farm

Creech Grange Arch

Portland – the entrance to the Verne Prison across the
artificial ravine (1860-67)

Burton Bradstock

Burton Bradstock

Entering Abbotsbury on the Bridport Road

Abbotsbury

St Catherine's Chapel, Abbotsbury

Abbotsbury Tithe Barn

Little Bredy

Little Bredy, where the Bride rises in the grounds of
Bride Head House

get the feeling that something is going on; something is being learned all the time; something functional and artistic is being created by each of those who live and work there in surroundings created by artists and craftsmen of the past.

7

Pigs and Eagles, Monks and Giants

WEST MILTON lies a mile to the west of Powerstock and between three and four miles to the south-east of Beaminster, off the A3066 that runs down to Bridport. The 'West' distinguishes this Milton from Milton Abbas and Milton-on-Stour. It is set snugly in a narrow, deep and lush valley on the Mangerton stream, or 'beck' as I have seen it written on a notice in the village. The bridge across the Mangerton had to be rebuilt in 1970 and very well done it was, because although the repairs were made in concrete, a facing of stone matching the original was added. The same care was taken with Dinkie's Bridge that crosses the Winscombe Water half a mile along the road to Bridport.

The church of St Mary Magdalene was built by Crickmay a century ago, to replace the old church of which nothing but the fifteenth- to sixteenth-century tower remains, some of the material having gone into the building of a school at Powerstock. But what a setting the old tower has! On the left is a house with mullioned windows, and straight ahead is the church tower, standing alone on a greensward except for some tilting or near-buried tombstones and an old yew tree. Across the fields, beyond the tower and the barn that stands on the left, is Eggardon Hill, bare and majestic. Looking in the opposite direction towards the village, the view is of leafy hills and sunken roads.

The water-mill at West Milton became a private house, which I knew in various seasons and aspects when it belonged to Kenneth and Betty Allsop. There was once a great summer party there—lights everywhere, the scent of strawberries and wine, a striped marquee and guests sitting around the stone-bordered pool which, when it was emptied later, turned out to contain an amazing variety of fish. But I also remember the house and garden in customary calm, as when the first snowdrops were out and a friendly donkey greeted me as another old ass, or discussing the habits of peacocks which reminded me to tell Kenneth of the board-clapping sound that I had once heard in a marshy meadow below Chilcombe Hill: I was sure it was a stork, a bird which I had often heard but never in England. That wooden clacking is a singular sound, but, as I never caught sight of the bird, I could not prove that it was in fact a stork. Kenneth thought it might have escaped from some gardens or had crossed over from Europe at the time I heard it, in early July of the previous year.

It was at West Milton that Kenneth Allsop wrote, among his many other books, the essays that were gathered together under the title *In the Country*. They were mostly about this part of Dorset, and the collection was published just after his death at West Milton in 1973.

King John comes yet again into the story of Dorset villages, building a hunting-lodge in the middle of Poorstock Forest in 1205. Perhaps King Athelstan hunted here too, and it is said that Powerstock (or Poorstock—both spellings are used) Castle, now a green mound, belonged to him. And long before Athelstan (AD 895–939) the Durotriges, the tribe that flourished in Dorset before the Roman invasion and survived through the occupation, were here.

The church stands on a knoll, overlooking most of the village in which the buildings are set on lesser knolls. The chancel has the finest Norman arch in Dorset, decorated with zigzags, lozenges and rope tracery. The south doorway, which may have been brought from some grander ecclesiastical building that stood somewhere else, is late-fifteenth century, and on either side of the doorway stands a figure in a niche. One is crowned and bearded and carries a book in one hand, a staff in the other. The second figure, on the right, is that of a young woman, also wearing a crown. She carries a loaf of bread in each hand and has a small child standing at her side, holding on to her dress. No-one seems to know who they are supposed to be, these two appealing figures in golden Ham Hill stone, but it has been suggested that the male figure is King Wenceslas and the female St Elizabeth, Princess of Hungary, noted for her charitable concern for children during her short life—she died in 1231 at the age of twenty-four.

Also much concerned with children was the Reverend Thomas Sanctuary, vicar of Powerstock for forty-one years from 1841. He was responsible for building, in 1848, Powerstock's first school, which is now a private house. In 1876 he had another school built, and it was into this that the relics of the old church at West Milton were incorporated. This school is now the village hall.

Two miles north-west of Powerstock five roads meet at a beautiful and lonely spot crowned by pines and a signpost with its name within the Dorset County Council circle—Mount Pleasant. Just below the crest of the hill the road to Powerstock passes below a grassy slope that rises to bracken and a line of spruce at the top: a place for wild strawberries, magpies and heath butterflies, and a view across woodlands falling away to Gray's Farm and beyond to Poorstock Common, a damp and jungly forest of gnarled oaks that in summer keep the light down to a yellowish green above the tangle of rushes, horsetail and brambles below. When, in 1971, Kenneth Allsop found a wide metalled road here, he began writing letters, telephoning, talking, obtaining the support of the Dorset Naturalists' Trust and *Dorset* magazine, to find out exactly what was happening. One hundred acres, as a result of this vigilance, were leased in perpetuity to the Trust, but the erosion of the Common had been noticed and notified only just in time. On the edge of the Common is Wytherstone Farm, a house of the seventeenth century, with a barn nearby that is probably of the sixteenth century. The front door of the house has an immense and beautifully carved shell hoodmould.

There is some confusion about certain Dorset villages because of the profusion of Winterbornes, Piddles and Tarrants. There are also Mappowder, Mappercombe and two Mappertons, the one north of Powerstock and the other half way between Bere Regis and Wimborne Minster. Mappercombe Manor is less than a mile south of Powerstock, and parts of the front of the house date from the fifteenth century with additions in the seventeenth century. Mappowder is the village in the centre of Dorset already described.

The Mapperton near Powerstock is a sixteenth- to seventeenth-century manor house with a small hamlet nearby. At the end of a long avenue leading to it, the house and the chapel attached to it are on the left—that is to say, the avenue does not lead to the front of the house. The courtyard in front of the house is entered between stone gate-piers surmounted by great eagles with spread wings. On the right, and facing the courtyard and the doorway, are two parallel stable-blocks.

The house was built in the reign of Henry VII, but, due to later changes and enlargements, its present appearance is that of the mid-seventeenth century. The interior has Elizabethan plaster ceilings, seventeenth- and eighteenth-century panelling and Jacobean overmantels of vast proportions.

The little church of All Saints is actually the south range of the house. It was built in 1704 and restored in 1846, and although I had seen it often from the outside, I had never been inside until one day Victor Montagu took us into the church directly from his house. The impact was startling—a few steep steps from the stone-flagged floor of a panelled room and one was in the chancel. The walls are pale blue, the carpet a lively red. The Communion-rail is eighteenth century, and the nave windows are filled with glass of the sixteenth, seventeenth and eighteenth centuries. Some pieces are heraldic, and some are medallions, including a Salutation, a Prodigal Son and a shepherdess and her sheep. This glass was brought from Europe by Richard Brodrepp or Broadrepp, a lord of the manor who died in 1737. There is a fine standing monument to him by Peter Scheemakers, and in the tower is a seat with a panelled back inscribed 'Ri. Brodrepp, 1711' and a shield inscribed 'IR'.

In the deep glen to the east of the house are the formal gardens in which there is a seventeenth-century summerhouse and a series of stepped ponds. At one end, an orangery was built about ten years ago which fits in perfectly with the atmosphere of the house and garden. Across the valley many trees have been lost to disease and many damaged by heavy snow.

Mapperton village, no more than a hamlet now, was deserted during the Great Plague of the 1660s. There is a lane nearby with an oak tree at the entrance to it. It is called 'the Posy Tree', for during the Plague posies were laid there to ward off the sickness that had killed those whose bodies were carried down that lane for burial. The present tree is a descendant of Posy Tree I.

Once upon a time there was a stream in Dorset called 'the Toller'. Somehow the name became subordinate to one particular feature of its course: from *hoc*, Old English 'sharp bend in a stream', it became 'the Hooke'. But Toller Down Gate remains as a crossroads where the A356 from Maiden Newton to Crewkerne crosses the B3163 from Beaminster to Evershot. Toller Down stands over eight hundred feet above sea-level. Towards Beaminster down the B3163, just before Dirty Gate (the origin of whose name I neither know nor care to guess at) and well nigh impossible to get to, is Toller Whelme. Here we get to 'the riverspring of the Toller'. The manor house is one in which I should like to live, not only because it is away from the main road and is difficult to find but because I love its appearance, mainly seventeenth century and incorporating a porch-doorway of *c*1470, its mullioned windows and the thick thatch of the roof.

Toller Whelme is in the parish of Corscombe, and the next Toller village is almost four miles downstream—if you can find the Toller-cum-Hooke stream at any time outside of the wettest winter. This is Toller Porcorum, the only Dorset village name in pig Latin. The name has gone back and forth between English and Latin, but the pigs remain. It was known as 'Swynesthoire' in 1259, as 'Tolre Porcorum' in 1340 and as 'Swyntoller' in 1457, and so on through the centuries, but those who live thereabouts have always called the village 'Great Toller'.

The font in the parish church is often described as a medieval bowl set on a Roman altar pillar or on a twelfth- or thirteenth-century capital, but I once met a local architect in the church who pointed out to me that the base of the font is the wrong shape to have been a capital; he thinks that it has always been part of a font. Although the ram's head on one side and the sign of the cross on the other are both recognizable, what are the other two symbols? "One ram's head and symbols between" is all that the RCHM will hazard. One of the symbols is, to me, totally baffling, but the other has more than a mere likeness to the phallus of the Cerne Giant.

A charity-board hanging in the church states that George Browne, on 24th January 1774, set aside money to be divided among the industrious poor in Porcorum and Fratrum. (He also endowed a school for the poor children of the parishes where they could learn the three Rs.) The board is curious in shape, being made up of planks that are broader at one end than at the other —obviously offcuts of coffin-lids.

The village of Toller Porcorum received an injection of modernity when the railway arrived about a century ago. There was a small flurry of Victorian building, which remains, together with some later refurbishing of old houses and new buildings, neat and solid, giving an air that Toller Porcorum is lived in by people who work elsewhere. Now the railway has been put down after having snaked its inoffensive and useful way for a hundred years from Maiden Newton to Bridport and West Bay—put down like a grass-snake under the heel of the giant Unprofitability. Therefore an intrinsic and very important part of the newer houses is the garage.

Teresa Masters is a potter who lives at Manor House Farm. Her working time is limited because she is the farmer's wife and has two small children with an immense store of energy between them. A sign in the village takes you over a bridge and up to the farm, where there is a pottery showroom in the barn.

Straight up the side of the down behind Manor Farm is a white chalky track that leads to Kingcombe, one of the farms isolated in the 1962–3 snows. Cyril Groves farmed there then, and he gave me a very graphic description of how he and his family and stock were marooned for weeks. Now he farms North Eggardon, which is also pretty much on the edge of beyond—"Not as much as Kingcombe though," he said as we stood looking up towards the rocky ledges and bare top of Eggardon from his farmyard.

There is no direct road from Toller Porcorum to Toller Fratrum, but in dry weather there is a pleasant walk along the bank of the Frome or, now that the railway has gone, along the old track. By road, go to the A356, turn right towards Maiden Newton and take the first right again, where a signpost states unequivocally 'To Toller Fratrum only'. After passing under the fossilizing railway-bridge a vision of the Middle Ages faces you. The house, Little Toller Farm, is of grey stone flecked with gold, with stone-mullioned windows, pinnacles with heraldic designs, and a great central chimney-breast with a gable finial depicting a monkey holding a looking-glass, the whole topped by two high twisted chimney-stacks. To the right of the house is a thatched stable-range with Tudor windows, one carving of the Samways initials and crest and

another of a boy playing the bagpipes. This may have been the
refectory building before becoming stables.

From 1300 until the Dissolution of the Monasteries in 1539 the
Knights Hospitallers of St John of Jerusalem were established
here. In 1540 Toller Fratrum came to the Samways family of
Martinstown, who built the present manor house. It was John
Samways for whom his crest of a hammer held in a claw and the
letters I.S. were carved.

Immediately behind the stables is the little church of St Basil,
a rare dedication in western Europe, a plain, rectangular building
with a tiny bell-turret and mainly of the nineteenth century. Toller
Fratrum is set on a ledge of the downs, and the churchyard (frequently occupied by a ewe and her lamb who keep the grass
around the gravestones in good trim) has a view of wide extent
and beauty across the downs. There is a twelfth-century font
carved with human heads, some of them upside-down, and other
figures including a monster with two bodies. In the east wall of
the chancel, above the altar, is a stone fragment of St Mary Magdalene washing the feet of Christ, mid-eleventh century, of great
strength and power to move. The Communion-rail is eighteenth
century, and on either side of the west door, on the outside, are
medieval heads that look across to the refectory of the Brethren.

In another bowl of the downs is Wynford Eagle. The original
centre of this settlement consists of the manor farm, the church
and some cottages. There are few trees here although the grounds
of Wynford House, up the hill towards Compton Abbas, are well-
wooded, and it is easy to believe that one is in the foothills of
mountains—in the Brecon Beacons, for example.

Hutchins reported that 'Winfrod' was said to belong to Gilbert de Aquila, and the manor has belonged to 'the Honour of
the Eagle' since the time of William de Aquila, a Norman. The
eagle is physically very much in evidence, not only in the name of
the village on surrounding signposts but also in the great stone
eagle atop the three-storeyed porch-gable of the Manor House.
The date on the porch is 1630.

From 1551 to 1709 the manor was owned by the Sydenham
family. During the Civil War five Sydenhams fought for Parliament, including Thomas, who later took his medical degree at
Oxford and, with his commonsense approach, did much to banish

superstition from medical practice. He is recognized as the father of British clinical medicine and was called 'the British Hippocrates'. There is a memorial tablet to him high up the wall to the right just inside St James's Church, Piccadilly. His brother William commanded the Parliamentary forces in Dorset, and another brother was a member of Cromwell's Council.

The Sydenhams and Wynford Eagle parted company in 1709 in bizarre circumstances. A Sydenham, also called William, held an appointment that was equally bizarre—that of Squire of the Body to William III, which cannot have brought him much material return because he ran into debt and devised a ruse by which he could raise some money. This consisted of putting up his house as the prize to be won in a lottery while, at the same time, making a secret arrangement with a young kinswoman for her to win the house and estate, and then sell it back to him. She won, dishonestly of course, but refused to sell and brought house and land to the husband she was not slow to find. Sydenham and his two daughters were removed from the house only by force and were taken to Dorchester Gaol where the unfortunate William, self-petard-hoisted, died nine years later.

Treves called St Lawrence's Church, set up on the hillside overlooking Wynford Eagle manor, "a modern building of daring ugliness". In fact, it is a fairly inoffensive plain building of 1842 of the Church Commissioners' type, incorporating the Perpendicular chancel arch from an earlier building. Reset in the west wall is a Norman tympanum carved with two long-tailed monsters facing each other like spitting cats. In a semi-circle above them a worn inscription states 'Mahad delegele' and 'Alvi me feci[t]'. There is more than a hint of eagles here. Under the heading 'Eponymous', Lord Wynford of Wynford Eagle contributed a letter to *The Times* when there was a correspondence about village names, begun by a reference to Leighton Buzzard. Lord Wynford wrote:

> . . . There are seasonal martins in Martinstown, brothers in Toller Fratrum and pigs in Toller Porcorum. A saint is remembered in Sydling St Nicholas, and we have maidens in plenty in Maiden Newton. But alas, never a recorded sighting of an eagle in Wynford Eagle, unless of course one allows Mr Taylor's buzzards, which are, after all, of the genus Falconidae. These abound.

And indeed they do. I saw a magnificent pair of buzzards over the downs a mile along the left fork from Wynford Eagle, near Shatcombe Farm, a house much added to and modernized but of which the core is from the seventeenth century. Just beyond here the road turns to the right and joins the ridge road close to Eggardon at Two Gates. This steep ascent to the Roman road has been metalled in recent years (in case your map is out of date and merely presents a dotty track). But at the foot of the hill is a cul-de-sac to the left of the road, and there is the hamlet of West Compton or Compton Abbas West to distinguish it from the other Compton Abbas near Shaftesbury. This 'valley farm', which is what its name means, belonged to Milton Abbey. It is hard to believe that there was ever more here than a farm and some cottages, yet a church was built here, not, as one might think, in the Middle Ages but in 1867 by the ubiquitous Dorset architect John Hicks. The cottages are now in very good order, but the church is threatened by the encroaching tall hedges and trees, and from the road up the hill it invites speculation about ruins. West Compton, Compton Valence and Wynford Eagle are all tiny pockets of habitation in these bare downs, unexpected when you come upon them and agreeably isolated in feeling when you are in them.

Leaving the Dorchester–Bridport road just before reaching Winterborne Abbas when coming from the east or, rather, keeping straight on, because the now minor road is the old Roman road and leads along the tops of the treeless downs to Eggardon, there is below and off to the left or north of the road the village of Compton Valence, seven miles west of Dorchester. Steep banks down to the village are planted with flowering shrubs and flowers, and to arrive there from the bare downs when the first daffodils are out or when the lilac is in bloom is to step into another climate and landscape after the descent of less than a mile.

Here, perhaps more than anywhere else, there is that feeling of being in what I have just called a pocket of habitation in the downs. The tower of the church of St Thomas of Canterbury is fifteenth century, but the rest of the church is a very rare and successful essay in the Decorated style by Benjamin Ferrey in 1839–40. In an earlier century the former church had been rebuilt by the priest, Thomas Maldon, and there is a brass of about 1440 to remind us of him, nearly a foot long, showing him from the waist up in Mass vestments and with two wing-like scrolls sprouting from his shoulders. The inscriptions on them are difficult to read as they were under the feet of the roughshod faithful for centuries before being rescued and set into the walls of the nave.

Immediately north of the church is the manor house, dating from the early-seventeenth century with some modern extension. Compton Valence House, hidden among trees, which is the home of those generous people responsible for the flowers and shrubs on the roadside banks, was built as the rectory in 1872.

One early spring day, as I was standing near the telephone-kiosk outside Compton Valence Post Office, trying to decipher a telephone-number I had written down, I was startled by a brisk nip in the calf of my right leg. I turned to snarl—or kick if necessary—at the impertinent mongrel and saw instead a robust cock-pheasant which first glared back at me and then gave another hearty peck. When I shouted and clapped my hands at him, he lowered his head and prepared to launch a serious attack. I made a craven retreat into the kiosk, and after he had given a few admonitory raps on the glass panes, he strutted off across the road. A black-and-white cat sitting in the wispy sunshine and minding its own business at the edge of the road moved off sharply, acknowledging who was cock of that particular walk. I doubt if this formidable bird fell to a local gun.

The road makes a circle through Compton Valence and climbs to the top of the down again, and that is the only way in and out of the village. In another year and another season I met a band of young men standing on the back of an ancient lorry, September afternoon sunshine gilding their horns that were blowing 'Honeysuckle Rose' to an audience of burdock and thistles.

This other end of the road does not join the Roman road again on its way to Eggardon but comes into yet another leading to Maiden Newton. Two miles along, it joins that from Wynford Eagle and then immediately links with the A356 by two prongs on either side of a triangle island of old brick and flint buildings at a point marked on the signpost as 'Tollerford'.

You could be excused, if you were in a hurry, for thinking that Maiden Newton was nothing much but a bent village street, some Victorian houses and a brick pub in green Devenish brewers' uniform, ending in a not uncommon way between petrol-pumps and

council houses. There is a lot more to Maiden Newton than that,
however. It is worth stopping there for a little while to look
round. The Castle Hotel has a tiny tower by a bridge over the
Toller, or Hooke, in its last few yards of independent existence
before it joins the Frome. Turn left at the very weathered stump
of the fifteenth-century market cross by the village store, which is
just beyond the mill that still makes carpets on the bank of the
river. This wide, curving, street, with an astonishing Gothic
Methodist chapel on the right and a great clock sticking out in-
congruously over the pavement, leads to the church, which is set
back on the outside curve of the street, surrounded by trees and
flowers, in a kind of timeless calm despite 'development' just
beyond on the road that climbs to the A37. These new houses are
of stone, well-planned and well-built. In Maiden Newton an argu-
ment has been going on for as long as I can remember about the
massive square chimney of what has always been known as 'the
milk factory'. From higher up the Cerne road, where there is a
punishing turn by the railway bridge, that chimney is an incon-
gruously industrial landmark. The plant no longer deals with milk
but has turned to light engineering, and not to everyone's delight
in the village.

The tower of St Mary's Church, less in evidence than the chimney, is late Norman, and there is a well-preserved Norman doorway that has been blocked up from the inside. There is no doubt
about the sentiments of Maiden Newton during the Civil War, or
at least as they came to be recorded later in the parish register:
"Mr Osborn, M.A., who was unjustly turned out by ye Rumpish
Triers, and afterwards restored by ye just hand of Providence. Mr
Bramhall, his base and unworthy successor, put in by ye scanda-
lous party, and turned out by God Almighty."

There is a narrow turning to the right off the road to Dorchester
called Frome Lane, which leads in a hundred yards or so to Frome
Vauchurch and crosses the river by an iron-railed bridge. This
road does not go much further but only to Cruxton and a farm,
where it ends except for those who walk and can find their way
along the hillside on the south bank of the Frome by way of
Notton, Frampton, Muckleford, Quatre Bras and Bradford Peverell,
by the remains of the Roman road and the course of the Roman
aqueduct to Poundbury ('Pummery') Hill and Dorchester. A short

lane beyond the bridge goes to the small flint and stone church of Frome Vauchurch, twelfth century, somewhat rebuilt in the seventeenth century and restored a century ago. Its single bell is dated 1631; the bellcote in which it hangs is seventeenth century; the font is late-twelfth century, as is the piscina, and there is a Jacobean pulpit. One afternoon in late summer we went there to a recital *a capelle* by some 'singing cousins' of the writer Sylvia Townsend Warner who lived close by and in whose garden that evening the singers turned their talents to old folk-songs.

Very early in World War II, when I was digging up unexploded bombs in Dorset, I used to bicycle from Came to Frome Vauchurch, where Sylvia brought me so much in conversation, encouraged me in my own writing, went over my poems and became my literary godmother. Throughout the rest of the war she wrote to me, and those of her letters that got through to a prison-camp in Germany sustained me by their wit, their comments on Dorset life and a skilful and knowing avoidance of any reference to the difficulties we were all undergoing. Our *boule de neige* roses were cuttings from her Fromeside garden promised to my wife in summer when they were in bloom and collected for planting on a cold day in early spring when she pointed out to me which to dig up. It was our last meeting.

Closer to Dorchester in the Frome valley Robert Browne had Frampton Court built in 1704. In the nineteenth century it was enlarged by Thomas Sheridan, son of the playwright, and in 1935 the house was demolished. The bridge built in Frampton Park to take the drive over the Frome to the house still remains: three arches, balustraded, its eighteenth-century elegance somewhat heavily earthbound by the four cylindrical pedestals, two at either end, that form the ends to the approach-walls. Robert Browne also had a tower built for the church in 1695, and its most astonishing features are the Tuscan columns that lead into rounded corners halfway up to the embattled summit.

The Reverend Everard Hall, his wife and two daughters were good friends of mine from the time he had the living at Oare in Wiltshire and I was in the army at Marlborough. At the end of World War II they found a cottage up a lane in Frampton for me at ten shillings a week, which for many reasons I was unable to take. It was, as Everard—a gentle and amusing man—pointed out to me, preferable to the almshouse called 'the Home of the Home-less'. Built in 1868, it incorporated in its appearance all the dis-approval of poverty that was the attitude of most Victorians who were not poor themselves.

For the most part, the village of Frampton is on the north side of the main road, and many of the cottages, stone-built and a large proportion of them thatched, are very much part of the Frampton estate. There was a south side to the street until around 1840, when the lord of the manor had the houses demolished and replaced by a line of trees that provided a more acceptable profile from the park. On a recent visit I was struck by the rich blue face of the church clock and the vision of boys and girls receiving lessons in bell-ringing in the gallery. As I wandered around the exceptionally wide church, in which two aisles of 1820 are each wider than the nave, looking at the many Browne memorials, one of the apprentice bell-ringers looked down and raised a hand to me with royal nonchalance.

Four miles downstream towards Dorchester is Bradford Peverell, on the other, south-west bank of the Frome. Among trees on high ground above the river meadows, it has only little lanes leading out of it apart from that over a bridge coming from the main road. One rough track, good enough for walking, goes up over Bradford Down to join the A35 between Dorchester and Winter-borne Abbas.

The east window of St Mary's Church has glass given by New College, Oxford, and in a north window there is a medallion of the arms of William Wykeham and the words "Manners Makyth Man". John Hutchins, the great Dorset historian, was born at Bradford Peverell in 1698. The first-century Roman aqueduct which I mentioned earlier ran from Notton through Bradford on its way to Dorchester, and although Bradford is close to the main road, to the railway and to Dorchester, it is calm and poised above the glistening Frome.

Between Bradford Peverell and Dorchester the Frome is joined by the Cerne, which flows from north to south. Having jumped over it in an earlier chapter, I will now return to its source and trace the villages that lie along its course. Going southwards from Sherborne through Long Burton and past Holnest church, the roads brings you to Middlemarsh, which is just what the name

says—a flat and low-lying place with nursery-gardens and a big
sawmill, where I have often bought timber and grubbed around
among the shavings for bargain offcuts that invariably turn out
to be half an inch too short for what I had in mind. Here the
A352 swerves sharply to the right, while the Old Sherborne Road
goes straight on its high and lonely way. Staying on the A352,
there is a sudden change of landscape less than two miles south
of Middlemarsh. At Lyon's Gate, steep, tree-covered slopes give
the feeling of the nearness of mountains, and, in fact, a sharp
right turn winds up the shoulder of High Stoy, a Dorset peak of
860 feet. If you follow the A352, you are forced into almost a
defile, which I find oppressive, particularly in early summer when
the greenery presses in from both sides. The village of Minterne
Magna crowds on to the road, and the tower of the church, dating
from 1800, is virtually on the carriageway. St Andrew's Church
has a seventeenth-century north chapel and many Napier and
Churchill memorials. General Charles Churchill, who died in 1714,
was brother to Marlborough and was described as "one of the best
commanders of Foot in Europe". Minterne House, the manor
behind the church, designed by Leonard Stokes for Lord Digby,
was built in 1904–6 in Ham Hill stone. If you take the track
going up to the left of the main road and almost directly opposite
to the turning to High Stoy (not a motor-road but a fine walk up
to the Old Sherborne Road), you will find a view of the park with
its lakes on a tributary of the Cerne, and the massed rhododen-
drons and the battlements of Minterne House which I find heavy
and vulgar and typical of the Edwardians' taste. The valley in
which it lies is a narrow pass between Dogbury Camp and High
Stoy, where the Cerne rises.

Cerne Abbas is, mercifully, spared the main A352 going through
it, whatever the map maintains, for no one in a hurry would
leave the straight road except to visit Cerne Abbas, a few hundred
yards to the east. From the Dorchester–Sherborne road one turns
into a lane called Folly, where a terrace of banded flint and brick
cottages stands on the left, followed by modern houses and beyond them some well-restored thatched cottages. To the right of
the road and hidden by trees is the tithe-barn that was built about
the middle of the fourteenth century. It is now partly a private
house and was converted into a dwelling in the eighteenth century

when pointed windows were put in. It is built of knapped flint and has ashlar buttresses and was originally longer than the nine bays that remain. To stand inside the part that is still a barn and look up at the roof and massive walls is to get an idea of the power and strength of the Church in the Middle Ages, to which farm produce was brought for the greater glory of God and all those concerned with Him. Now there is a lawn and a view out to the downs, and a sharp turn in the drive by a holly tree ensures that you come suddenly upon the barn's great archway.

The Folly crosses the Cerne, which then gurgles on its way beneath a couple of wooden bridges connecting two segments of the same garden. To the right, just beyond the road bridge and the grass triangle on which the telephone-kiosk stands, is Back Lane, which has come forward with carefully restored houses on either side. Straight on brings us into the main street, Long Street. On the right are some Georgian houses and a schoolish stone building and then the oldest public house in Cerne Abbas, which is naturally called 'The New Inn'; it has original seventeenth-century stone-mullioned windows and a carriage archway built in the eighteenth century.

Opposite the New Inn is Duck Street, with what used to be the saddler's shop on the corner. On the bank of the Cerne in Duck Street stands a hopeful sapling, *Melus Tsarniscuii*, planted on 10th November 1977 by Colonel Sir Joseph Weld OBE TD JP, Lord Lieutenant of the County of Dorset, to commemorate the Silver Jubilee of Her Majesty Queen Elizabeth II. At this point the Cerne passes under Duck Street to emerge on the other side close to 'The Elephant and Castle', a pub older than it looks. Over the door of 'Green, Family Butcher' the date 1784 probably refers to repairs or to a new front. On the other side of the road there is a solid plank across the river, leading to tennis-courts and a football-pitch and on to a path alongside the Cerne where tributaries and off-shoots bubble all over the place. The path runs at right angles into another lane, where there is a sturdy stone bridge with what looks like an abnormally narrow passage for the river to force its way through. The track over this bridge comes face to face with a barn made of chalk and stone rubble with a brick and stone porch that was added later. The barn is certainly of medieval origin, but its collar-beamed roof has been much repaired, and on the outside it is covered with corrugated iron as rusty red as cayenne pepper. The building is probably fifteenth century, and in the end wall there is a pointed doorway, which surely came from some part of the abbey buildings, with above it a stone decorated with a thirteenth-century leaf design.

This track runs into the farmyard behind the Abbey Farm House, at the back of which stands the porch to the Abbot's Hall, often incorrectly called 'the Gate House'. It is a four-centred arch with a fan-vault inside and a two-storeyed oriel window. There it stands, alone, surrounded by trees, the rest of the buildings gone from the Abbey that was founded in the ninth century and re-founded as a Benedictine abbey about A.D. 987. The only other building that has survived is the guest-house built by Abbot John Vanne between 1458 and 1470. It has a reset oriel window, but much has been blocked up, shored up and held together by various means. It was here that Margaret of Anjou sought sanctuary in 1471 and from here that she left to fight the battle of Tewkesbury—which she lost.

The Abbey Farm House, standing magnificently high up at the end of Abbey Street, incorporates what must have been the main gateway of the Abbey, which, after a fire in the mid-eighteenth century, was partly reconstructed to accommodate the great window of the central gabled projection. Facing down Abbey Street and immediately to the left, there is a gate in the wall, an archway surmounted by three obelisks. This leads into the graveyard where the Abbey church once stood. Beyond the tombstones is St Augustine's Well, which William of Malmesbury (1095–1143) said was a spring that gushed at the saint's command when he wished to baptize the local population.

On the way down Abbey Street is the Town Pond which is generally decorated by some handsome ducks who are very sensible of the tourist trade. Across from the pond is the fine Georgian Andrews House and beside it Andrews Lane that leads down to the Cerne. Towards the lower end of Abbey Street there are, on the right, some houses of c1500, timber-fronted and of two storeys with an overhang. The last house of the row is called 'the Pitchmarket', not a place where pitch was sold but one where grain was brought and displayed for sale on a pitch.

St Mary's Church is at the end of Abbey Street on the left. On

the west face of the fifteenth-century tower there is a statue of
the Virgin and Child. The church is Perpendicular, except for the
chancel, which is Early English with a very large fifteenth-century
East window that may have come from the Abbey. The church had
fallen into disrepair and was carefully restored in 1958–61. On
Whit Sunday, 21st May 1961, the Bishop of Salisbury conducted
a 'Service of Thanksgiving after Restoration'. For fourteen months,
while the major repairs were being carried out, the Congregational
Chapel was lent to the Church of England parishioners—a fine
example of ecumenical neighbourly feeling. The restoration continued until 1967 under the guidance of Messrs Potter and Hare
of Salisbury and cost in all about £20,000. There are some fine
gargoyles. Look out particularly for the one to the left of the
south door: through its mouth escaped the smoke from the stove
that used to be in the porch. And in the churchyard there is an
open stone coffin that seems to have been made for an immense
corpse.

The Cerne is crossed at the end of Andrews Lane by a narrow
footbridge at a point where the stream was forced between stone
banks to break into a waterfall that powered the crushing-mill in
Mill Lane that ceased working in 1933. In Mill Lane, just before it
joins Duck Street, is the Cerne Valley Forge, which may be visited.

It is in these back lanes of Cerne Abbas that one gets an idea
of the thriving little town it once was. It had a tannery and produced gloves, boots, saddles and harness. There was a malt-house,
a Rural District Council and a Magistrates' Court. The decline
cannot have begun as far back as the Dissolution, but whenever it
began, it was later hastened by the Railway Age, which left Cerne
Abbas out of its network. The last stage-coach ran through Cerne
Abbas in 1855, and by the end of the century the town was being
described as a run-down place where the inhabitants lived in
hovels and grass grew in the streets. Although it has not regained
any of its former importance, and none of the traditional industries has been restarted, it is today a neat and well-to-do little
place that is visited by many tourists in the summer but has in
no way been vulgarized as a result.

The presence of the Abbey that used to be the centre of the
village and the Cerne Abbas Giant that remains unchanged above
the village on a westward-facing escarpment of what I have called

the Central Highlands, is an example of 'if you can't beat them, join them.' The giant was there before the Abbey, but exactly when it was cut into the turf is not certain. He is described by the RCHM as

> . . . a nude man striding towards the left; he holds a knotted club in the right hand and has the left arm stretched out; the nipples and ribs are boldly represented, as is the phallus. The figure has been repaired and recut at various periods, a general repair having taken place in 1887. Whether the outstretched left arm originally carried a lion-skin is difficult to say: but the general resemblance of the figure to that of a Roman Hercules is sufficient to suggest the probability of a Romano-British origin.

He is depicted in outline in trenches roughly two feet wide and two feet deep, which has allowed, in the words of Jacquetta Hawkes, ". . . the representation of internal features, including facial features (with the nose modelled in relief), nipples, ribs shown with a Roualt-like emphasis, and the erect phallus and testicles which are the source of so much interest and so little open comment".

The giant is 180 feet tall, and his phallus is thirty feet long. John Hutchins, clergyman as well as historian, writing in the mid-eighteenth century and mindful of his cloth, spoke vaguely of letters and figures scrawled between the giant's legs. John Sydenham, in his idiosyncratic study *Baal Durotrigensis* (1842), gave the giant calf-muscles, a navel (which has since grassed over) but no phallus at all. Yet the figure is obviously the pictorial celebration of a fertility cult, and a line taken vertically upwards along the phallus takes the eye to the east and the rising sun. Between the giant's head and the top of the down is the site of an ancient camp known as 'the Trendle', 'Trundle' or 'Frying Pan'. Here that phallic symbol the maypole was erected each May Day until, in 1635, the churchwardens paid "Anthony Thorne, and others, for taking downe ye maypole, and making a town ladder of it". There was a snakes-and-ladders symbolism in that act too—a practical Puritan version of 'if a member offend thee, cut it off.'

Through the centuries there have always been those, clergy and laity alike, who have protested about the giant and tried to have his chalk virility removed. It could easily have come to pass in

Victorian times, but fortunately the land belonged to that splendid man General Pitt Rivers, archæologist and Inspector of Public Monuments, and in 1921 the Pitt Rivers Estate presented the Giant to the National Trust. It is the fence around this hexagon of National Trust land that gives the Giant the 'frame' that is so apparent in photographs taken from the air. The best view undoubtedly is from an aeroplane or helicopter, but the next best is from near the former workhouse, a grim block just to the north of the village on the road to Sherborne.

Here are two of the legends connected with the Giant. One is that he used to catch and eat sheep, and the local people waited until he had gorged himself and lay sleeping to creep up and slay him (you don't merely 'kill' a giant, do you?) and then traced his outline in the chalk to commemorate the size of their victim. Another legend is that women wishing to conceive children should sit on the Giant's phallus or, better, lie there with their men.

Who put him there is still something of a mystery. Now it is most often supposed that he represents Hercules and was traced there in the time of the Emperor Commodus, who proclaimed himself a reincarnation of Hercules in A.D. 191. Or was he adapted from a much older figure, the somewhat rubbery and jointless looking arm holding the 120-foot club being added on orders from the Roman Army of occupation or by the inclination of those whoring after strange new gods?

He was obviously too close, both physically and in folk tradition, for him to be eliminated by the Christian Church, so the Church took over at Cerne, the Abbey was built, and the well that had probably been connected with the Giant cult was given the name of 'St Augustine's Well' and a chapel built round it.

All of which makes Trendle Hill and Cerne places of continuing ancient magic and faith that go on like the River Cerne, whose force has been harnessed at different times for different purposes and which here and there runs underground only to appear again, never drying up or deserting its valley.

Nether Cerne, 1¾ miles south of Cerne Abbas, consists of a house, a church and a few cottages, all standing on the bank of the Cerne. Nether Cerne House and All Saints' Church are set down together on a greensward. The house late-seventeenth century and added to in the eighteenth century and again during the last two centuries, is of stone and flint and has a slate roof. The church is of local rubble banded with flint and dates from the second half of the thirteenth century. The tower is late fifteenth century and instead of the usual gargoyles has angels' heads. The font is Norman and shaped like a water-lily. Until recently the church was neglected, and brambles crowded to the doorway. Now it has become the responsibility of the Redundant Churches Fund and is very well kept. Steps behind the church lead up to a track and a line of farm buildings and cottages, used, when I last saw them, as store-houses. The track climbs steeply and eventually reaches the Old Sherborne Road, from which one can look along the Cerne Valley, which is wide, deep and impressive for so small a stream.

Less than a mile down the road towards Dorchester is God-manston, 'Godmanstone' on many maps though it is more correctly spelled without the final 'e' because the origin of the name is 'Godman's Farm' and has nothing to do with stone. This village too is on the Cerne, five miles north of Dorchester, and the guide-book cliché about it is that its inn, 'The Smith's Arms', is the smallest pub in England and was granted its licence when Charles II—that busy traveller through Dorset—stopped there and asked the smith for a drink when what is now the bar was the smithy. The smith had no licence, so Charles granted him one on the spot. What with knighting drunken revellers, dressing up as a servant, listening to church bells announcing his own demise, racing up and down the lanes of West Dorset, sleeping in what would seem to be about three houses each night and turning smiths into inn-keepers, the Merry Monarch made sure that he would not be forgotten in Dorset. Whatever the truth of the exchange between King and smith, the bar of 'The Smith's Arms' measures only ten feet by twenty feet.

On 8th February 1827 it was announced in the *Dorset County Chronicle* that "A penny post is established between Dorchester and Cerne Abbas by which the regular delivery of letters, etc. daily is ensured at those places, and in the intermediate villages of Charminster, Godmanstone and Nether Cerne."

Charminster is *not* on the River Char, which is at the western end of the county and reaches the sea at Charmouth, but on the Cerne or Churn, and the village is 'the church on the Cerne', which, just south of here, joins the Frome in a maze of water-meadows, gullies and runnels. The village is close enough to Dorchester to risk becoming a suburb, but it is these water-meadows that have discouraged 'development' that would have made Charminster contiguous with Dorchester.

The village is dominated by the early-sixteenth-century tower of St Mary's Church, built by Sir Thomas Trenchard, and reminders of this fact are spread liberally around in the form of Ts. There are twelfth-century arcades to the nave and a small chancel of about 1838. There are a number of Trenchard memorials and a kneeling effigy of Grace Pole, a member of the Trenchard family by marriage, who died in 1638. The Trenchards came to Wolfeton House nearby, through a marriage, in 1480, and added much to the house during the next hundred years.

In 1496 Philip, Archduke of Austria, surnamed 'the Handsome', had married Joanna, daughter of Ferdinand and Isabella, rulers of Aragon and Castile. In 1504 Isabella died, bequeathing Castile to her daughter, and Philip assumed the title of King of Castile, setting out for his kingdom in January 1506 with Joanna from Middleburg, one of the Zeeland ports of the Netherlands. A storm drove their ship into Weymouth, and they were taken to the greatest house in the district, which was Wolfeton. There they were welcomed by Sir Thomas Trenchard, who regretted that he had no Spanish in which to converse with his illustrious guests and sent for a young kinsman who farmed Berwick, between Litton Cheney and Burton Bradstock, and who, having travelled widely, spoke Spanish. Philip was much taken with young John Russell and asked him to go with him to Windsor, to which the couple had been invited—an invitation close enough to a summons—by Henry VII. Henry in turn took notice of Russell and kept him at Court. In 1540 Russell was made a baronet, swiftly acquired Woburn Abbey at the Dissolution of the Monasteries and was made Earl of Bedford in 1550, five years before his death. The dukedom was created in 1694.

The Trenchards were staunch Protestants, and when the Jesuit priest John Cornelius, who had been sheltered by the Roman Catholic Arundel family, was arrested at Chideock, he was taken to Wolfeton. Among those who talked with him there was Sir Walter Ralegh, and it is said that he and Cornelius argued through the night. Cornelius was later tried, found guilty of treason and executed in Dorchester.

Only the gatehouse and the south-west corner of Wolfeton remain, but the house is at times open to the public, and there are helpful signposts on the Dorchester–Maiden Newton road. The size of the gatehouse with its two massive towers of unequal size is impressive and unexpected as one emerges from the rather overgrown drive. Inside there is a fine stone staircase and a great carved oaken chimneypiece in the drawing-room. The east drawing-room has giant wooden Corinthian columns, unusual not only in size and material but in their corded decoration.

The building north of the house was usually described as a barn but has been identified by the RCHM as "... the earliest surviving riding-house known in England. ... Prince Henry's riding-house at St James's Palace, built c1604, was in many respects similar to the present building although larger. ..."

Although the house is now only a fragment of its former self, it is impressive in its medieval strength and aloofness. It seems isolated among its trees, its farm beside it, and one is surprised to emerge in a couple of hundred yards or so into the narrow back lanes of Charminster with their carefully-tended gardens and sprucely painted houses. The other side of the hedges is centuries away, with Russell interpreting his way to an earldom, the Jesuit arguing for his faith, knowing that he would die, and Ralegh, who at that time had no idea that his life too would be ended by execution.

8

Behind the Great Dorset Barrier Reef

THERE is only one eastbound road from Bridport or West Bay and that is the B3157 that leads to Burton Bradstock and eventually to Abbotsbury and Weymouth. There is a very pleasant walk of about three miles along the clifftop to Burton, starting from the seaward side of Bridport Golf Course. The first break in the cliffs is Burton Freshwater, where the River Bride (not to be confused with the Brit which gets to the sea through Bridport and West Bay) forms itself into a pool and fights to get to the sea intact before sinking into the shingle. It loses the fight in a sludgy pond just beyond the Burton Freshwater caravan-camp. What used to be marshy meadows is now a large holiday site with a prodigious summer population. Over the hill is Burton Bradstock where the Bride is still a river and is crossed by a bridge on a bend at the eastern end of the village. Burton's one-sided street looks across the Bride meadows towards the Dove Inn and a row of thatched cottages with the hill ascending to the clifftop behind them. The main road to Abbotsbury turns sharply to the left just beyond the bridge, and a turn to the right leads between new small houses and bungalows to the car-park, which is in the National Trust area of these cliffs on either side of the gap. There is a walk back to Freshwater, to the west, below the orange cliffs that are the home of thousands of seagulls and of the many jackdaws who constantly mock and attack the gulls and try to steal their young as well as their eggs. To the east of the gap the cliffs are lower, greyer with clay and eventually give up altogether the pretence of being cliffs.

Between Burton and West Bay there are frequent cliff falls, particularly after a period of prolonged heavy rain, followed by a severe frost and then a sudden thaw. We gathered some fine ammonites there after a heavy fall in the winter of 1961–2. Because of the increasing summertime invasion, some plants have been in danger of extinction—the yellow horned poppy and the centaury, for example. Near Burton I found the deepest crimson yarrow that I have ever seen. I raised some plants from seed, and they crossed with both the more common white and lilac shades, but the original crimson one perished in the great snow of early 1978.

A right turn, just after Burton Bridge, leads into a cul-de-sac called 'Southover', which in turn leads to 'The Dove' and the cottages seen from the main street. Until early 1978, when Mrs Jean Day retired, the Dove had been in her family for about thirty years. First her father had been landlord, and then her husband, Charlie Day, who had formerly been butcher to Burton Bradstock took over. 'The Dove's' Greenfingers Club raised thousands of pounds for charity from behind its ramparts of giant marrows and leeks and prodigious barrels of rough cider and organized bonfire celebrations on top of the cliff. Through many years, day and evening, winter and summer, I have called in at 'The Dove' and sat in the bar that was furnished with stout deal tables and benches. There were Greenfingers photographs from years back on the nicotine-brown walls, and a Taunton Cider 'weather-clock', probably fifty or more years old, with an old man or an old woman emerging according to the barometric pressure. There were also some gigantic lobster-claws hanging over the bar.

An old friend first met at 'The Dove' is Des Gape. His surname is Old French for 'a weakling', the last of the litter, but everything about Des contradicts the origin for he is a burly man with curly black hair and bright blue eyes. For many years I have bought fish from him at West Bay where it is landed. Other 'Dove' regulars were Douglas Northover, who knows more about the history of Burton Bradstock than any man alive; Stan, that pillar of the Greenfingers, who would sell me paraffin-oil long after he had closed up for the day; Bob Cammell, who had lost a leg when a soldier in Germany and who used to go out on the fishing-boats until cider and melancholy ravaged both that once handsome face behind the beard and any will to do anything again until he faded out of living and out of life. His ashes were taken in a boat and scattered in Lyme Bay by his friends. Years ago, too, there was old Jack Way, chuckling over stories that were difficult to follow but were often about the days when he was a corporal in the army. When I knew him, he lived in the one-man encampment he had built for himself below a hedge. He drew water from a farm tap, and one frosty day I found Jack wrestling with a blown connection in the plastic pipe. "Bugger me," he said, " 'tis jumpin' like a snake," as the hose whipped around. We fixed the two ends of the pipe together, got soaked in doing so, had a pint of cider, and then Jack set to adjusting the saddle on his incredible bicycle that was both brakeless and lightless. It was on that bicycle, some years later, that old Jack was killed by a motor-car while on his cider-fuelled and unlit way through the West Dorset lanes.

Not much of the real Burton Bradstock is seen from the main road because the village lies behind in a labyrinth of lanes. In Grove Road, Monique and Hugh Stevens have turned what was once a butcher's shop into a house for their children and themselves that is a fine example of what thoughtful conservation and good taste can do. Working mostly by themselves, they uncovered and restored the late-medieval features of their house, demolishing the Victorian and later additions, bringing to light the beams and open fireplace and the best of what was originally there. Monique is a Frenchwoman with a great personality that helped her to survive the early death of her first husband and, some years later, that of a young son. She and Hugh design and print fabrics for their business, called 'Human Beings'.

St Mary's fifteenth-century church is golden stone with a central tower resting on four panelled arches, and a clock that comes from Christ's Hospital, London. There is a small, triangular village green by which stands the White House, bearing the date 1635, and nearby the Wesleyan Chapel, dated 1825, which is now a branch of the Dorset County Library. Beside the self-explanatory Church Road, Mill Lane and Grove Road, Burton has Donkey Lane, Darby Lane and a street called 'Shadrack' which is also the name of a Burton farm. Church Road ends at a little bridge and the entrance to a large seventeenth-century house surrounded by trees and appropriately called 'The Rookery'.

Leaving the coast road just before the right-hand turn to the beach, a narrow road runs parallel to the River Bride, usually only a meadow away on the left. Two miles along this road there stand on the right a stone house and some farm buildings that include a massive and half-hidden barn. This is Berwick Farm, from which young John Russell set out in 1506 to translate from the Spanish for the tempest-stranded Archduke Philip at Wolfeton and thus started on the road to his own translation from country gentleman to belted earl. It is now just the farmhouse, some buildings and cottages, set beside the valley road—probably much as it has always been but touched less now by history than by the giant silver cigar-tubes of silos.

Down on the bank of the Bride opposite Berwick a dam has made an artificial lake of several acres, which I saw for the first time on a June day. Years before, I had often walked these meadows and banks, but this was new to me: I had never imagined a lake in that place. So I went down to where the hay hung out to dry on tripods—a very unusual sight in Dorset—and met Peer and Ella Pratt, who have set up Water Lane Fish Farm to produce carp, a fish that must have been very familiar to the Russells in the Middle Ages. Peer told me that the demand was principally from restaurants catering for customers of European origin or tastes. Did the carp fall out of favour, together with the monks, in the mid-sixteenth century, and was there a Dissolution of the Carp Ponds?

John Russell's father James and grandfather John were both buried at Swyre, a village to the south of Berwick, on the Bridport–Weymouth coast road. On both sides of the church door are brasses that were originally laid in the pew belonging to Berwick House. The son remembered here died only four years after his father but already in the next reign. John Russell and his wife Elizabeth are recorded as follows: "Here lyeth John Russell Esquier and Elizabeth his wyfe daughter of John Frocksmer Esquier which deceasyd the XX yere of King Henry ye VII Ao 1505," and James their son: "Here lyeth James Russell Esquier and Alys his wyfe daughter of John Wise Esquier who deceasyd the first yere of King Henry VIII Ao MCCCCCIX." Was the engraver paid by the letter and so decided to revert to using Roman figures?

John's daughter Ann married James Napier, son of the Scottish

Sir Alec Napier of Merchiston in Midlothian who had settled in Dorset at the next village of Puncknowle—sometimes written 'Punknoll' but however spelled always pronounced 'Punnel' to rhyme with 'tunnel'. Here Dorset, Scotland and the carp of the Bride probably all come together. The memorial to James Napier states that he supplied fish to the adjacent abbeys. Maybe it was carp he provided for the monks' table.

The Napiers, who sometimes spelled their name 'Napper' (as did Sir Robert Napper of Middlemarsh, who established in 1616 the almshouses for ten poor men in South Street, Dorchester, known to this day as 'Napper's Mite', were three centuries, until the early part of the eighteenth century, lords of the manor a mile inland at Puncknowle. Their manor house delighted Treves, who spoke of it as "hidden in a garden behind the church . . . one of the daintiest and most beautiful manor houses in the county, a marvel of dignity and peace". One of the later tenants of the house, in the early-nineteenth century, was Colonel Shrapnel, who gave his name to a shattering invention and died a general in 1842.

St Mary's Church, standing on raised ground beside the manor and overlooking the one-sided village street, is predominantly Norman, with a north aisle added in 1891, and has many Napier memorials, a helmet, gauntlet and spurs of the early-seventeenth-century tablets of 1616 and 1620 and another that is undated but of about 1700 when Sir Robert Napier died, although, curiously, he was given only his initials in an inscription in Greek, Latin and English: "Reader when as thou hast done all thou canst, thou art but an unprofitable servant. Therefore this marble affords no roome for fulsome flattery or vaine praise. Sr.R.N." The inscription is signed, rather more flamboyantly: "*Johannes Hamiltonus Scoto-Britannicus fecit.*" This Robert Napier was High Sheriff of Dorset.

Puncknowle is close-composed of church and manor house set in trees overlooking the village street and the Crown Inn. The houses are stone, mostly thatched, with the exception of two in provincial suburban style in nineteenth-century red brick, complete with first-floor bay windows and a little decoration here and there in ceramic tiles. Next door to 'The Crown' there used to be a bakery where I collected bread hot from the oven in the early morning. The baker was a compact man with a white crewcut, built like Jean Gabin, rarely seen without a pipe in his mouth, called Fonso Bartlett. When I walked into his bakehouse from out of the bright sunshine or the sleety murk, according to the season, he would say "I've got two roughs for 'ee, young maan," handing me the aromatic wholemeal loaves. If I called later in the day, when Fonso had left on his rounds in a square old motor-van, I collected bread and a scrap of local news from Mrs Bartlett, who sat, however hot and sunny the weather outside, in the dark, low-ceilinged bakehouse, in an armchair near to the cooling oven, her cat and a glass of something comforting close by.

Five roads lead out of Puncknowle. One turns sharply to the right, passing the post office perched on the side of the hill, and climbs sharply over Swyre Knoll. A path past a plantation leads to the crest and the little square stone coastguard lookout. It consisted of one room on the ground floor with another room above, but it has been vandalized again and again, the rafters torn down and burned, the inside covered with graffiti. Yet I remember, within the past twenty years, when it was in habitable condition.

Shortly after dawn one summer morning, I surprised a doe and her fawn lying close to the landward wall of the stone hut. It was one of those still pauses before cloud came in from the west to turn the day to rain. I could still see across Lyme Bay to Beer Head and beyond, in all about seventy miles to Start Point on the Devon coast, a point from which to watch out for the French during those years when Boney's ships and soldiers were expected from one day to the next. Dorset was alert to the threat of Johnny Frenchman long before that, however. In a raid in 1440 the French destroyed Bexington church apart from some remnants that eventually found their way into Swyre church.

Returning to the end of Puncknowle street and taking the left-hand fork at the old village school, you will find a narrow road that runs over hedgeless pastures and down and into a farmyard. This is Look Farm, the solid and well-kept stone buildings standing squarely around the concreted yard which is sometimes gated off when the cows are waiting there to be milked. The house can easily be missed, half-hidden behind both iron railings and a lot of farm machinery, unless you keep a look out for the four decorated chimneys that rise from it and add an English eccentricity to its French façade. The house is dated 1700 and has semi-circular pediments to the windows and a generous amount of stone fruit hanging about the door. It is a very pretty house but dwarfed by the big farm buildings, and in part its uncomfortable appearance is explained by the absence of trees and gardens around it.

The road turns left through the farmyard and crosses a stream which was a water-splash but is now a solid concrete bridge. On the bank stand some massive stone cottages, probably as old as Look Farmhouse, whose blocked-up and milk-chocolate-painted dormer windows lend them the air of an ecclesiastical building or fortified barn. To the left of the road, where it emerges again into unfenced pastures, there is a modern stone house aptly named 'Outlook'. In less than a mile this road reaches the village of Litton Cheney.

Of the three remaining roads out of Puncknowle, one is the continuation of that which comes from Swyre, and the two others run down to the Bride Valley road from Burton Bradstock to Litton Cheney. The eastern one goes past Golly Knap Farm but, taking the westernmost one of the two, which is a continuation of the road from Swyre, the Bride Valley road is crossed, and a high-banked lane leads down to the first of two narrow bridges. To the left lies Berwick farmland, and in the centre of the first field to the immediate left there is a spring of brackish water whose rise and fall in level is said to correspond to the tides on the shore nearly three miles to the south. The road rises from the valley to run between Rudge Farmhouse and its pair of council-house-style cottages, up to a clump of trees on a knoll where there is a turning to the right. On this south-facing bank I have found primroses on New Year's Day. A plateau opens out beyond this point, and a hundred yards to the right is Chilcombe, once a hamlet with a Tudor manor house that was demolished in 1939. A stone from above a door in that house was inscribed: "John Bysshop, Elnor Bysshop. Anno dni 1578." It is now in the chancel of the church, which, with the eighteenth-century farmhouse, the farm buildings, the studio of the painter who lives in the farmhouse, and two cottages along the lane, comprise Chilcombe today.

The twelfth- to fourteenth-century church, one of the smallest in England, has a Norman font and a trefoil-headed piscina of the early-fourteenth century. There are memorials to the Strong and Bishop families. A Bishop daughter married the German Dr Sagittary who built, around 1660, that extraordinary brick house in the Plocks at Blandford. In the chancel stands a chair belonging to the Bishops engraved "R.B. 1642". During the reign of Charles II one of these Bishops was MP for Bridport, but later, through various marriages, it passed to the second Earl Nelson, Horatio's nephew, in 1832.

On the north wall of the nave is a panel of dark golden wood incised with scenes of the Flagellation, Crucifixion and Resurrection, the designs being outlined in poker-work. It has long been thought to be a chest-front from a Spanish Armada ship. It is probably of the seventeenth century, but it is unlikely that the Hispanophile John Russell was still alive to see it.

The churchyard in spring is kept trim by a ewe and her lamb, but the farmhouse garden on the other side of the wall has a more orthodox lawn across which are the steps, flanked by black iron handrails, leading to the modest front door of the house. House and farm are now parted, the former belonging to the painter whose studio is across the farmyard, and the land to a nearby farmer.

Chilcombe Camp is an unexcavated hill-fort from the top of which are extensive views to the sea, eastwards across the valley to Coombe Plantation and Hodder's Hill, while westwards Shipton Hill lies like an upturned boat beyond the pasture and copses of Lower Sturthill Farm. The road past Chilcombe continues through more gates and over cattle-grids to come out on the A35 Bridport–Dorchester road.

Leaving Puncknowle by either of the two northbound roads out of the village, and turning right along the Bride Valley road for two miles, Litton Cheney is reached, a deceptively large village of which not much shows at any one place. Half way along the road from the Puncknowle turning, the Bride is crossed, and at the next turning to the right is 'The White Horse', surprisingly Litton's only pub, with tables in the garden by which a tributary of the Bride bubbles by. Architecturally, 'The White Horse' is built of red brick in a turn-of-the-century railway-tavern style. Just around the corner, down the turning, is Litton Cheney Youth Hostel.

Along the main road, beside which the little stream runs, is a disused water-mill on the right, now turned into a private house. On the left are stone and thatched cottages with, at a T-junction, a farmyard and buildings. Here the stream bubbles under the road, and if you follow it up a rough lane and into a field sloping up to the top of the downs, you will find that this and other streams are made use of by the Water Board which has a small pumping-station there, looking like a tiny chalet and well-concealed in an angle of the field with trees behind. There is an air of secrecy all around, and the tall trees beside the lane shade the garden of the Old Rectory where the streams have also served to make a small lake. Years ago I found a solitary primrose on the bank of the stream which was iced over on that particular Christmas Day.

On the other side of the Old Rectory garden a path leads up beyond a battered turnstile gate under overhanging branches to the upward-sloping downside on which St Mary's Church stands. Predominantly of the fifteenth century, it was heavily restored in 1878. There is a Norman font, and George Dawbney's memorial of 1612 has his bright coat-of-arms painted on it. A naïve painting on wood of David and his harp bears the legend, "I will sing with understanding". A brass in the nave has an inscription lamenting Anna Henvill who "went off ye stage" in 1681.

A tombstone in the churchyard is marked with appropriate simplicity: " 'The Lord is my Shepherd, I shall not want.' In loving memory of Alfred W. Feist, died 12th January 1976, aged 62 years. Beloved husband of Inga, Much loved father of Stephen and Wendy."

Alfred was born in Silesia, where, until the Second World War, he was a smallholder. He served on the Russian front, escaped from Stalingrad, was taken prisoner in France and sent first to Colorado and then to England, to work on a farm at Burton Bradstock. As his former home was in the Russian zone, he chose to stay in England and went to work at Chilcombe. In 1950 he married Inga, also German, and theirs was the first marriage-service performed in Chilcombe church for thirty-six years. (It was also the last because Chilcombe lost its licence to marry parishioners.) For the last fifteen years of his life Alfred worked at Coombe Farm across the valley from Chilcombe. He was a superb plough-man and a good shepherd. Many a load of wood he sawed for me, and many a cold morning at lambing time I gave him a hand

Winterborne Came: this farm building under Came Down was
Roland Gant's study in 1941

Plush: a font put out to grass as a bird-bath

Hilfield: a calvary near the Franciscan Friary

Plush: not a kiln or a bake-oven but a hydraulic ram in a farm water-system

Piddletrenthide, lying just under the snow-line when this photograph was taken

Portland – Easton's main street, known as 'Wakeham'

Hilfield church

Toller Fratrum church

Hermitage – the
church bellcote
with a ball on top

Studland church

The Cobb, Lyme Regis

The Smugglers' Inn, Osmington Mills

West Bay Harbour and E. S. Prior's 1885 Bay House Hotel

West Bay: retailer of local history and local fish, Des Gape

Little Bredy church

while we talked of the Russian winter and told old soldiers' tales. I went to the German Embassy on his behalf when he applied for compensation for loss of his German property and we used to laugh about the way his children cheered on the British against the Germans in war films on television.

Three roads go down to Litton Cheney from the A35. One crosses Martin's Down just to the west of Winterborne Abbas and also takes you to Long Bredy. The most direct is called 'White Way' and is steep and straight between beech trees on high chalky banks, always reminding me of my small son's cry of surprised delight on his first sight of a fox as it padded across the road in the headlights of my slowly-climbing 1937 Riley Kestrel at five on a September morning. At the foot of this hill there used to be a great elm set in a triangular island in the middle of the junction. It was felled when it became dangerous, and a succession of saplings has struggled to take its place since. At this T-junction there is a forge and the village shop, which has been there so long that the road has risen high above its doorstep. This shop huddles very much to itself, an impression reinforced by the solid wooden privacy it obtains when its green shutters are closed and locked.

The third road from the top of Askerswell Down descends sharply and then makes a right-angle turn at the old chalk-pit, which is gradually being filled up with rubbish that is periodically bulldozed over with soil. Through the gate opposite the pit is Pin's Knoll where there was a small Iron Age farmstead. There were burials here in the second half of the first century A.D., and I saw a small skeleton exposed there during archæological excavations in 1959. A small Romano-British building stood here in the fourth century.

The little River Bride, which ends its course in the shingle of Burton Freshwater but whose name means 'a gushing, surging, torrential stream', gives its name to Long Bredy and to Little Bredy, close to its source on the Bride Head estate three miles south-east of Litton Cheney. Before getting away on its eight-mile course, it is dammed to feed a lake in Bride Head Park, which is elegantly landscaped around a house built in the early- and mid-nineteenth century in Tudor style on the site of an earlier house. The whole of Little Bredy is a triumph of estate landscaping and

L

building and adaptation of what was already there when the main work took place between 1830 and 1850. The Gothic farmyard, developed from some Jacobean buildings, dates from this time and stands close to the road where it forks into two, one going around the foot of the down with the park on the right and the other climbing steeply between beech trees to the top of the down. Above the principal part of the village there is an irregular green from which an unmade road goes sharply down to the diamond-paned stone and flint cottages on the banks of the Bride. A shaded path leads off to the left to St Michael's Church, into which Benjamin Ferrey, in his 1850 restoration, incorporated the thirteenth-century chancel and fourteenth-century tower, to which he added a spire.

The narrow road winds down from the green and along the wooded valley, beside an immense red brick wall that encloses the manor vegetable-garden, and then the road turns up the hill between woods that have been thinned in recent years and climbs over the down to reach an isolated farm called 'Fox Earth'.

All views along the main valley road are pleasing, and Bride Head and Little Bredy have the air of a well-kept secret in this bowl in the downs that are marked by other, very much earlier, occupation. A mile to the north there is a Bronze Age burial-ground, containing forty-four round barrows, known as 'Poor Lot'. A mile to the south are the remains of a megalithic long barrow, and a few hundred yards to the north-west is the Kingston Russell stone circle that dates from about 1500 B.C. and was certainly used for religious purposes. Although the stones are fallen now, the eighty-foot diameter of the circle gives some idea of how impressive it must have been when all were still standing. Less than a mile and a half to the south-west of Bride Head is the Valley of Stones. Why there is this large collection of massive sarsens along the bottom of the valley is a matter for speculation. Treves, as usual, gave a good description:

> . . . a mysterious glen among the downs, on whose grassy slopes many huge stones are scattered. Lower down the hollow are clumps of trees, under the cover of which the strange valley curves out of sight. If it was along this vale that the dead were borne for burial, then no processional road could have been more awe-inspiring. The tribesmen might have gathered on the lonely heights and watched

the shadows below the trees for the first sight of the slowly-moving company. It is said that the stones were once covered by a barrow fifty-four feet long, twenty-five feet broad, and five and a half feet in height, and that the sepulchre was rifled and broken up years ago by men incontinently searching for treasure.

This district is rich in memorials of all kinds. On Black Down, to the south-west of Little Bredy, is a 4000 B.C. dolmen wrongly put together in 1866. Known as 'the Hell Stone', it has nothing to do with Hades and is more likely to have a meaning similar to that of 'heeling in', as when covering potatoes, though it might come from Hel, the goddess of the dead, or from Halig, meaning holy. And a little over a mile to the south of Little Bredy church are the remains of a megalithic burial-chamber given the inappropriately fanciful name of 'the Grey Mare and her Colts'.

On Black Down is a famous Dorset monument that can be seen from almost every high point in the county. The Hardy Monument, often thought by tourists to commemorate the novelist, was put up "on his own land" in memory of Admiral Sir Thomas Hardy, Nelson's flag-captain, in whose arms he died. It is a seventy-foot-high octagonal stone tower built in 1844. Treves said: "Afar off it may be mistaken for a factory chimney, and when seen nearer at hand it bears a strange resemblance to a telephone-receiver placed on end"—he was writing at the time of the 'daffodil' or 'candlestick' telephone, and he had a point about the similarity. John Hyams, in his fresh and lively book on Dorset, likened it to "a factory chimney with a crinoline", and it has also been said to resemble a chess pawn and a pepper-mill. But there it stands, seven hundred feet up on Black'on, a strong sea-mark that would have pleased Thomas Masterman Hardy, who had been born less than three miles to the north-west of his monument, in the Bride Valley at Kingston Russell House, which was built of Portland ashlar in the seventeenth to eighteenth centuries and lengthened at the ends in 1913, so that from the road it looks like a shoe-box on its side, set on the nearly treeless greensward. The future Admiral was born there in 1769, that vintage year for martial babies that also saw the births of Bonaparte and Wellington.

A mile to the south of the monument is Portisham (often spelt

'Portesham'), Admiral Hardy's beloved 'Possum', where he first lived as a boy and again, late in life, in the seventeenth-century manor house that stands close to the road west of the church. Portisham has many old cottages of grey stone and an ever-increasing number of modern houses and bungalows of all sizes, shapes, styles and materials. It also has one of those sad, abandoned railway bridges, the central section over the road gone, the sides remaining like useless walls supporting the amputated stumps above. This branch-line from Upwey on the Dorchester–Weymouth line, operated for only half a century from its inauguration in 1885, one of the wilder optimistic but unprofitable products of the Railway Age euphoria. Abandoned at the time of the First World War and never revived was the week-long fair in early August known as 'Possum Fes' Wik', where there was dancing, including the ancient ring dance, until the early morning.

Just over a mile from Portisham on a narrow road that leads to Upwey is Waddon Manor. There was a Tudor house here to which an addition was made at the end of the seventeenth century. The Tudor part has gone, but the well-proportioned addition remains, set somewhat oddly endways into the down and looking across towards the sea. On the same side of the road a few yards along are thatched barns of 1702 which, with the manor, make a harmonious group that has survived practically unchanged through nearly three centuries.

Possibly the most dramatic section of road in Dorset is that part of the B3157 between West Bay and Abbotsbury. From Burton Bradstock to Swyre it runs along the top of the downs at a distance of between half a mile to a mile from the shore. Down below, on the seaward side, the golden to orange Chesil Beach shingle lies, with now and then at low tide patches of sand and, according to what seas are running, breakers and a line of white surf. In one place the dark green below, changing to mauve and fawn in winter, shows the extent of Burton Mere, whose reeds shelter a variety of marsh birds, and at another point a track runs down to Cogdon Beach where there is a grassy car-park for which the local farmer or his tenant collects parking-fees in summer. In summertime those who want to picnic on a beach that is not too crowded come here, and at all times of the year, night and day, there are anglers watching and waiting for the mackerel.

When the mackerel are 'straying', the professional fishermen come to take them in seine nets, and I have helped to haul in the long arm of the seine with friends from Burton and West Bay. I have taken garfish there too, those miniature swordfish whose bones turn a poisonous-looking bright green when they are cooked.

As along the whole length of the Chesil Beach, bathing is dangerous. You can be in six feet of water as many feet out from the edge, and there is often a powerful undertow. Each summer there are warnings, and each summer they are ignored, and people are drowned there. I have swum for many years at various spots along this coast, in winter as well as summer, and familiarity breeds an ever-increasing respect, because the Chesil is ruthless with both men and boats.

In spring and summer the landward side of the Chesil is bright with mallow, sea poppy and sea holly, and the rich green of sea-spinach or sea-beet, which I prefer to garden spinach for its succulent fleshiness and salty tang. Up on the hillside, just below the road, is a dark patch of conifers that shield completely a house belonging to a community called 'Othona'. Just east of here the coast road dips into a tree-lined valley at Swyre where the Bull Inn displays on its terrace two immense sea-mines that were real enough in their time and a 'wishing well' that *is* real to the small children who throw pennies into it. Swyre church, described earlier in this chapter, is a few yards down the road going inland to Puncknowle from beside 'The Bull'.

The B3157 is particularly rewarding when travelled from east to west in clear weather and when the setting sun strikes the top of Golden Cap, and the curving coast beyond Lyme begins to turn violet in the shadow of evening; or again, when going eastwards as the sun rises and throws Portland into grey relief, like a bird's head resting on the sea, as Victor Hugo described it. At the top of Wear's Hill, nearly seven hundred feet above the sea that lies a mile to the south, is a parking-place on the seaward side and almost opposite a track going inland over the down that is marked 'To Ashley Chase only'. A few hundred yards beyond this turning there is a gate with a rough path leading up to a triangular hill-fort that has never been excavated and is known as 'Abbotsbury Castle.' From the hilltop of the Castle another hilltop can be seen to the east and closer to the sea and on top of it is perched a stone building. Beyond that is a lagoon separated from the sea and, nearer at hand, a great tree-filled hollow between the downs and the sea.

To begin the story of Abbotsbury at the beginning, or near enough, the Danes—after years of raiding and plundering Dorset —arrived in force at Poole under Cnut in A.D. 1015. Cnut's troops spread out over the land and eventually besieged London. In 1017 he was recognized as King of England and, like many of his followers, became a Christian. One of these converted followers was Urk or Orc who, with his wife Thola, founded the Benedictine abbey at Abbotsbury on land given to him by Cnut. The abbey stood there for five hundred years, until the Dissolution of the Monasteries, when the buildings were demolished and some of the stone incorporated into the house of the new owner, Sir Giles Strangways. Nothing remains of the abbey buildings but the south wall of the nave and parts of the gatehouse. Now the Strangways house in its turn has gone because in the Civil War Colonel Strangways declared for the King and resisted the Parliamentary troops under Sir Anthony Ashley Cooper in September 1644. "The business was extreme hot for about six hours," said the besiegers' report. They fired the house, but their own soldiers were plundering it, reckless or ignorant of the gunpowder stored there, and were blown sky-high. Nothing but a wall remains.

The church of St Nicholas was also defended for the King, and the fine panelled Jacobean pulpit has two bullet-holes in it from the battle. The second window in the south aisle is of fifteenth-century painted glass, a beautifully delicate face of a woman, usually supposed to be St Catherine but more likely the head of the Virgin from a Crucifixion window. The fragments of old glass in the south and north aisle windows are of most subtle colours. There is the effigy of a late-twelfth-century abbot, of Purbeck marble, in the porch.

The chapel of St Catherine, that building crowning the bare hill seen from the Castle, is some seven hundred yards seaward of the church. The stone walls are four feet thick, and the interior of the chapel measures only forty-five feet by fifteen. Every part, including the panelled ceiling and roof, is of stone, and the chapel has withstood the gales blowing in from Lyme Bay since 1370. Built at about the same time, and also still standing, is the Great

Tithe Barn, and great it is, measuring 272 feet long by thirty-one feet broad. It used to store the grain and wool brought to the abbey in tithes from the surrounding manors and farms. Built like a church, with transepts and lancets, it is one of the largest barns in England and stands at the foot of St Catherine's Hill and close to the ruins of the abbey with a small pond, populated by ducks and a large and alarming drake, standing between.

The swannery at the western end of the Fleet, that lagoon behind the Chesil, has existed unchanged since the end of the fourteenth century. The swans, ducks and other water birds caught in the decoy used to be eaten by the monks, but the birds are now caught and ringed for records kept by the Natural History Museum. The Swannery is open to the public at certain times.

West of Abbotsbury are the Sub-Tropical Gardens, first planted by Lord Ilchester in the eighteenth century. They are open to the public through spring and summer, and there you may see magnolias, camellias, azaleas and a wide variety of sub-tropical trees and water plants. The gardens are sheltered from the sea winds by ilex trees, and the beach is approached through an avenue of them, but the sea slips out of sight the closer one gets to it, hidden behind the Chesil Beach, the great bank of pebbles that rises to twenty feet between the marshy coastal strip and the sea.

'Chesil' is an Old English word for 'shingle', and the Chesil Beach is a bank of pebbles—"a prodigious riffe of beach," Defoe called it—that is, separated from the Dorset mainland for ten miles by the Fleet, a narrow sea loch, or lagoon, as I have called it earlier, whose width varies from two hundred to a thousand yards. The Beach continues westwards from Abbotsbury for seven miles as part of the main shore to West Bay. This is a natural formation, unique in Europe, a Dorset barrier-reef with a reputation for mackerel, shipwreck, dangerous currents and a variety of cast-ashore objects, from ships' boilers to silver ingots, exotic plants from the Americas and, in 1757, a mermaid—"no beauty", commented those who saw her.

The Beach was at its most impressive when I walked the twelve or thirteen miles from Abbotsbury to Chesil in Portland on a day in February just after a great gale. A heavy sea was still running, and waves the height of Abbotsbury barn were bringing in great balks of timber from a ship that had gone down off Guernsey, tossing them onto the steeply shelving shingle like cabers. I found no mermaids, but far along the Beach I saw hares scampering around. Did they survive on the sea-spinach and sea-holly and the patches of heath? And what did they drink? Presumably the brackish water of the Fleet, although an old Dorset farmer told me that he had seen hares swimming, and he believed that the Beach colony commuted to the vegetable gardens on the mainland on calm summer nights. There are a few shacks used by fishermen to store their gear, and some boats opposite Fleet House, and at one spot I found the corroded remains of a World War II bomber engine. It is a hard slog over the pebbles which can only be relieved by walking on the shore of the Fleet where a tangle of dead weed lies like thick coco-matting.

Between Abbotsbury and Portisham there are only three villages, none of them on the shore of the Fleet. Rodden, two miles east of Abbotsbury, is a small hamlet gathered about a stream and its manor, a 1750 stone house of three bays with a pediment over the central bay. Rodden may yet be developed into a bungalow and ranch-type dormitory village for those who work in Dorchester and Weymouth.

Langton Herring is closer to the sea and yet in the middle of nowhere and on the way to nowhere, the one road that leads to it from Rodden curving back to join the same Abbotsbury–Chickerell road again. The Herring part of the name comes from that same family whose name survives in Chaldon Herring, Winterborne Herringston, Herrison etc. The village is prudently set on a ridge above the Fleet, secluded among trees, architecturally unremarkable but decent and pleasantly stone in appearance. Between the middle of May and the middle of September the Western National 412 service from Weymouth to Bridport operates an open-top bus along the coast road, which makes a detour through the winding lanes to Langston Herring and Rodden. When the weather is fine, this is one of the best ways of seeing the Chesil coastline.

The third village is Fleet, which consists in total of Fleet itself, Fleet Common, West Fleet, Fleet House and East Fleet, from Old English *fleot*—meaning 'water, inlet, estuary'.

On 23rd September 1824 there was a great storm in Lyme Bay,

and the sea breached the pebble reef of the Chesil about three miles north-west of Weymouth, rushing through the gap to destroy most of the village of East Fleet and the church of Holy Trinity. In 1897 a man of eighty-seven who had been there at the time told the Reverend W. Miles Barton:

> At six o'-clock on the morning of the 23rd I was standing with other boys by the gate near the cattle pound when I saw, rushing up the valley, the tidal wave, driven by a hurricane and bearing upon its crest a whole haystack and other debris from the fields below. We ran for our lives to Chickerell, and when we returned found that five houses had been swept away and the church was in ruins.

This great storm became known as 'The Outrage' and there have been fears of a repetition ever since. In 1839 the October gales hoisted the 500-ton *Ebenezer* onto the top of the Chesil, from which it was later hauled into the Fleet and towed to Portland Roads.

Only the chancel of the old church remains and is used as a mortuary chapel. There are two brass plates to the memory of members of the Mohun family, those same Mohuns who came over with William the Conqueror and settled at Hammoon. One brass is to Robert Mohun and his wife Margaret, dated 1603, showing them kneeling at prayer, with nine sons behind the father and eight daughters behind the mother. Having borne seventeen children, Margaret lived to the age of ninety. The other brass is of 1612, to Maximilian Mohun and his wife Anna, with five sons behind the father and eight daughters behind his wife.

Holy Trinity new church was built five hundred yards further inland, at the expense of the vicar, George Gould, in memory of his son John who died in 1818. The ashlar is reddened now by lichen and this is a pretty church in a Gothic style deriving from the eighteenth-century Gothic Revival, surrounded by beech trees and iron railings.

In the 'old church' there is, in addition to tablets to the Mohuns, a brass memorial to John Meade Falkner, author of *Moonfleet*, now familiar to an even wider audience through a television version. It was in this churchyard (and *not* that of Holy Trinity where so many tourists believe the story to be placed) that young John Trenchard used to sit on a tomb above the Mohun vault where the smugglers hid their kegs of spirits.

Fleet House, now the Moonfleet Manor Hotel, is mostly Georgian, in a unique setting, with a large, heated swimming-pool, riding-stables and rowing-boats on the Fleet, which is narrow at this point though beyond it rears that formidable wall of shingle on which the sea can be heard pounding and, even on the calmest day, ceaselessly shifting millions of pebbles.

9

Heath and Furze are Everything

THAT Dorset may be divided into three parts is still to a great extent true. In 1907 Frank Heath, author of the first *Little Guide to Dorset*, commented that "The terms the old geographers applied to Arabia, although hackneyed, fit [Dorset] perfectly": that is, the designation *Petraea* of the North Downs that run through the north of the county from Shaftesbury to Pilsdon Pen and Lewesdon Hill and out to the Devon coast at Beer Head, and the South Downs that run from Eggardon through the southern part of Dorset into the Isle of Purbeck—North and South Downs accounting for roughly half of the county; *Felix* is the land of clays, principally the Vales of Blackmoor and Marshwood and the fertile river valleys, forming a quarter of the county; and the remaining quarter is *Deserta*, or 'Bruaria' as it was described in the Domesday Book. Bruaria is an area that has always been described as a roughly equilateral triangle of twenty-one-mile sides, the extremities being Cranborne, Dorchester and Studland.

For nearly a century this triangle has been called 'Egdon Heath', a name invented by Thomas Hardy in his novel *The Return of the Native*, (1878). In a preface reprinted in the current New Wessex Edition of *The Return*, Hardy explained that

Under the general name of 'Egdon Heath', which has been given to the sombre scene of the story, are united or typified heaths of various real names, to the number of at least a dozen; these being virtually one in character and aspect, though their original unity, or partial unity, is now somewhat disguised by intrusive strips and slices brought under the plough with varying degrees of success, or planting to woodland.

That was written in 1895. Since then the heathlands have been changed even more from the wastes of black heather—purple for only two or three weeks in the year, patches of scrub and bog and clumps of stunted trees, which was the landscape Hardy evoked, making it both harsher and more extensive than it was in reality even in his time. But then he was poet and novelist, treating landscape as a character.

Agricultural man and military man have both contributed to the change. During World War II many parts of the heaths were made to yield, with the help of fertilizers, both cereal and root crops. In World War I the Army tested a new-fangled weapon on the heath, and tanks have been at Bovingdon ever since. The Army has encroached in other areas, notably in the Purbeck Hills and on the Purbeck coast. During the Second World War, farms, dwellings and a complete village were taken over and made derelict and have been held ever since. The changes brought about by the Army are obvious when one looks down on the area from any height—the criss-cross scars where the tanks have torn up the heather and bracken and where the barren subsoil has been brought to the surface.

When Hardy wrote of Egdon in *The Return of the Native*, he was sitting in a room of a semi-detached house that overlooks the Stour and its meadows at Sturminster Newton, a landscape totally different from that of the heath. But immediately before starting the novel, he and his wife Emma had spent Christmas with his family at Higher Bockhampton, where his childhood impressions had been recharged by new contact with the heath and by the conversation of his mother and other older people. In his earliest known poem, 'Domicilium', Hardy had written of his birthplace, a long, low house both larger and more substantial than the average 'cottage' of the period (which is a label that has often been stuck on it by those who have no idea of what a Victorian Dorset cottage was really like). The house looks towards the fertile lands watered by the Frome and its tributaries—a vision of the Dorset *Felix*, but the almost blank rear wall is only yards from the heath that stretches, with a few fertile interruptions, towards and into Hampshire.

Hardy wrote of the land at the back of the house:

> Behind, the scene is wilder. Heath and furze
> Are everything that seems to grow and thrive
> Upon the uneven ground. A stunted thorn
> Stands here and there, indeed; and from a pit
> An oak uprises, springing from a seed
> Dropped by some bird a hundred years ago. . . .

Higher and Lower Bockhampton are in the parish of Stinsford
—a name derived possibly from 'stint', Old English *stynt*, meaning a limited piece of pasturage—limited by the heath, perhaps?
The heaths are dotted with natural pits called 'swallow' or 'swal-
let' holes, which were formed by the subsidence of the chalk
beneath the subsoil, or in some cases by the shifting of running
sand beneath the surface. It was probably in one of these pits that
young Hardy saw the oak growing. Close to the road on Briantspuddle Heath there is a pit a hundred yards in diameter and
forty feet deep with trees growing in the bottom. It is called
Culpepper's Dish'—spelled like that on the signpost at the
crossroads—because of a fancied resemblance to a pestle and
mortar.

As Hardy is responsible for Egdon Heath, let us see where it
first made its impact on him a child who was not expected to
reach maturity, and where he took the first steps of his eighty-
seven years. Of Stinsford and his imagination he made 'Mellstock',
and his heart is buried here among his ancestors where he had
wished his complete and unmutilated body to lie—his ashes are
in Westminster Abbey where he, the unbeliever, had not wanted
to lie. Stinsford churchyard was for him consecrated ground because his parents, his sister and first wife Emma lay in Dorset earth
at the edge of the heath. Close to the Hardys lies a Poet Laureate,
Cecil Day Lewis.

There are many descriptions of Hardy's birthplace, now administered by the National Trust, and of St Michael's Church
there is little to say. There remain the thirteenth-century arcades
and the square Norman font and the battered but impressive
Saxon relief of St Michael with spread wings on the outside of the
tower. As in so many other churches in which an organ was installed, the musicians' gallery has gone. In 'A Church Romance,
Mellstock: *c*1835', Hardy wrote:

> She turned in the high pew, until her sight
> Swept the west gallery, and caught its row
> Of music-men with viol, book, and bow
> Against the sinking sad tower-window light.

One of the music-men was Thomas Hardy senior, a self-employed mason in his mid-twenties, and the woman who turned in her pew to look for him was Jemima Hand who, five years later, became the writer's mother.

The local big house, Stinsford House, is immediately to the west of the church and is something of a mixture. The basement and ground storeys are mostly of the original seventeenth-century structure but from there up the building is early-nineteenth century, put up after a fire. And there are two other big houses nearby, Kingston Maurward House, a few hundred yards east of Stinsford church, and Kingston Maurward Old Manor House. The former was built in brick in 1717–20 and was faced with Portland stone in 1794. Arthur Oswald, in *Country Houses of Dorset*, recounts how, when the owner proudly showed his house to George III, visiting from Weymouth, the King crushingly commented, "Brick, Mr Pitt, brick." So George Pitt had his house encased in Portland stone and did the same with a brick temple in the grounds. The house is now the Dorset Farm Institute, and the county council also owns the Old Manor House, a late-Elizabethan E-plan house that was the seat of the Grey family (for whom the bridge over the Frome at the edge of Dorchester is named), whose last heiress married George Pitt, who then built his new house and linked the two by an avenue. The old house became a farmhouse, went downhill over the years, was saved by public appeal from demolition by the county council and has now been restored.

There are few villages on the poor heath soil itself because of the difficulty of getting a living out of it, excepting gravel or china-clay extraction. Most of the settlements are on the chalk or clay fringes, and those villages give their name to the heaths. Through the centre of the heathlands runs the Frome, which is joined by the South Winterborne at West Stafford, two miles east of Dorchester. The Piddle, sometimes marked on maps as the Trent, also comes down from the chalk downs in the centre of the county and runs for twenty-five miles, giving its name to eight villages before running parallel to the Frome in its last few miles and reaching the sea as an independent a few hundred yards north of the Frome's mouth east of Wareham.

Eight miles to the west of Dorchester the A35 road cuts through that group of forty-four round barrows (mentioned in the preceding chapter) called 'Poor Lot'—which refers more to the quality of the soil than to the barrows, I imagine. Half a mile before Winterborne Abbas (often spelled with a *u* in it), and immediately to the right of the road, is the circle of Nine Stones. All of them have been standing since about 1500 B.C., and the circle is twenty-five feet in diameter. In the wood behind the stones is the source of the South Winterborne.

St Mary's Church, Winterborne Abbas, has kept its musicians' wooden gallery, dated 1701. The chancel is Norman, and a carved piscina was dated by Sir Owen Morshead to just before the Black Death of 1348. The church, like the houses on the south side of the road, is reached by a footbridge over the stream that bubbles brightly between its banks beside the road. While the road winds up to Knowle Hill on its way to Dorchester, the Winterborne goes south-east almost immediately into a village gathered close about its banks. Winterborne Steepleton Manor was built of Portland stone in 1870 but looks older, and there is a stone and gabled rectory of 1850. Manor Farm is banded limestone and flint, from the seventeenth century, with a round arched window of the following century, and there are farm buildings of the same date and in the same architectural style. The Steepleton part of the village name derives from St Michael's fourteenth-century spire, one of the three medieval spires in Dorset, the others being at Trent and Iwerne Minster. The rest of the church is older, twelfth- and thirteenth-century, for the most part, with traces of wall-paintings and a Saxon nave with a flying angel of the tenth or eleventh century set into the south wall. A fine brass is to the memory of Daniel Sagittary, who died in 1756. Was he a son of the German doctor of Blandford?

The next village along the valley is Winterborne St Martin, or Martinstown, where the road widens into a broad village street with bridges over the Winterborne to the gardens of the stone and thatched houses. The fourteenth century was energetically restored in Victorian times, but the twelfth-century font was left in place.

A very narrow lane turns off the B3159 under the southern slopes of Maiden Castle to Winterborne Monkton, a huddle of houses of little architectural interest, some modern farm-buildings and the church of St Michael and St Jude, late Perpendicular with a Norman doorway, and with a very original and touching plaster figure of a long-haired young girl lying in bed. She was Ellerie Williams of Winterborne Herringston, the next place downstream, and the memorial is signed 'Alex Elliott, 1875'—apparently Major-General Sir Alexander Elliott, an amateur painter and modeller.

The meaning of 'Mai Dun' or 'Maiden' Castle is still uncertain. It could mean a flat-topped hill, the settlement on a hill in the plains or merely the great mound. It lies just to the north of Winterborne Monkton and two miles south of Dorchester. To say that it 'lies' there is to give little idea of how this great earthwork (enclosing 130 acres and in itself covering more than forty acres with some of the ramparts that are still standing rising some sixty feet high) dominates the surrounding plain and dwarfs both the tree-lined roads leading out of Dorchester and the housing estates spreading from the town. The fort was built during a series of occupations, beginning somewhere around 4000–3000 BC as a Neolithic camp. This was followed by an Iron Age fort around 350 BC, in which a sophisticated system of defences, pierced by gates, enclosed the village of timber huts. In the first century BC it was enlarged and fortified still more by invaders from north-west France. Mortimer Wheeler, who directed the excavations in 1938–9, believed that just before the Roman invasion Maiden Castle may have had a population of four to five thousand, who kept both sheep and cattle and tilled the soil. Vespasian's Second Legion stormed the fortress in AD 45, and in the 1938 excavations the skeletons of those killed in the battle or in flight were found just outside the eastern entrance. The ammunition used by the defenders, then and for long before, was round pebbles brought from the Chesil Beach and Portland. Huge stores of these sling-stones have been found at Maiden Castle. The fortifications were partly dismantled by the Romans but there was further sporadic occupation, and the Romans themselves built a temple at the top, the foundations of which are still visible. Maiden Castle has a powerful atmosphere at any season, weighing on the senses without imparting anything. It is as strong on a summer's day when the larks are singing and the gulls and rooks weave black and white patterns in the air as when the mist hides the roads and soggy fields below or the moon lights a snow-powdered landscape clear away to the post office masts to the west, which also seem insignificant and transitory beside the giant ramparts. In a very dry summer I collected from the chalky gullies between the banks a great variety of snail-shells, coral, toffee-and-chocolate striped, and sulphur or daffodil yellow.

The South Winterborne passes under the A354 just to the east of Winterborne Monkton and flows to Winterborne Herringston, where there is no hamlet, just a house or two and the tree-studded parkland that enclosed Herringston House, which stands on the bank of the stream. Given a Gothick façade at the beginning of the nineteenth century and a new east wing in 1899, Herringston retains much of its sixteenth- to seventeenth-century origins, including the tunnel-vaulted plaster ceiling in the Great Chamber, overwhelming in the number and variety of birds and beasts in the mouldings, with elaborate panelling and chimneypiece.

Winterborne Farringdon is merely a remembered name and a rebuilt wall—all that remains of St German's Church, incorporating a fourteenth-century window and fifteenth-century stones. Yet there was a village here in the Middle Ages, and probably its population was decimated by plague and the village was never resettled. There is not much of a village a quarter of a mile to the east at Winterborne Came either. On Came Down is Dorchester golf-course, from which there is a magnificent view over Weymouth Bay to Portland. In Came Wood at the top of the Down patches of grass-pierced concrete under the beeches show where much pre-invasion equipment was hidden in 1944 to await shipment across the Channel on D Day.

Just along the lane from the right-angle turn at the foot of Came Down there used to stand two Nissen huts in a field: I lived in one of them in 1941; and a hundred yards further along the lane there used to be a farmyard building, formerly carters' quarters, where I used to go to read and write.

It stood next to the stables, and the door had to be left open

M

to let out the pungent horse-ammonia that combined with the fumes of the paraffin-lamp to provoke instant tears. The cottage was hung with old harness, and up in the loft rats scuttled and jackdaws prattled. A friend used to come there to paint and some-times to practise the trumpet, when we had finished the day's work of digging up unexploded bombs anywhere from Yeovil to Wool, from Wooden Cabbage Farm's mud to the pebbles of the Chesil. And right there on Mr Cake's Came Farm we dug up a stick of hundred-pounders. Came Farm is south of the Winter-borne, whose course turns north-east-by-east to run through the grounds of Came House, built in 1754 by Francis Cartwright, whose memorial is in Blandford church and depicts Came House as his finest achievement. The house was constructed for John Damer, younger brother of that Damer who became Lord Milton. This Palladian mansion has barely been altered except for the addition of the north porch and a fine cast-iron conservatory of the early 1840s.

St Peter's Church is almost hidden by trees and the high walls of the gardens of Came House. A small Perpendicular church with a little tower, it was pleasantly refurnished in Victorian times. Nothing changes very much here, and only recently I saw something that reminded me of the year I lived in the parish—a notice dated 1940 hanging in the porch warning that village names must be removed from church documents on the notice-board. This was to confuse German parachutists disguised as brass-rubbers.

In the churchyard a simple Celtic cross is inscribed: "In memory of William Barnes. Died October 7th 1886 aged 86 years. For 24 years rector of this parish." The rectory where he lived and died is about half a mile away, on the Dorchester–Wareham road. Thatched and pink-washed 'estate rustic' of the early-nineteenth century, it is now marked on Ordnance Survey maps and is clearly named on the wall beside the gate, 'Came Old Rectory'.

Edmund Gosse recorded that

Hardy and I went on Monday last to Came Rectory, where [Barnes] lies bedridden. It is curious that he is dying as picturesquely as he lived. We found him in bed in his study, his face turned to the window, where the light came streaming in through flowering plants, his brown books on all sides of him save one, the wall behind him being hung with old green tapestry. He had a scarlet bedgown on, a kind of soft biretta of dark red wool on his head, from which his long white hair escaped on to the pillow; his grey beard, grown very long, upon his breast; his complexion, which you recollect as richly bronzed, has become blanched by keeping indoors, and is now waxily white where it is not waxily pink; the blue eyes, half shut, restless under languid lids. I wish I could paint for you the strange effect of this old, old man, lying in cardinal scarlet in his white bed, the only bright spot in the gloom of all these books.

A few months earlier Barnes had dictated to his daughter Lucy the moving poem of the recollection of life at the approach of death, the poem that ends:

> An' oh! it is a touchen thing
> The loven heart must rue,
> To hear behind his last farewell
> The geäte a-vallèn to.

A mile towards Broadmayne on the Wareham road is Whitcombe—a limestone farmhouse and buildings surrounded by a wall, a few thatched cottages and a little twelfth- to sixteenth-century church, now in the keeping of the Redundant Churches Fund and much as it was when Barnes preached there. Whitcombe was linked with the Came living, and it was there that he preached his first and last sermons. Whenever I sit in that quiet church, with its clear glass, its early-fifteenth-century wall-painting of St Christopher and its old bleached wood, Barnes is very close.

The Winterborne crosses the Wareham road north of Whitcombe and joins the Frome at West Stafford, where St Andrew's Church stands on a rise above the road, flanked by a barn and farm-buildings. The former rectory, of red brick, dated 1767, is now called 'Glebe Court'. In Stafford House, a few hundred yards to the north-West, a west front by Benjamin Ferrey of 1850 harmonizes with and is in the same limestone and ashlar as the east façade of 1633. Close by, the Frome celebrates its acceptance of the South Winterborne with a weir. Stafford House was the 'Froom-Everard House' of Hardy's story 'The Waiting Supper', and the weir or waterfall was the scene of a drowning in this 'Valley of the Great Dairies.' Denys Kay-Robinson, in his *Hardy's Wessex*

Re-appraised, makes a very convincing case for Lower Lewell Farm's being the Talbothays Farm of *Tess*. Just east of West Stafford is Talbothays Lodge, the villa Hardy designed for his brother Henry in 1893.

The North Winterborne rises in the highlands of central Dorset to the north of Milton Abbas. The first two villages along its course, Winterborne Houghton and Winterborne Stickland, have appeared in an earlier chapter. A mile south of Stickland is Winterborne Clenston, probably derived from 'the farm of Roger de Clencheston', patron of the church in 1312. Clenston's present St Nicholas was built in 1840 on the site of an earlier church and stands on a slight rise above the Winterborne, by itself on a greensward and backed by trees. It is in two shades of light grey, with flint and stone bands, and has a slender tower surmounted by a spire. The windows have the original bright glass of 1840, and the chancel ceiling is pale blue and decorated with gold stars.

The de Winterborne family's Clenston Manor has been neither bought nor sold since AD 1230, and the present house dates from the late-fifteenth- to early-sixteenth century, built of Portland and Purbeck stone, with flint courses and stone roof-tiles, and with mullioned windows dressed with Ham stone. The west side has a striking gabled staircase turret, built in the early-sixteenth century, projecting from it, and the whole house shows a satisfying continuity that has not masked the original Tudor house. Near the road is Clenston's tithe-barn of grey stone and flint, roofed with nineteenth-century red tiles set in a checkered pattern. Under these tiles is a magnificent hammerbeam roof with fine mouldings that may have been brought from Milton Abbey at the time of the Dissolution.

Winterborne Whitechurch is a place that can be rushed through too easily on the main road. Little is likely to halt the determined traveller but 'The Milton Arms', set end-on to the road and looking towards the one-sided village green that stands between two side turnings, one leading to Clenston and Stickland and the other to Milton Abbas. Here are thatched cottages, a post office and some sheltering trees standing back from the traffic changing gear to climb the hills.

St Mary's is as near-white as a church built of light grey stone and flint can be. Most of it is thirteenth century, including the central tower, but the nave was rebuilt by Benjamin Ferrey, and around 1882 a parson's lady, who had been caught up in the medievalizing of the period, stencilled the arches of the nave— by no means an outrageous idea as there was colour in the original chancel. The font is mid-fifteenth century, and the pulpit came from Milton Abbas church when Lord Milton had pulled it down.

John Wesley's grandfather was rector of Whitechurch for four years under the Commonwealth but was ejected in 1662. Like Pinney of Broadwindsor, he became an itinerant preacher but had less good fortune and a less influential family, being repeatedly imprisoned in various Dorset towns and dying eight years later, in 1670. Born in Whitechurch was George Turberville, poet and translator from the Latin, who served at Queen Elizabeth's embassy in Ivan the Terrible's Russia.

The road south from Whitechurch follows the eastward-curving line of the stream to Winterborne Kingston, which manages to have four roads running in and out of it and a triangle of houses in the middle of the village. It is always associated in my mind with small children. Whether or not there are many of them there or that they just happened to be in evidence when I have been there, I do not know. Just beyond the Greyhound Inn are the Batchelor Farm Supplies buildings, where, one hot day, a half-dozen small naked children splashed around with noisy glee in the water of a large trough set on the ground. Another time I went through the Norman-seeming doorway into St Michael's Church and found a dozen or so little children clambering around the pews at the same time as they sang a hymn, punctuating their singing with cries for a different hymn. The grey-haired lady in charge took them calmly through to the end and then let them launch vociferously into their top of the *A and M* pops for that week.

The grey and brown stone and flint church is mostly Decorated but was helped out by much restoration in 1872, when the Norman appearance of the doorway and of some of the interior was scalloped and plastered in most effectively. Four Henry VIII windows are more like those set into the walls of houses than in churches of the time. A mighty old yew grows in the churchyard, which overlooks back gardens and a landscape of scarlet runners, dahlias and beehives. Kingston is something of a muddle but a very friendly muddle.

Winterborne Muston, half a mile to the east, is just a large cottage built to look like a miniature manor house in the seventeenth to eighteenth centuries.

Another half-mile downstream is Winterborne Anderson, usually called just 'Anderson' or, in the past, 'Anderstone'. This manor house—for there is little else—was built in 1622 for the third John Tregonwell of Milton Abbas of rich dark red brick, every third course being of vitrified headers of an even darker, Burgundy red, dressed with white limestone. The five-sided and three-storeyed porch has a gable behind it to match the two flanking gables. The exterior of the house has remained unaltered through three-and-a-half centuries, but now it is almost completely screened by trees from the narrow private road that leads to it by a bridge over the Winterborne.

By the bridge is St Michael's Church, in flint and banded stone, 1889, and incorporating the south chapel of 1755. When I first saw the church, it was in the fading light of evening, and I thought that the shape of the bellcote was an optical illusion. But when I next went there, in strong summer light, I found that it is in fact assymetrical. A purple-and-gold-lettered notice-board states: "This building, formerly the parish church of Winterborne Anderson, has been appropriated to use as a private chapel." This has a ring of the age of Lord Milton, but it took place quite recently and should at least guarantee that the church does not become derelict.

This Winterborne village was distinguished from the rest by its 'five ash trees' spelled in a dozen different ways, including a good Dorset-sounding 'Vyfasshe'.

If Five-Ash Anderson has one of the manor gems of Dorset, Tomson has a treasure church. It is small and compact with twelfth-century nave and chancel all in one. The apse is Norman too, and the interior fittings are from the first half of the eighteenth century—a plastered wagon-roof, a two-decker pulpit with tester, Georgian pews and gallery. For many years this church was abandoned. Treves calling it ". . . a lowly church . . . a wizen old building, curiously small, with no more architectural pretence than a barn . . .", but it has been carefully restored. An inscription cut by Reynolds Stone records that it is

In memory of Albert Reginald Powys 1881–1936 CBE, Architect and Writer, the devoted servant for over 25 years of the Society for the Protection of Ancient Buildings, who was buried in this churchyard as he desired. This church, greatly loved by Thomas Hardy, was saved from ruin by the sale of certain of his manuscripts which paid for work done here 1929–31. As they shared life, love and death, this stone is set by Faith, wife of A. R. Powys.

Near the church is one thatched cottage, and just over the churchyard wall is a farmyard, part of Tomson Farm, a house of the sixteenth to seventeenth centuries with a hipped roof and mullioned windows. From the farmyard one can appreciate its impressive size, the two great chimney-breasts and the gabled three-storeyed porch.

Tomson is off the main road and not easy to find, a small and serene island on which the tiny Norman church seems to have been left like a boat on the land by some receding tide.

Winterborne Zelston (from Henry 'de Seles', fourteenth century) is most cunningly set on a looping road that follows a bend of the Winterborne to the north of the A31 where there is a pub called 'The General Allenby'. Zelston lies in this cul-de-sac, and the only road that runs out of it goes to Bushes Barn, about a mile to the north. I was once curious enough to walk the track running along the western side of Great Coll Wood to Combs Ditch, an Iron Age and Romano-British boundary-ditch bank which was excavated in 1965 and revealed successive enlargements over many centuries. The Ditch is nearly three miles long and crosses the A354 on Whatcombe Down.

Zelston has thatched cottages and modern bungalows; the banks of the stream between the bridges are planted with flowers. and there is a feeling of a community spirit among commuting or retired residents. After Anderson and Tomson, Zelston is tight-knit and cosy, neither a typical heath-border village nor a typical valley village but attractive in its own manner.

The road from Dorchester to Wimborne Minster, the A31, takes a northward turn shortly after Zelston, and it is soon obvious why. It runs beside a high brick wall that seems to go on for ever

—in fact for two miles—and encloses 650 acres of Charborough Park. The road was re-routed in 1841 to provide a larger park for the landowner, John Sawbridge Erle Drax.

There are three gateways into the park: Lion Lodge Gate, whose triumphal arch is topped by a lion; Stag Gate, which bears a stag above a high brick arch; and a gate at East Almer Lodge that made do with a simple pediment. There was a fourth gate, now inside the park as it was built in 1790 before the park itself was enlarged. This was the Peacock Lodge, but there is no peacock, just another stag.

Charborough was destroyed during the Civil War and rebuilt in 1661 by the Parliamentarian Sir Walter Erle, and it is said to contain timbers from Corfe Castle, which had been blown up by Sir Walter's forces. The house was extended early in the eighteenth century and again at the beginning of the nineteenth century. A small church was built behind the house for Thomas Erle Drax in 1775, but it was much changed in 1837 when it was filled with sixteenth- and seventeenth-century Flemish and German carved wood.

In Charborough Park stands the 120-feet-high folly tower that was the inspiration of Thomas Hardy's *Two on a Tower*. Treves did not approve of it: ". . . at a distance [it] looks like a factory chimney—can be see for miles. It was originally built in 1796, was struck by lightning in 1839 and unfortunately re-erected. It has been described as an example of the most distinctive and aggressive Strawberry Hill Gothic."

The present head of the Drax family and owner of Charborough, H. W. Plunkett-Ernle-Erle-Drax, is one of the patrons of the benefice of Red Post which was created in 1976 and comprises the parishes of Morden with Almer and Charborough, Bloxworth, Winterborne Zelston with Tomson, Anderson and Kingston.

The main gate to Charborough House, as distinct from the gates to the park, is Morden Round House, polygonal and thatched Gothic of around 1820, and on the other side of the road is the village of Almer, half a mile along a looping triangular road from Dorset's second Mapperton (the other is close to Beaminster). Almer House is a small, well-proportioned Elizabethan manor with mullioned windows and a five-sided projecting porch. The church of St Mary is set close to it but always seems to me to be waiting in the wings for its final place to be chosen. Of brown stone, it has a fifteenth-century tower and Norman arches in the north arcade where the north window has a mixture of glass from the fifteenth to eighteenth centuries and includes a Last Judgement that is Swiss and of 1610. Outside the church and west of the porch is a cross with the inscription, "This shaft is the base of an ancient cross and dates from about the year 1400. It stood for 400 years on the south side of Almer Manor House and was moved here in the year 1933."

Better known to travellers is Almer's World's End Inn, large, pleasant and thatched, standing back from the south side of the A31.

In St Mary's Church, Morden, the Charborough families are much in evidence. The most striking monument shows Thomas Earle on one knee in homage, his enormous thighs and buttocks recalling that heroic worker-style seen in Eastern European Communist countries. Whatever kind of Stakhanovite he may have been, there ". . . lieth buryed the bodie of Thomas Earle, the sone of Walter Earle, who departed from thes lyff the sixteen daye of Marche in the yeare of our God 1597".

Lytchett Matravers (perhaps 'Lychett' is more correct) is north-west of Lychett Heath and stands a couple of miles east of Morden on the same belt of woodland, more fertile and higher than the heath. Matravers was largely depopulated by the Black Death in 1348–9: the cottages were abandoned, and their occupants moved to higher and what was probably considered healthier ground. Even Lytchett Manor was deserted for a long time. But the creeping of modern building is doing more than repopulate the village 650 years later, because it is turning rapidly into a suburb of the Bournemouth–Poole conurbation.

The church of St Mary is almost a museum of Lytchett's past. There is a thirteenth-century chancel window, an early-sixteenth-century north arcade, and, in the fifteenth century, Margaret Clements, who died in 1505 but about whom not much is known, carried out some restoration. The village takes the second part of its name (the first is possibly 'grey wood') from Sir John Matravers, Maltravers or Mautravers, who died in 1365 and who is suspected of having been the murderer of King Edward II. True or not, the Matravers fret and the Arundell rudder are much in evidence in the church. The Arundell family came into possession in the four-teenth century by marriage, and at the end of the sixteenth century the property passed to the Duke of Norfolk and thence to the Trenchards in 1567. There are two interesting monuments, that to Sir John Maltravers, a grave-slab of black marble nine feet long and four feet eight inches broad with a few fragments of the original brass left, a few words of the marginal inscription in black letter; and the other a shroud-brass, the only one in Dorset, fifteen inches high and showing Thomas Pethyn, his shroud knotted on top of his head and falling to his heels but leaving his bony shanks and large feet bare. The shroud is draped over his left arm, his hands being placed palm to palm in prayer.

The roads around Morden are particularly baffling. Many of the hedges are mostly tall bracken, and at one spot there is a row of cottages called significantly 'Cold Barrow'; when I last saw the signpost to East Morden Grove, it pointed straight at a brick wall. But Morden is certainly north of Morden Heath, just as the village of Bloxworth is north of Bloxworth Heath and just south of Bloxworth Down, which again shows clearly that the villages are on the chalk rim of the heath.

The Red Post of the parishes now gathered together under that name is an actual red-painted iron signpost that stands where the road from Anderson and Tomson crosses the A31. In white lettering on red arms it states: "Winterborne Tomson ¼ mile, Anderson ½ mile, Winterborne Kingston 1½ miles, Winterborne Whitechurch 4 miles." It was at the crossroads that a crier used to call, "Oyez, oyez, oyez; this is to declare that a Court Leet will be held at Anderson Manor this day at twelve o'clock noon" on or near St Martin's Day, 11th November; the Court Leets were held there until the beginning of the present century. After the Court Leet the Lord of the Manor visited the cottages on his estate, and at that time the question of repairs would be discussed.

From the crossroads the road leads southwards to Bloxworth, which lies just to the north of the A35. To the south of that main road are Bloxworth Heath, Bere Heath, Morden Heath, Lower Hyde Heath, Decoy Heath, etc.

A few hundred yards down the road from Red Post there is Botany Bay Barn. Was it named in memory of the Tolpuddle exiles or because it is so far from its parent farm? And it is easy to get exiled on the way to Bloxworth if you head towards a giant water-tower thinking that it is the church, as I remember doing when the trees were in leaf and only part of the water-tower could be seen clearly. Bloxworth is built on several crossroads, and there is a pub that looks like a school. Council houses are no more architecturally attractive than usual, but there are some solid, well-thatched cottages dotted about as well as newer houses and bungalows in a variety of styles. St Andrew's Church was originnally a small Norman church belonging to Cerne Abbey. Only the south doorway remains of the Norman building, and most in evidence is the late-seventeenth-century restoration.

John Morton, who was born at Milborne St Andrew and rose to become Henry VII's Cardinal Archbishop of Canterbury, was rector here and was called "the fighting parson of Blokesworth". (There must once have been a homestead here that belonged in the Middle Ages to a bloke named Bloc.) A later rector than Morton is remembered thus:

> Here lies that reverend orthodox divine.
> Grave Mr Wellstead, aged seventy-nine.
> He was the painful pastor of this place
> Fifty-five years complete, during which space
> None justly could his conversation wound
> Nor's doctrine taint, 'twas so sincere, so sound,
> Thus having his long thread of life well spunne,
> 'Twas cutt, November's tenth in fifty-one.

The grave pastor, more painstaking than painful, I hope, died in 1651.

While the South Winterborne only just gets into the heath, the North Winterborne breaks through the chalk rim and then somewhat perversely runs north-east to join the Stour at Sturminster Marshall, thus forming a rough north-eastern boundary to the heaths. But the river that enters the heathland near its western end is the Piddle, which gives its name to the heath at the back of Hardy's birthplace, Puddletown Heath, and to the village of Puddletown. The Piddle crosses the heaths diagonally from northwest to south-east, disdains to join the Frome and enters Wareham Channel independently, divided from the Frome's mouth by the few hundred marshy yards of Swineham Point—which is no point at all but a muddy hammerhead.

I shall quote Treves once more:

A clear, bright stream, libellously called the Puddle, runs . . . across the Heath. On its way it gives to each of the many villages along its banks the unhappy cognomen of Puddle. The traveller who has crossed the Heath to Bloxworth and Bere may well return to the side of this rush-shaded river. Its course is marked by many trees, by many water-meadows, by endless flowers, so that it makes a path of generous green across a poor and famished country.

The libel was more general in Treves's time than it is now, but it still exists. I have heard elderly people and schoolchildren talk of 'Puddletrenthide' and 'Puddlehinton'. The stream was called 'Pidelen' stream in 966, a name of Germanic origin, and the spelling has varied through the centuries. On the church tower of Piddletrenthide it is spelled 'Pydel', and from the name of that village, meaning 'the Piddle village of thirty hides' (a measurement of land), the river was given the alternative name of 'Trent'. Since the 'small stream' meaning of piddle became a euphemism for 'piss', the Victorians referred to the river and those villages incorporating its name as Puddle. Ralph Wightman, born in Piddletrenthide, pleaded in his book *The Wessex Heathland* for a universal return to 'Piddle', and in that book he stoutly referred to 'Piddletown', 'Affpiddle' etc throughout. But some years later, in *Portrait of Dorset* (1965), he wrote: "The voters' lists, when I last saw them in 1946, still referred to Briantspiddle and Piddletown, but some six years ago a long County Council debate decided Piddletown should be Puddletown"—none of which changes the river or the villages.

In fact, there is nothing puddly or piddling about them. The Piddle rises in roughly the same latitude as the Cerne, just over two miles to the east, in the chalk near Alton Pancras, and follows a southward-flowing parallel course for over four miles before it turns eastwards.

The first village to which it gives name is Piddletrenthide, a long single street except at the northern end where there is less of a squeeze by the chalk downs. There is a space between the road and the Piddle, on the west bank of which stands All Saints', a church basically Norman and fifteenth century with some nineteenth-century restoration, built of stone in a variety of shades from buff to grey, and with an exceptionally beautiful tower.

"By purchasing this book you will help to preserve Piddletrent-hide's beautiful twelfth-century church. £10,000 is required to ensure that it will be preserved for the worship and enjoyment of future generations," wrote the vicar, the Reverend Derek Parry, in his foreword to the *Piddle Valley Cook Book*, a collection of recipes contributed by parishioners to help raise funds. It has been sold in pubs and grocery shops as well as in bookshops, and I used it as a kind of Christmas card for friends in the United States. It has sold very well to the gourmet who wants to know exactly how to make Southcombe Syllabub in the fashion of Mrs Girdwood, Mrs Baker's Piddle Apple Cake or Flirtation Tartlets by The Piddle Heart-Throb. Heather Parry, the vicar's wife, had the last word in one of her poems:

> In order to forestall a riot
> And keep the whole family quiet,
> I have said I will cook
> All the things in this book—
> And then we'll all go on a diet.

—not quite the last word because a London publisher did a hard-cover edition and pushed Piddle delicacies out into the wide world.

In the vicarage attic is a military museum collected and cata-logued by Nicholas Parry, the younger son of the family: uni-forms, weapons, posters, gas-masks, a wide variety of militaria on display under the rafters.

Piddletrenthide is full of surprises. I do not know of another pub called 'The Poachers', nor do I know of another village school with railings from Westminster Abbey. The railings were made in the sixteenth century and were the gift of John Bridge, of the London silversmiths Rundell and Bridge, who also gave the village its school in 1848 in memory of having been born in Piddletrent-hide, whose manor house the Bridge family acquired. Further down the valley from 'The Poachers' are 'The Thimble' and The Euro-pean Inn.

Piddlehinton is contiguous with Piddletrenthide, and at the right-hand turn westward to the Old Sherborne Road there is a venerable but ailing ash in the centre of the road. Opposite is the short path to St Mary's Church beside a house that has a finial from the church tower standing on the grass in front of it like a hitching-post. The Perpendicular church was restored in 1867, and there are two early brasses inside which are worth looking for. One is to William Golding, 1562, discovered in 1910 to be a palimpsest, showing on the reverse the lower part of a priest, the habit, cloak, girdle and staff thought to be of around 1500. A copy of this is shown beside the brass. The other brass is of Thomas Browne, 1617, a priest but portrayed in a large striped coat with leg-of-mutton sleeves and a ruff, wearing a high-crowned hat and carrying a walking-stick and a book.

Between Piddletrenthide and Piddlehinton, just to the west of the road that runs through them, is a hamlet called 'White Lackington', a farm and a few houses set on the banks of the Piddle. There is a bridle-path that goes from White Lackington to the top of the down near where that long straight road from Piddlehinton joins the Old Sherborne Road. The view from the top is splendid, and beyond Piddlehinton, up a long cul-de-sac running from the ash tree and war memorial in the middle of the crossroads, is the surprising sight of a tall thin chimney from which a plume of white smoke or steam rises straight up over the downs on calm days. In this somewhat unlikely setting is a plant for making cattle-food. On the top of the downs above White Lackington I have had some enjoyable skiing under a cobalt sky and a blazing sun that still brought the temperature nowhere near up to freezing-point. A mile south of Piddlehinton the road, the B3143, carries straight on to join the A35 just beyond Grey's Bridge at the edge of Dorchester. But the Piddle makes a sharp turn to the east, and another road, the B3142, follows its course to Puddletown. To the left of this road, and with the Piddle running through its grounds, is Waterston Manor which Hardy used as Bathsheba Everdene's house, 'Weatherbury Farm', in *Far From the Madding Crowd*. It is a fine manor of the early-seventeenth century which a fire in 1863 did not destroy but damaged. The exterior was carefully repaired, but there is little of the original interior left. It is a warm, calm and pleasant house which I used to enjoy visiting some years ago when it was owned by a friend, the writer Constantine FitzGibbon.

The B3142 joins the A354, the Dorchester–Blandford–Salisbury road, at Puddletown. There is a pub, 'The Blue Vinny', from whose corner can be seen, to the right and a few hundred yards away, the T-junction with the A35 Dorchester–Bere Regis road. There is a pub on this corner, too, the King's Arms Hotel, guarded by urban-looking traffic-lights and advertising itself by lettering on the stable roof. But Puddletown is much more than a meeting between two main roads. The Square has a row of thatched cottages built in the nineteenth century and a Tudor cottage of banded flint and stone, built in 1573; the brick vicarage is of 1722. Some two hundred years earlier, however, Cardinal Pole, the last Roman Catholic Archbishop of Canterbury, was vicar there for three years. St Mary's Church has a fine Norman font, and there is a stone memorial in the form of a cross-legged knight and his lady of *c*1300. There is a brass of 1517 to Roger Cheverell, one to Christopher Martyn of 1524 and another to Nicholas Martyn, 1595. In the south chapel of the church is the burial-place of the Martyn family. Their badge was the ape called Martin, just as the badger was Brock and the fox Reynard. Their motto was: "He who looks at Martyn's ape, Martyn's ape shall look at him." There is a chained ape at the feet of the alabaster effigy of Sir William Martyn, who died in 1503. He was Lord Mayor of London in 1493, and at about that time he had a new house built for himself at Athelhampton just to the east of Puddletown.

The Martyns lived at Athelhampton through eight generations. One of the finest houses in Dorset, it is crenellated and has a fine oriel dating from the end of the fifteenth century and a Great Hall with a magnificent timber roof, a great Chamber and a State Bedroom. Both house and gardens are open to the public at certain times. In the garden, on the greensward to the north of the house, is the early-sixteenth-century circular dovecote that has a ladder suspended from a *potence* (French for 'beam' or 'gibbet'), which can revolve around the dovecote to allow those collecting the pigeons' eggs to go from pigeon-hole to pigeon-hole without dismounting.

To the south of the A35 there is a walk of over two miles through Puddletown Forest, beginning and ending at the start of the Rhododendron Mile, brilliant in colour in late spring—for those who like them, which I do not. Behind the twenty-foot-high hedge are Forestry Commission plantations, regimented but not aggressive.

Downstream from Puddletown is Tolpuddle, a small village on the main road where the Piddle veers slightly south. From the lane to Affpuddle, which crosses both the Piddle and a subsidiary loop of the stream, one can obtain the best view of Tolpuddle, looking up towards the main road and beyond to rising land dotted with trees.

The story of the Tolpuddle Martyrs is too well-known for anything here but the broadest outline. Six Dorset farm-labourers formed a rudimentary trade union, administering an oath in the process, to keep wages above the starvation level to which they had fallen. They met in Tolpuddle under the sycamore tree whose trunk still stands, held together by cement. They were arrested, tried at Dorchester, found guilty and sentenced to seven years' transportation and were shipped to Australia in 1834.

These men were guilty of trying to keep their families from starvation, and they were the victims of those who lived in fear of revolt by the miserable masses in both country and town. It was only some forty-five years since the outbreak of the French Revolution and less than twenty years after the final defeat of Bonaparte. But there was a public outcry against the severity of the sentences, and the condemned men were pardoned and allowed to return to England. The Old Shire Hall in Dorchester, where they had been sentenced, is now a TUC memorial, and in Tolpuddle the Dorset men are remembered in the gateway to the Methodist Chapel (the Established Church and social protest rarely went hand in hand in Victorian England) and in the six cottages for pensioners built in 1934 as a centenary memorial by the TUC.

The Piddle goes on its vaguely south-eastern way, reaching Affpuddle in a mile. Aelfrith, whoever he was, gave the land hereabouts to the Abbey of Cerne in AD 987, but Cerne lost the lands at the Dissolution of the Monasteries in 1539 when the manor and advowson (patronage) were granted to Sir Oliver Lawrence of Creech Grange; and then for about 250 years the land passed back and forth between Lawrences and Framptons until, in 1914, Harry Frampton sold the property to Sir Ernest Debenham, London draper and founder of Debenham's stores. Debenham put into action the then 'modern' farming methods, reclaiming much land that had lain barren, building good solid cottages and the

great 'milk factory' on the Dorchester–Blandford road just outside Milborne St Andrew, equipped with concrete cowsheds and a
piped water-supply. Debenham brought life and organization to
the ten square miles of his estate—capitalism's answer to the
TUC along the valley, perhaps—which was broken up and sold
off on his death in 1952.

The Piddle bounds Affpuddle churchyard and the Garden of
Peace that adjoins it, beside the millrace of the now disused mill.
The control of water in the water meadows around was studied
and rationalized by George Boswell who lived at nearby Waddock
Farm and who published a book on irrigation control in 1779. It
was probably George Boswell who changed his early-eighteenth-
century house in 1797 so that it faced south instead of north.
Waddock is red brick and thatched, and if you go round to the
back you will find a more formal front than that on the
south.

St Laurence's Church in Affpuddle has a fine west tower of pale
grey stone and flint with a pediment and pinnacles in golden Ham
stone. The 1547 benches have poppyhead ends, and on one bench
in the north aisle is the carved inscription: "Thes seyts were
Mayd in the yeare of our Lord God MCCCCLVII the tyme of
Thomas Lylynton, vicar of this cherche." Lylynton had been appointed to the living in 1534 when he was a Cerne Abbey monk,
and as he stayed on after the Dissolution, he must have been
diplomatic, adaptable, acceptable or lucky. On the north wall of
the chancel is a monument bearing the Lawrence coat-of-arms,
said to have been the inspiration for the flag of the United States
of America. George Washington's mother was a Lawrence, and
her arms were quartered with the stars and stripes.

Briantspuddle is spelled in many ways on maps and in books,
'Briant', 'Bryant', 'Brian' and 'Bryan' figuring in the first part. In
the thirteenth and fourteenth centuries the village was called
'Pidel Turberville', but around the middle of the fifteenth century
it was changed in order to preserve the name of Brianus de Tur-
bervill among whose descendants Thomas Hardy placed 'Tess'. The
houses and cottages of the old village have been well restored with
white walls and good thatch, and mixing with them unobtrusively
are twentieth-century cottages and houses. Most striking of all
are those of the symmetrical Ring, a linked group sporting jaunty

N

thatched turrets, put up by Sir Ernest Debenham in 1919. A few hundred yards west is the hamlet of Bladen Valley, begun during the First World War and finished just afterwards, at the time the great war memorial by Eric Gill was erected: no tin-helmeted infantrymen going over the top here but a Virgin and Child on one side and on the other Christ holding in gashed hands a sword pointed to the ground.

Just over the hill to the south of Briantspuddle is Cloud's Hill, the cottage of that controversial folk hero of the First World War T. E. Lawrence. He first rented it when serving in the ranks in the Tank Corps at Bovington, a mile to the south, and he used it as a holiday home until he left the Royal Air Force (which he had later joined under the name of Shaw) in 1935 and lived there for only a few weeks before his fatal motorcycle accident. Cloud's Hill is now a National Trust property and is still much as Lawrence left it. He was buried in the cemetery at Moreton, across the road from the Georgian Gothick church of St Nicholas, 1776, which was damaged by a bomb in 1940. The five new windows were designed and engraved by Laurence Whistler (1958). The recumbent figure of Lawrence in Arab dress, by Eric Kennington, is often looked for here but is in St Martin's Church at Wareham.

Bang in the centre of Wool Heath, south of the desert warrior's cottage and of Eric Gill's war memorial at Briantspuddle, is Bovington Camp, one of the largest villages actually on the Great Heath. The *Shell Guide to Dorset* comments that the buildings are in ". . . the conventional style of military architecture—too hot for the tropics, too cold for the UK: unsightly in both. The heath is scarred with erosive tracks. Attempts are being made to heal some of the grey desolation by blocks of pine afforestation." There is little to add to that except to say that there is a fine Tank Museum, open to the public.

Why should Turner's Puddle be spelled in two words when Briantspuddle is spelled in one word? This village is on both banks of the Piddle, and its origins are more likely to be from the name 'Toner', 'Tonere' or 'Tonnerre' than 'Turner'. The two sides of the village are connected by Piddling bridges that flank fords. The largest house is a tall old farmhouse, and the church of the Holy Trinity was for a while in a state of bad repair with only the chancel waterproof and in use. I seem to remember it in this condition during and after World War II, but now the sixteenth-century nave and the chancel have been restored, and the stubby west tower of the same period holds up well after the repairs following a storm in 1758.

Bere Regis could be assumed to be the capital of the Dorset Heath villages. It gives its name to a heath but is not on but at the apex of the heathlands, on a chalk stream that rises near Milton Abbas and flows due south to Milborne St Andrew, hugged by the road. It carries on south-east then turns due south before flowing under the A35 through the ancient farm that used to be marked on maps as 'Shitterton' but has become 'Sitterton' and sometimes 'Shutterton'. In 1086 it was *Scetre* and inescapably derived from Old English for dung or manure. There was an attack of the Victorian piddles at some time, and Sitterton Farm, a fine early-eighteenth-century brick and thatched house, is decorously but illogically so-called.

Bere Regis was Kingsbere-sub-Greenhill (Woodbury Hill) in *Far from the Madding Crowd*. 'Regis' comes from Queen Elfrida, *not* one of the most lovable queens of England, who had her stepson Edward, thereafter known as 'the Martyr' stabbed to death at Corfe Castle so that her own son Ethelred (Unready because he could never make up his mind) could ascend the throne. Elfrida later stayed briefly at Bere Regis, and King John, ever in pursuit of some quarry or other, almost certainly hunted here when it was a royal demesne. In AD 1270 one half of the manor was granted to the Abbey of Tarrant and the other half to the Turberville family, who also acquired the first half at the time of the Dissolution.

The Norman arcade of the church of St John the Baptist has some lively carvings of heads, one of them said to be that of King John. Others are of men suffering from afflictions other than kingship—toothache and headache, and above the chancel is a boss carved into a hideous caricature, one does not know of whom. The wooden nave roof is elaborately carved with near-life-sized figures of the Apostles, and there are heraldic bosses representing the triumphs of Cardinal Morton, Henry VIII's Lord Chancellor and Archbishop of Canterbury. Morton, who died in 1500, founded a chantry here and was born, as I said earlier, in Milborne St

Andrew. His parents lie buried beneath the floor of the north
aisle, the Morton Chantry. The south aisle is the Turberville
Chapel, and their crypt lies beneath it.

The extensive watercress beds outside Bere Regis rely on artes-
ian wells which go a hundred feet below the chalk for the water
that bubbles under its own pressure at a constant temperature of
fifty degrees centigrade throughout the year.

Woodbury Hill, a mile east of Bere Regis, used to be the site
of a great fair that lasted five days. It was held yearly from about
AD 1267 and was the largest fair in Dorset. The first day was
called 'Wholesale Day', the second 'Gentlefolks' Day', the third
'Allfolks' Day', the fourth 'Sheep Fair', and the last day, a Friday,
was 'Pack and Penny Day', when the remaining goods were sold
off cheap.

As Thomas Hardy has figured so often in this chapter on the
Great or Egdon Heath villages, which, as I have shown, lie everywhere except on the Heath itself, here is a last quotation which
is from *Far From the Madding Crown*:

Greenhill was the Nijni Novgorod of South Wessex; and the busiest,
merriest, noisiest day of the whole statute number was the day of
the sheep fair. This yearly gathering was upon the summit of a
hill which retained in good preservation the remains of an ancient
earthwork, consisting of a huge rampart and entrenchment of an
oval form encircling the top of the hill, although somewhat broken
down here and there. . . .

When the autumn sun slanted over Greenhill this morning and
lighted the dewy flat upon its crest, nebulous clouds of dust were
to be seen floating between the pairs of hedges which streaked the
wide prospect around in all directions. These gradually converged
upon the base of the hill, and the flocks became individually visible,
climbing the serpentine ways which led to the top. Thus, in a slow
procession, they entered the opening to which the roads tended,
multitude after multitude, horned and hornless—blue flocks and
red flocks, buff flocks and brown flocks, according to the fancy of
the colourist and custom of the farm. Men were shouting, dogs
were barking, with greatest animation, but the thronging travellers
in so long a journey had grown nearly indifferent to such terrors,
though they still bleated piteously at the unwontedness of their
experiences, a tall shepherd rising here and there in the midst of
them, like a gigantic idol amid a crown of prostrate devotees.

The fair has not been held since before the First World War, and Egdon Heath, by Hardy's own admission, never existed as a single entity, but both fair and Heath and much more of Dorset now beyond reach still live in Hardy's words.

10

Semi-Detached Islands

THE Piddle, to the north of Swineham Point, and the Frome, to the south of it, reach the sea, which around the corner of the Arne Peninsula becomes Poole Harbour. Gigger's Island (there was a John Gigger, 1584), together with another silty dot in Lychett Bay, Pergin's Island in Hole's Bay, which is nearly landlocked and surrounded by Poole, Long Island, Round Island, Green Island, Furzey Island and—largest of all—Brownsea Island make up the dozen or so Dorset islands. Far better known are the Isle of Portland and the Isle of Purbeck, neither of which is an island, the former being a peninsula at the south-eastern extremity of the Chesil Beach and the latter an area bounded on the south and east by the English Channel, to the north by Poole Harbour and the River Frome and to the west by marshes and streams which often made Purbeck an island in past winters.

There is nothing else like Portland in Dorset. This almost tree-less block of limestone rises from the sea to a height of nearly five hundred feet at the Verne Citadel and is girt by precipitous cliffs except at the southern tip, Portland Bill, where stand the modern lighthouse, the triangular Trinity House obelisk of 1844 and the Pulpit Rock, which emerged a century ago as a result of the cutting-away of blocks of stone around it.

The 'island' is the shape of a lung, nine miles in circumference, four miles long and not two miles wide at its broadest point. Two hundred years ago Portland was often a complete island, and Ferry Bridge, where one now leaves the mainland, was in fact a ferry. The peninsula has suffered repeatedly from the battering of the sea, most recently in February 1979 when the waves smashed through the Chesil and swept through houses at Chiswell, piling high rubble and motor-cars, tearing up the road and making many homeless.

Portland's isolation from the mainland, the hard life of prising millions of tons of stone from under their feet, keeping at bay the sea, being raided by the Danes, threatened by Napoleon and having the island turned into a naval, military and prison fortress, gave the inhabitants a very special character of their own. Even now the islanders have beliefs, customs and turns of speech considered to be closer to the Channel Islands than to Dorset. Mainlanders as well as any other strangers are called 'kimberlins', and there is still the tradition that to call *Oryctolagus cuniculus* by its common English name is to invite bad luck. I once let it slip out inadvertently when talking with Reg Gill, a man much-versed in local lore and history. Knowing that I was a kimberlin, he forgave me, and in any case we were standing in St George's Church at the time. But, respecting Portland's tradition, I solemnly warn visitors to speak of 'bunnies', 'conies' or 'little furry creatures'.

From the mainland end of Portland the road climbs sharply up to and through Fortuneswell, Portland's largest village and the main shopping centre. Thomas Hardy gave a memorable picture of the island and of Fortuneswell in *The Well-Beloved*:

> . . . that Gibraltar of Wessex, the singular peninsula once an island, and still called such, that stretches out like the head of a bird into the English Channel. It is connected with the mainland by a long thin neck of pebbles "cast up by rages of the sea", and unparalleled in its kind in Europe . . . the ancient Vindilia Island, and the Home of the Slingers. The towering rock, the houses above houses, one man's doorstep rising behind his neighbour's chimney, the gardens hung up by one edge to the sky, the vegetables growing on apparently almost vertical planes. . . .

Fortuneswell is as vertical as a Mediterranean hill-town. Yet higher, up a left fork out of the top of the village, is the Verne Citadel, built by convicts in the 1860s as a fortress (growing French naval power alarmed the British Government), now HM Prison Training Centre entered by a bridge over a convict-dug ravine 120 feet deep and seventy feet wide. From the top of the

Verne Hill there are magnificent views of the Chesil Beach, with the West Dorset and Devon hills beyond. Below lies Portland Harbour, to the east St Aldhelm's Head, and Sandsfoot Castle over at Weymouth partners Portland Castle built by Henry VIII in an earlier fear that the French might invade this royal manor.

There are two other castles in Portland. Half-way down the east coast is Rufus Castle, which was already there in the twelfth century but which since then has mostly slid down the cliff into the sea. All that remains of Rufus or Bow-and-Arrow Castle is a single fifteenth-century pentagonal block and an archway. The public path passes it and goes down to Church Ope Cove, one of the few coves on the Portland coast where one can picnic and bathe with reasonable safety. At the top of the path is the Portland Museum, restored and given to Portland by Dr Marie Stopes. The building, two cottages dating from the seventeenth century, was 'Avice's cottage' in Hardy's *The Well-Beloved.*

Close to the Museum is the entrance to a different kind of castle, Pennslyvania Castle, built in 1800 by James Wyatt for John Penn, Governor of Portland and descendant of William Penn, who gave his name to an American state. It is now an hotel, almost hidden in the summertime by the trees which surround it. In these grounds are the sparse ruins of the old church of St Andrew's. The present Portland church dedicated to St Andrew is at Southwell and is known as 'the Avalanche Church'. This is not because, in addition to the gales and tidal waves, Portland suffers from heavy snowfalls (in fact, stray threads of the Gulf Stream keep its climate a fraction milder than that of the mainland) but because the church, designed by the ubiquitous Crickmay, was built in 1878 by public subscription as a memorial to the 106 men, women and children who perished in the collision, some twelve miles south-west of Portland Bill, between the clipper *Avalanche*, bound for Wellington, New Zealand, and the full-rigged sailing ship *Forest*, bound for the USA. Portlanders in two lerrets, Portland's own distinctive boats, brought twelve survivors out of the mountainous seas. Relatives and friends of those who were drowned donated money to raise a memorial church, which was consecrated on 3rd July 1879 by the Bishop of Salisbury. There is a stone inside the church stating that it is "In memory of the Portland men who rescued the survivors of the *Avalanche* and the *Forest*, 12 September, 1877. First boat, John Flann, Thomas Pearce, Joseph Shaddock, Lewis White, Thomas White, John Pitway, Thomas Pitway. Second boat, William Flann (Senior), William Flann (Junior), George Byatt, John Byatt, John Way, John Bennett, George White." This gives an idea of how the lifeboats were manned by close-knit families. Beneath these names appears: "Look to the rock from which you were hewn, to the quarry from which you were dug. Isaiah LI: v.I." There is a model of the *Avalanche* made of matchsticks by a prisoner in the Verne Prison, set in a recess above the brass plate that records: "This church, erected for the glory of God, was built by public subscription, in memorium of the Captain, passengers and crew whose names are here recorded beneath, of the ship *Avalanche* lost by Collision with the *Forest* in the Channel opposite this spot on the night of September 11th 1877." Opposite the church is Avalanche Cottage in Avalanche Road, so a century later the disaster is by no means forgotten.

St George's Church, Reforne, now usually called 'Portland St George' was abandoned long ago, and much of the interior, including the organ pipes, was ripped out by robbers. It was declared redundant on 16th April 1970 and was vested in the Redundant Churches Fund on 20th October 1971.

The church stands on the very top of Portland, surrounded by the stony desolation that is the legacy of a once-flourishing stone-quarrying industry that no longer flourishes. St George's was designed and built by a Portland mason, Thomas Gilbert (1754–66), who used Portland stone as Inigo Jones had done for the Banqueting Hall at Whitehall and as Christopher Wren did for St Paul's Cathedral. Cruciform in plan, the church has a central dome over the crossing, a west tower and a splendid interior with twin pulpits and galleries in both transepts and in the west end.

A particular memory of St George's is of Christmas carols on 12th December 1977 (when the box-pews were decorated with holly garlands) with the ecumenical participation of a captain of the Salvation Army and the priest from the parish Roman Catholic church.

'Tophill' is an apt geographical name for the plateau of Portland. Reg Gill, in whose presence I had mentioned the long-eared animal and who wrote a booklet about the *Avalanche* and the memorial church, told me in a letter that: "Mr Tompkins and I will be pleased to talk more with you. He has more knowledge of the stone and top hill—I was more naval and under hill." There are several local historians in Portland, gifted raconteurs to a man, such as Skylark Durston, who, as a mason, worked on the Cenotaph in London, on Whitehall and other public buildings. He has been fisherman and fireman too and is a living encyclopædia of all things Portland.

Some idea of Portland history is gained from a look around St George's churchyard, a plantation of gravestones many of which record the toll that the sea has taken. Here is another aspect of Portland life: "Sacred to the memory of Mary, daughter of John and Mary Way, who was shot by some of a press gang on 2nd April 1803, and died on 21st May the same year." And as another reminder of the great storms: "William Hansford aged 61 years who was killed on the 23rd November 1824, by the sea overflowing the village of Chissel, his leg was broken in attempting to make his escape. Afterwards the house fell on him." That storm was the 'Great Outrage' which smashed through the Chesil and demolished the old church at Fleet.

Easton's broad village street is bordered by pollarded trees and grass verges.

Sometimes the number of names for the same place seems confusing in Portland, for example, 'Chesil', 'Chesilton' and 'Chiswell', and this street of Easton is also called 'Wakeham', the name used by the Post Office for addressing purposes.

The new (1905) lighthouse at Portland Bill may be visited, its spotless and gleaming efficiency a welcome change from the huddle of black tea-shacks and souvenir-shops close by. Two earlier lighthouses, of 1716, were replaced in 1869 by the Old Higher Light, later a summer home of Dr Marie Stopes and now an hotel, and the Old Lower Light, now a Bird Observation Centre.

At Grove, on the most easterly part of the coast, is HM Borstal, formerly the 1848 prison built for convicts employed in the stonequarries to produce the stone for other convicts to built the breakwater to enclose four miles of sea in Portland Harbour. Prince Albert dropped the ceremonial stone into the sea on 25th July 1849, and the Prince of Wales laid the stone commemorating the completion of the work in August 1872. Convicts also built the church of St Peter at Grove in 1870–72—presumably as light and dry relief from work in the harbour. Its mosaic pavements were laid under the supervision of Constance Kent, who had acquired her knowledge of ceramic and mosaic at the Couvent de la Sagesse at Dinan, Brittany. When she was twenty-one, she confessed to having murdered her half-brother when she was fifteen. Her home-life must have been bizarre, because earlier, when she was twelve, she had chopped off her hair, dressed in boy's clothes and absconded with another, younger, brother. Found guilty of murder, her death sentence was commuted to twenty years' penal servitude, and while in Shepton Mallet gaol she was taken to Portland to direct the mosaic work at Grove. After release from prison, she went to Australia, where she became a dedicated nurse and nursing instructor and later ran a nurses' home until she retired at the age of ninety.

On returning to the mainland from the harshness of Portland, one plunges into Weymouth's suburbs, the Georgian façades of the town centre, the mixed blessings of a seaside resort in summertime, and one of the most confusing traffic-systems ever imposed on a small town. This makes Weymouth a town to walk in rather than ride in. There are quays, the Nothe Gardens high above the harbour, a ferry to the Channel Islands and France, and on the promenade a spirited 1809 statue of George III, not to be taken too seriously, and the 1887 Golden Jubilee clock-tower in the same genre. Both are full of colour and good fun to look at. And Weymouth is a cheerful and colourful town—if you can once get into it and park somewhere!

George III, remembered by grateful Weymouth, was also depicted on horseback in a chalk design 280 feet long and 323 feet high, the horse cut into the down in 1808 and the King hoisted on its back seven years later—riding away from Weymouth, it has been said ever since. For ever trotting towards Cockaigne, 'King Jarge' is immediately above Osmington, a stone village in a glen or dell, with many thatched houses and the White House which, with its 1830 bow windows, recalls Lyme Regis, Charmouth and Weymouth. The date 1697 is over the doorway of East Farm, but with its stone mullioned windows and hoodmoulds it seems to belong to an earlier architectural style. Charity Farm, at the north end of the village, has stables and byre built into the same range as the house. In the chancel of St Osmund's Church is a seventeenth-century memorial to a member of the Warham family, one of whom was Archbishop of Canterbury in the time of Henry VII and Henry VIII. Three inscriptions are crudely cut, as if by someone unlettered who merely copied clumsily something written down for him. One is in Latin and states defiantly: "I have come into harbour. Farewell Hope and farewell Fortune. I am done with you. Sport now with others." The second records: "Man's Life. Man is a glas: Life is as water that's weakly walled about: Sinne brings in Death: Death breakes the glas: So runnes the water out. Finis." The third announces: "Here is not the man who in his life with every man had law and strife."

Osmington Mills is a tiny hamlet squeezed into the valley of the narrow stream that bubbles around the Smuggler's Inn. The Dorset Coast Path runs through the pub garden and along the side of the house, and there is a fine cliff-top walk from Overcombe, just to the east of Weymouth. The view of Weymouth Bay from the beach is the one which Constable painted while on honeymoon at Osmington, when he also painted 'Osmington Village'.

The next two villages along this road to the east now suffer from 'development', but each has a carefully-concealed manor house as a tangible link with the past. Poxwell, or 'Pokeswell' as it used to be spelled and is still pronounced, shows its whereabouts by a pretty brick gatehouse, hexagonal and with a pyramidal roof. The house is early-seventeenth century, and in Hardy's *The Trumpet Major* it is Squire Derriman's Oxwell Hall. The manor house at Owermoigne, Moigne Court, dates from 1270, and its Early English traceried windows give it much more the air of an ecclesiastical building than a manor house protected only by a moat at one time. It is far more ecclesiastical and much less of a fortress than Woodsford Castle, three miles away to the north and on the road to Athelhampton. Woodsford was built sixty years before Owermoigne, in 1337, was allowed to be crenellated, still has a square tower with arrow slits in it and, for all its peaceful charm under its enormous spread of thick thatch, still looks very fortified. Not so Moigne Court, which by comparison, appears open and defenceless—but not, one hopes, against the besieging developers.

Just to the east of Owermoigne a road leads off south of the main road and loops around to West Chaldon and East Chaldon or Chaldon Herring and Winfrith Newburgh before rejoining the A352. The 'Herring' in Chaldon is the name of the same family remembered in Winterborne Herringston, Langton Herring and Herrison. West Chaldon was also called 'Chaldon Boys' from the family of Boys or Bosco who held land there in the thirteenth century.

In the present century East Chaldon has attracted both literary residents and allusions. T. F. Powys lived here for many years and used the village under the name 'Folly Down' in his novel *Mr Weston's Good Wine* (1927); the youngest of the Powys brothers, Llewelyn, lived and wrote in a cottage on the downs close by; David Garnett used the name of East Chaldon's inn for the title of his novel *The Sailor's Return* (1925); Sylvia Townsend Warner lived here before moving to Maiden Newton, and she and the poet Valentine Ackland are buried in St Nicholas's churchyard. I once noticed, during a service in the churchyard, a dead fox grinning from the hedge—a vision that would have intrigued Sylvia and T. F. Powys and David Garnett—author of *Lady into Fox*.

This sweeping countryside of downs with the sea beyond has a long history of human occupation. There are over thirty round barrows in East Chaldon parish, a line of them just north of the church is known as 'the Five Marys', two of which were found to contain skeletons in a sitting position with stag's antlers on their shoulders.

North-east of Chaldon is Winfrith Newburgh, where on another occasion, I saw under a yew tree in the churchyard a tibia, a radius, two phalanges, a split flint and a rusted sickle blade gathered into an earthy and haphazard heraldic grouping. Something in this district brings death easily to the surface.

Winfrith church stands at the southern end of the village, farm buildings close by and lime-trees surrounding it. The tower is fifteenth century; both doorways are Norman, and the north aisle was added in 1854 because the church had become too small for the congregation. The village street begins at the church, and just along from it is a brick manor house with outbuildings that include a sixteenth-century barn. Winfrith House is eighteenth century and hides behind a very tall brick wall. This self-contained village with many thatched cottages has its own stream—the Winfrith, 'the bright stream' of the Celts, that flows north across Winfrith Heath to the Atomic Energy Establishment that sits clean and functional to produce its own bright stream of energy and whose buildings are dwarfed by the immensity of the heath. Perhaps more than anything, it is the Steam Generating Heavy Water Reactor and its two cooling-towers that show up in reality the scope of Egdon that Hardy gave it in fiction.

Three-quarters of a century ago Treves called Wool ". . . once a pretty village enough, but the railway has contaminated it". Wool cannot win because the railway is still there, and it is now also the meeting-place of a number of roads. The real village has to be looked for away from the main road, and in Spring Street there are thatched cottages standing well back from the road beyond a broad grass verge.

Wool Bridge has crossed the Frome since the sixteenth century, and Woolbridge Manor, now an hotel, has stood beside it since the early-seventeenth century. A mellow mixture of stone and brick, it was once the home of the real-life Turbervilles and also the house where Hardy set Tess's honeymoon. On the landing at the top of the stairs are the portraits, now somewhat debased by ill-advised retouching, that frightened Tess. To the east of Wool is the site of Bindon Abbey—but further than Hardy placed it— where one can still see embedded in the ground the stone coffin in which Tess was placed by Angel Clare.

Woolbridge Manor remains the aloof and calm house it has been for centuries—well, not always calm, because it may have been damaged during the Civil War—set low beside the Frome away from the motor traffic which in summer often becomes one long traffic-jam when the railway-crossing gates are closed.

On the B3071 due south of Wool is Coombe Keynes, a few thatched cottages with a farmyard-range on the left of the road turned into a dwelling-place. Opposite is a tiny triangular green with a signpost pointing "To the Church of the Holy Rood". But the thirteenth-century church, of which the west tower and the chancel arch remain while the rest was restored by Hicks in 1860–61, seems abandoned, although the windows have been shuttered, and in general it looks to be in good condition. A bearded young man in the village told me that the key of the church is now with the priest at Wool and that it was hoped that the church would be handed to the village so that local people could look after it. Apart from my informant, the village at 2.30 p.m. on a bright March day, was totally deserted, and it was like having stepped into a painting.

To the right of the road to Lulworth and only a short walk away are the North Lodges to Lulworth Castle, 1785, ashlar-faced but now in poor repair. Also in the grounds of Lulworth Castle but in the parish of Coombe Keynes are the Clare Towers, a gateway of rubble and brick, late-eighteenth century and in a ruinous state but worth walking to see.

Three roads lead into East Lulworth, and one road describes an ellipse around the village, which has a very 'estate' feeling and aspect. The big house here was Lulworth Castle, now ruinous after a disastrous fire in 1929. It was built just before 1610 for the third Viscount Bindon, whose seat was at Bindon Abbey near Wool. As it was his second house, the work did not proceed very urgently, and the interior was still unfinished when it was sold to the Roman Catholic Weld family. The outside was finished, and despite the building being a shell now, it still looks the same— that is, a four-square battlemented building with four-storeyed round towers at the corners, the whole built of brick and faced with Purbeck and Portland stone. It must always have been more impressive than attractive, and now that it is an ivy-clad ruin very much knocked about by the fire (it had also been stripped of its lead and iron in the Civil War), it has the look of a back-drop to a Gothic drama.

The parish church of St Andrew has a fifteenth-century tower but is mostly by Hicks, 1864, and could never have been of close concern to the Welds who asked, and were granted, permission by George III to build a Roman Catholic church for their own use. Perhaps the King's mood was favourably prepared by the Welds putting his food before him on gold and silver plate and having the fifteen Weld children sing 'God Save the King' for him. It is said, nevertheless, that George III told Thomas Weld to make the building look as little like a church as possible. John Tasker designed and built St Mary's, 1786–7, in a most attractive form, like a theatre lifted bodily from pre-Revolution Versailles. The interior has galleries on Tuscan columns and a great central dome painted like a sky in which float a few serene clouds. It is a most elegant little church which Fanny Burney called "a Pantheon in miniature".

Both West Lulworth and Lulworth Cove are best visited outside the main holiday months if you want to look around the village, which has many interesting cottages of the late-eighteenth and early-nineteenth centuries and some of earlier date. The second or third on the left-hand side of the road as you enter the village from the Lulworth Camp direction has set into an end brick wall two terracotta plaques, one the head of Anne Boleyn wearing the crown and the other her personal badge of a falcon with outspread wings, also crowned and holding the sceptre. At the Cove end of the village street is a mid-eighteenth-century cottage, and a little further along one of about 1840. The Doll's House on the right, with its one downstairs room, lean-to and two tiny rooms above, merits its name.

The nearly circular bowl of Lulworth Cove is open to the sea through a four-hundred-foot-wide breach in the Portland stone cliffs, through which has been washed out the softer rocks, sands and clays. To the west is Stair Hole, narrower and even more dramatic, another inroad of the sea that shows clearly the tremendous past pressures in the tortured strata now startlingly revealed. In maybe only a few hundred years the sea will batter through from Stair Hole to the Cove.

During World War II the Army took over a vast area of Purbeck for training purposes, evacuating 225 people from their homes with the promise that they would be allowed to return when the war ended. But those exiles who survive are still exiles, and about a thousand acres, from $5\frac{1}{2}$ miles of coastline between Lulworth and Brandy Bay and extending five miles northwards, is still crawled over by tanks and fired over by artillery. For nearly thirty years a campaign was waged to get the Army out, or at least to get the area opened up occasionally to the public. In 1974 Lord Nugent's Defence Lands Committee report was published, and on the same day a public trust was founded, Friends of Tyneham Limited, ". . . ready to step in when the the ten square miles of the Dorset coastal army ranges are released. Meanwhile it is raising funds towards projects to protect Dorset's most outstanding wildlife refuge and to help restore Tyneham's battered historic buildings."

The Lulworth Range Walks are now open during the whole of August and at each weekend during the rest of the year from Saturday noon to Sunday evening. Work has proceeded to make safe those buildings damaged by shellfire, and the church has now been leased by the Army for twenty-one years from 1977 as a museum. The length of that lease indicates a determination to continue in occupation, I think.

The first time I saw Tyneham was in 1943 after scrambling ashore from a bumpy and puke-streaked landing-craft. I can remember little about this exercise or why we parachutists were involved in a mock-up of a seaborne invasion. I recall sleeping on the floor of an empty house near the church, which I have not been able to identify on subsequent visits, but the old concrete telephone-kiosk, of a style that was even then very rare, still survives.

To get to Tyneham village, take the road eastward out of East Lulworth just beyond White Gate Lodge. Follow it up Whiteway Hill and over Povington Hill—on whose north slope rises the stream known as 'Luckford Lake' which flows north over Holme Heath to the Frome and forms the western boundary of Purbeck Island—until you get to West Creech Hill, where a signposted road to the right doubles back westward to Tyneham, the only road in and out of the village.

The boards have at last been taken down from the windows of St Mary's, a small cruciform church with central bellcote and a fourteenth-century south porch that at some time was dismantled and re-assembled at the west end of the church. Part of the chancel and north transept are also Early English, and in the north transept there is a stone cross memorial of 1487 to Thomas Mohun, another member of that family who settled on the banks of the Stour at Hammoon and by the Chesil at Moonfleet. There are also memorials to the Bond family of Tyneham House, whose seat was at nearby Creech Grange; it was they who gave their name to Bond Street in London. The earliest part of the house is fourteenth century, and the rest is from 1583. Pre-war photographs show a dignified three-gabled house set around with level lawns and terraces and shielded by trees. Now the house, much deterior-

o

ated, is hidden in a jungle. But Tyneham, village and house, should be seen for an idea of what remains still barred to the civilians of this country and what may, it is hoped, be free again and give everyday access to the Iron Age fort of Flowers Barrow and the sea at Worbarrow Bay.

After the turning down to Tyneham from the top of the ridge, the next turn to the right over the crest of West Creech Hill leads down to Steeple and Kimmeridge, while the left-hand fork goes north to Creech Grange and Creech and eventually straight north to Wareham. It is easy to overlook Steeple, which is just a church, the manor house and farmhouse, all on a small knoll in the Steeple stream valley south of the ridgeway. It is virtually unspoilt and mercifully remains just outside the military occupation area. The fifteenth-century church has a Norman south doorway and the same Lawrence arms, the stars and stripes, of those collateral ancestors of George Washington, to be seen in Briantspuddle church. Here the arms appear in the barrel-vault built by the Lawrences, from whom the lordship of the manor passed at the end of the seventeenth century to the Bond family. The manor house was begun in about AD 1600 but has had many additions, the north-west front being dated 1698 and bearing the crest of the Clavells.

Creech Grange is Elizabethan in origin, has a Palladian south front of 1740 and 1847 alterations and additions, including the east front. A chapel was built in 1746 and incorporated a Norman arch from Holme Priory. In the 1850s–1860s a neo-Norman church was built around it, consecrated in 1859. As this church was in Steeple parish, the curate had to cross the ridgeway to conduct services. This journey from St Michael's, Steeple, to St John Evangelist, Creech, came "very near mountaineering" in Ralph Wightman's words. I have done it, and it is! Paul Hyland in *Purbeck the Ingrained Island* tells how one curate spent a summer cutting steps up the ridgeway's flank to make his wintertime progress a little easier. It is still a spectacular journey because at the top of that punishing climb, at about 650 feet, stands Grange Arch. Built in the 1740s, this is a battlemented arch of Portland stone ashlar with openings on either side topped by pyramidal finials. Sometimes called 'Bond's Folly', it was just that—another example of the eighteenth-century passion for follies. It was an eye-catcher designed to be viewed from Creech Grange, which lies below ilexes and yews, with its three rectangular lakes and the Italianate white tower of St John Evangelist. The Arch and an acre of ground were given to the National Trust by Mr J. W. G. Bond in 1942.

Gerald Plant patrols a great stretch of this part of the coast for HM Coastguard, and he once gave us a lift from Gaulter's Gap up to the ridgeway to shorten the walk to Corfe Castle, where there was a bus to catch. On that summer evening he pointed out from the Arch a great deal that we would have missed. He belongs to a family evacuated during the war and now lives in West Lulworth. Very little in that district and along the cliffs and shore misses his eye.

A quarter of a mile east of Steeple there is a right-angle turn to Kimmeridge, a mile to the south. This well-kept village of stone cottages of the seventeenth to nineteenth centuries, some stone-roofed and some thatched, has a post office-cum-general stores with the dual attractions of a plastered barrel-vaulted ceiling and excellent teas that can be served on the terrace just above the village street. The church is of unknown dedication, the nave twelfth century in origin, and there is a Norman south doorway and a fifteenth-century bellcote. Much restoration was carried out in 1872. East of the church is the Old Parsonage, built in 1837 in the style of two hundred years earlier, complete with a stone roof and stone-mullioned windows. Kimmeridge Farm is near the church and almost in the village street, with the Mansel shield-of-arms over the front entrance and at the back a stone let into the wall with the date 1829, which must have been the date of alterations because the house is much older than that.

Kimmeridge has a surprising industrial history, a good deal of it abortive. The village lies mostly on Kimmeridge clay, which is rich in fossils. One of them, *Pliosaurus grandis*, holds high its seven-foot-long head in Dorchester Museum. The clay has in it layers of bituminous shale, the hardest of which is called blackstone or 'Kimmeridge Coal'. In prehistoric and Roman times this blackstone was fashioned into ornaments, and the discs found in profusion and called 'coal money' are the waste material from lathes turning amulets. The Romans made salt here, and in the 1620s Sir William Clavell boiled sea-water to obtain salt, using

the shale as fuel for the fires. In the middle of the previous century Lord Mountjoy had obtained a patent to make alum here.
This had come to nothing, but it gave Clavell another idea, and he
set up an alum-works, but he ran into trouble with the London
alum-merchants, to whom Charles I had granted the sole patent
for making alum in England. These merchants seized Clavell's
property and extracted £1,000 a year from him—a kind of protec-
tion-racket—before returning to wreck the works and rustle
Clavell's cattle. He failed in an action he brought and then tried
to turn Kimmeridge into a port, building a pier which fell into
ruin and finally collapsed in a storm in 1745. Blocks of stone
from it can still be seen on the east side of Kimmeridge Bay,
together with bits of two separate sea-walls. Clavell also tried
making glass at Kimmeridge, but this failed too, and he spent
some time in prison before dying in 1644.

In the mid-nineteenth century, when oil was extracted from the
shale, tramways, inclined planes and causeways were built, under
an Act of Parliament of 1847, to bring shale from the workings
for transport to Weymouth where naphtha, dyes, pitch, varnish
and other commodities were produced from it. There was even a
contract to light Paris with gas refined from the shale oil, one
great problem could not be overcome: both oil and gas stank of
sulphur when burned. But it was not the end of Kimmeridge as
a non-boom town. In 1959 an oil-well went into operation on the
cliff to the west of Gaulter Gap. The tale of Kimmeridge has at
last lived up to its ancient beginnings and prosperity. The oil has
been pumped from the cornbrash strata over fifteen hundred feet
below the surface, at up to more than 100,000 gallons a week,
producing 200,000 tonnes of crude oil between 1961 and 1974
alone. There are no derricks, towering tanks and sheds here, no
traditional oil boom-town, and one has to look carefully for the
machinery, which is painted green to blend into the background
and which stands in a small enclosure behind its fence, nodding its
head gently and looking like a toy donkey. 'The Donkey' is what
it is called, and it is steadily plodding and nodding its way towards
acceptance as a piece of industrial archæology.

On Hen Cliff, on the opposite, eastern, side of Kimmeridge
Bay, stands Clavel Tower, built around 1820 by the Reverend
John Richards who adopted the name Clavell on inheriting Smed-

more, the nearby big house, in 1817. Why his tower lost an 'l', I do not know. It is circular, consisting of three storeys with a colonnade around the bottom and mock machicolation and a parapet at the top. Not only is it a folly but it is near becoming a ruined folly, is unsafe and protected by barbed wire.

Kimmeridge Bay is not an ideal spot for bathing or picnics because there are many rocks on the shore, and the lowering aspect of the dark grey cliffs is like a disturbing shadow on all but the brightest day. There is a toll-road down to the grassy car-park near the sea, and in summer there are plenty of visitors—some, perhaps, disappointed at finding a black beach in place of golden sands. Great slabs of flat rock lie on the shore, fallen from the cliffs as the clay strata were washed out. A long and impressive line of these slabs runs along eastwards beyond Clavell's Hard and Rope Lake and are called 'the Kimmeridge Ledges'.

A private road leads from Kimmeridge village for a mile southeast to Smedmore House, built by Sir William Clavell at the time he set up his alum-works, his "little newe House" he called it in 1632 when he moved there from Barnston Manor near Church Knowle. The original parts of the house are visible at the back (the house is open at certain times to the public) from the secluded courtyard and garden. The west front of Smedmore is eighteenth century, and the entrance has the date 1761 on the rainwater heads. On either side of the doorway are astonishingly large window-bays that pout like cherub's cheeks. There is some fine eighteenth-century plasterwork inside and an oak staircase of the early-eighteenth century with balusters alternately twisted and turned. Smedmore estate has been in the hands of the Clavells and their descendants the Mansels for six centuries, although it was touch-and-go at the time of Sir William's disastrous experiments with industry.

Church Knowle is a small village of Purbeck stone almost at the centre of Purbeck. At the beginning of the village, and to the right of the road, there is the New Inn, which was built in the seventeenth century, and added to in the eighteenth. Further up the street on the same side is 'The Old Cottage', which is also seventeenth century. St Peter's Church, at the other end of the village is thirteenth century and the west tower of 1741 is a triumphant addition. Inside, much is made of St Peter's keys in

stone carvings and in the windows. A painted wooden gallery runs
over the north aisle of 1833–4, in which there are pews and at the
chancel end a place for children whose drawings are exhibited
there, sketches of ships and fish accompanied by poems about
Jesus and His love for children of all colours. The chancel arch
has some interesting leaf decoration. A well-preserved altar-tomb
of 1572 shows us John Clavell (1541–1609) and his two wives,
Myllicent and Susan. Clavell is wearing Elizabethan armour, his
helmet and gauntlets beside him as he kneels in prayer. His first
wife Myllicent kneels with her three sons and daughter, while
Susan—at that time just married and without issue—kneels
alone.

Corfe Castle, a mile and a half to the east, stands at the only
gap (*ceorfan*, Old English, 'a cutting') in the ridge of the Purbeck
Hills that separates Purbeck from the heathlands to the north. In
addition to being placed in this strategic position, the castle was
built on a conical hill in the centre of the pass it guarded. The hill,
crowned by the towering ruins, has become as much a visual
symbol of Dorset through reproduction on calendars, teacloths,
beermats and so forth as the Eiffel Tower is of Paris and the Acro-
polis of Athens. But however familiar its photographed and printed
outlines may seem, each time the castle is seen in the stone, it
comes as a new shock even without knowing anything of its long
and violent history. I find there an atmosphere akin to that of
Mycenae. Perhaps it is because both places seem to hold in the
ruins of massive masonry so much cruelty and bloodshed.

Because of its position, it is possible that there was always
a settlement at Corfe protected by some kind of fortifications.
What is certain is that Aelfrith, or Elfrida, widow of King
Edgar, had a house or hunting-lodge there in 978. Edgar
had ruled England wisely and well from 957 to 975, but
Dunstan, Archbishop of Canterbury, had delayed his coronation
until 973 because Edgar, after the death of his first wife, wished
to marry Aelfrith and could achieve this only by killing her husband, Aethelwold, while hunting near Andover. Edgar's son by his
first wife was called Edward and came to the throne when he was
thirteen and his half-brother Ethelred, Aelfrith's son, was seven.
While hunting in Dorset one day, Edward became separated from

his companions and called at his stepmother's house. Still in the saddle, he accepted a glass of wine from Aelfrith and as he drank was stabbed or shot with arrows. It is not known if Aelfrith struck the regicidal blow herself or if Edward was killed by a servant on a signal by her, but the King's right arm was held and broken, the horse bolted, he fainted and fell from the saddle and was dragged by the stirrup for a considerable distance, being horribly mutilated by the stony track, and was killed.

From there on, conflicting legends begin. One is that the young King's body was placed in the hovel of an old blind woman and that during the night the hovel was filled with holy light and the old woman regained her sight. Some men of Wareham were led to the body by a light in the sky and took the King and buried him in the Priory of the Lady Saint Mary at Wareham. Three years later he was exhumed and taken to Shaftesbury for re-burial. When Aelfrith tried to set out for Shaftesbury, her horse, and several subsequent mounts, refused to move. This equine recalcitrance seemed to move her, however, and she retreated for the remainder of her life to the Priory of Wherwell in Harewood Forest, where her first husband had been murdered. Her son, brought to the throne by her murder of his half-brother, ruled badly—not for nothing was he called 'the Unraed' or 'ill-advised'. Edward was proclaimed saint and martyr, and in 1008 the Witan, the Council of England, under Ethelred, decreed that the Feast of St Edward be celebrated on 18th March, the anniversary of his martyrdom. In 1978, the Millennium Year, a service was held in Corfe Parish Church of St Edward on that day, and throughout the year there were celebrations including the performance of plays written around Edward's murder and Aelfrith's penance.

After the Norman Conquest Corfe was held by the King, and the building of the castle began about 1080 and continued for the next two hundred years, with the addition of towers named 'Plenty', 'Cockayne', 'La Gloriette', 'Malemit', Sauvary' and 'Butavant'. The last three were for prisoners, Butavant being a dungeon entered by a trapdoor and presumably never left alive. Among the many who died there were twenty-two French knights left to starve by King John, who kept his niece Eleanor of Brittany and the two daughters of the King of Scotland prisoner at the castle. Edward II was also held here, and although he was murdered in

Berkeley Castle by, among others, Sir John Matravers, his death was probably planned here. Sir John is himself buried at Lychett Matravers.

Corfe Castle passed out of the hands of the sovereign when Queen Elizabeth I sold it to Sir Christopher Hatton, that handsome and accomplished dancer who became Lord Chancellor. He had no legal training but became a favourite of the Queen from the time she had seen him dancing in a masque. But he died in debt to the Queen, with whose money he had raised a great house, Kirby Hall in Northamptonshire, and in 1634 his nephew's widow sold Corfe Castle to the Bankes family. At the beginning of the Civil War Sir John Bankes was Lord Chief Justice of the Common Pleas under Charles I and was a Privy Councillor. His wife repelled the Roundheads and held out during two different sieges of Corfe, the second ending by the castle's being delivered into the hands of the Parliamentarians from within by the treachery of Lieutenant-Colonel Pitman. Parliament voted to 'slight' the castle in 1646, but although it was mined and blasted, the massive towers did not tumble down but sank into the mines and still remain, ruined, leaning but upright. With the Martyr's Gate, which is split in two, and the massive keep, the castle is still an awe-inspiring sight.

Corfe Castle village is still largely unspoilt and retains something of a medieval air about it. The church has its original Per-perpendicular tower, and the remainder of the building is mostly by T. H. Wyatt, 1859–60, in thirteenth-century style, and is very well carried out, so that it fits easily into the village. The west door of the tower is flanked by carvings that include a man playing the bagpipes and a monkey—Martyn of Athelhampton perhaps? The courageous Lady Bankes must have seen it as it had been there for a couple of centuries before she went to Corfe, and, as she was the daughter of Nicholas Martyn of Athelhampton, she may have had a friendly feeling for Corfe's monkey. The present owner of Corfe is a direct descendant of Lady Bankes, which shows that neither treachery nor kegs of gunpowder can part that particular family from its home.

The village is formed of two prongs which converge at the market place immediately below the southern slope of the castle mound. The Greyhound Inn forms the eastern corner of the market place, and above its porch which projects over the street on which it is supported by Tuscan columns is the incision 'I.C. 1733', but much of the building is of the seventeenth century. The two-storeyed eighteenth-century Town House is now the Westminster Bank. The upper floor was the mayor's robing-room, which was entered directly from the churchyard—made possible by the rising of the ground behind the house. It is a most unusual stone house, roofed with stone tiles, the whole of the upper part of the central bay one great timber-framed window behind which the robing-room suite extends through to the back of the building. John Uvedale was mayor in 1582 and, possibly in the flush of civic pride, had a house built in 1575 just north-east of the Market Place. Uvedale's house has been altered and divided up since his day, but the two six-light mullioned windows that look out on to the road give an idea of what an impressive house it must have been originally.

The Town Hall in West Street is a small building which, like the Town House, backs into the churchyard. The ground-floor walls are of Purbeck stone and the walls of the upper storey of brick with ashlar dressings. This upper storey is the Council Chamber and has round-headed windows and a plaster ceiling with decorated cornice and is entered direct from the churchyard by a doorway which was blocked up for many years but has recently been opened again. The ground floor of the Town Hall was the lock-up and has since done duty as a museum.

The eighteenth-century almshouses are made up of eight single-room dwellings, four on the ground floor and four on the floor above, to which an external stone stairway leads. An E-plan Elizabethan house of Purbeck stone—Morton's House—seems to have strayed into East Street from more spacious and rural surroundings.

At the height of the stone-industry, Corfe was a town, and on Shrove Tuesday the Ancient Order of Marblers and Stonecutters still meets in the Town Hall. In the past this was the time when men brought their sons to be entered on the apprenticeship records, and the new apprentice had to dash across the road with a pint of beer in his hand and evade all those who set out to prevent him. There was also a tradition of kicking a football along the track over the heath to present the ball, with a pound of pepper, to Ower Farm before crossing Ower Heath to Ower Quay, where only a landing-stage remains, from which Purbeck marble was shipped over to Poole.

From the time in the eighteenth century when the local china clay began to be exploited—and in 1791 there was a contract to supply Josiah Wedgwood with Purbeck clay, there have been workings in the heath to the north of the Purbeck ridgeway. Many of the abandoned sites have filled with water and formed lakes, of which the best-known is the fifty-feet-deep hole, now surrounded by conifers and with all mod cons close by, known as 'the Blue Pool'. Particles of clay suspended in the water give the pool a greenish colour in shadow and turquoise in sunshine. It is all very un-Dorsetish in its parkiness, which is rather like that of reservoirs such as Vyrnwy which are costumed and rehearsed to play the part of lakes. But the Blue Pool has an Alpine beauty about it and is a great improvement on other clay-pits I have seen, which remain like oozing eye-sockets poulticed with slices of raw and rusty motor-car under dressings of ancient mattress. And then there are others which can be found by exploring on foot and where sphagnum moss and purple moorgrass have appeared again and a covering of scar-tissue vegetation is beginning to take over, as it does in the gashes left by torn-up railways and tramways which green over cuttings and embankments, turning them into make-believe Stone Age fortifications. From just east of Wareham a branch line operated to Corfe Castle and Swanage. Now it has gone, and so also have the lines laid to move shale, clay and stone to landing-stages and quays along the deeply-indented Purbeck shore of Poole Harbour.

The northernmost village in Purbeck in fact lies marginally north of Purbeck's northern boundary, the River Frome. This is not quite as contradictory as it sounds, because Arne is in the middle of the Arne Peninsula which protrudes north from the main body of Purbeck into the Wareham Channel, into which the Frome runs. And on the northern shore of the peninsula, opposite Hamworthy is Gold Point, from which a ferry used to cross to the Hamworthy shore, and Hyde's Quay on the western coast of Arne Peninsula was a loading-point for china-clay at the end of the eighteenth century.

There are but two roads in and out of Arne Peninsula and to

Arne village. Leaving Wareham, one turns left at Stoborough, and once the marshes to the north have been left behind, the road crosses a heath which always seem to me unlike any other in Dorset and more like Breton Finistère. There are birches and bracken, conifers and brambles, and between the road and the mouth of the Frome is the Arne oil-well where a donkey nods away to itself among the conifers.

This road ends at the cluster of houses and a church standing on slightly raised ground, the first hillock on this heath. St Nicholas's church was built around AD 1200 of reddish-brown stone taken from the heath, some of it now cement-rendered. Nave and chancel are in one, and the church is just under fifty feet long and sixteen feet wide. The windows in the east and north walls are early-thirteenth century, most of them lancets. The altar-stone may well be the original and has five incised crosses. The font is fourteenth century, the organ of 1842 and the painting over the south doorway an early-sixteenth-century stencilled design in red of pomegranates or apples. The church is lit by candles set in sockets on hoops of iron, 'rowels' or 'coronas of lights'—presumably from the crown usually placed at the apex of the hoop.

A walk of under two miles from Arne village leads to the shore of Poole Harbour at Shipstal Point. A Nature Trail board with a map gives the information:

> The Arne Reserve is a Royal Society for the Protection of Birds Reserve and is leased from David Scott, Esquire. The Reserve is a site of special scientific interest . . . and it is also designated as an area of outstanding natural beauty . . . a fine example of lowland heath, mainly dry heath, lying on the sands and gravel of the Bagshot Beds, dominated by heather and substantial areas of gorse. . . . The most important bird is the Dartford Warbler, much in need of protection due to the continuing reduction of this lowland heath habitat.

The shore itself is silt, gravel and mud, and at Shipstal point there are thick layers of oyster shells, testimony to those oysters eaten twice a day by Henry Hastings, Squire of Woodland, until his death in 1650 at the age of ninety-nine. Whether or not the revival of Dorset longevity is the aim, the oyster-beds are going to be cultivated again.

From this low-lying and marshy shore there is a view across Poole Harbour to the towers of Poole and Parkstone, Brownsea Island and Long and Round Islands. Brownsea Island has been in the care of the National Trust since 1962, and there is a nature reserve, administered by the Dorset Naturalist Trust, in the northern part of the island, which can be visited April–September. Brownsea was where Baden-Powell established the first Boy Scout camp in 1907, and the island is like a floating park safely out of reach of the Poole–Bournemouth conurbation. If Colonel Waugh had found china-clay here in the 1850s, as he hoped, Brownsea would now be a hole in the bed of Poole Harbour. But as he did not find it, he went broke—but not before having built St Mary's Church which is a mixture of ecclesiastical architectural styles filled with panelling, sculpture, brass, plate etc from many centuries and countries.

Brownsea Castle was yet another of Henry VIII's chain of forts, built in 1548 to guard Poole Harbour. It was changed and added to in the eighteenth and nineteenth centuries, and Waugh added more stone to turn it into a mansion. After a fire in 1896, some further refacing was done, this time with brick, and there is little of the original castle left. It is now the summer holiday residence of the employees of the John Lewis partnership. The castle—and perhaps the old name of 'Branksea Castle', which is now appearing again on O.S. maps, is more accurate—and Waugh's pier of 1852, flanked by white stucco octagonal turrets, the brick gatehouse and the wall around the Castle estate are all crenellated, and this and the early-nineteenth-century quayside buildings make up Brownsea's only village. There is an information office, a shop and a restaurant, and in the dry weather an ever-present fear of fire which is the island's scourge. Brownsea is a conservation and nature reserve with two lakes, a wilderness, red squirrels, golden pheasants, peacocks, a colony of terns, the second largest heronry in Britain, acres of daffodils left from an attempt to grow the flowers commercially, beech and rhododendron. It is part of Purbeck and in Studland parish.

While Arne, on its heathy peninsula, is the most northern of Purbeck villages, Worth Matravers is the most southern, high above the sea at the head of Winspit valley which, narrow as a ravine, rises from the shore in giant steps between cliff faces riddled with caves, for this was one of the great quarries worked until the end of World War II. It was at this point, between East Man and West Man clifftop downs that the East Indiaman *Halsewell* was driven aground on 6th January 1786. 168 people were drowned, and seventy-four were saved from the quarries and caves into which they had been swept by the waves.

Worth Matravers has a heart of stone and a body of stone as well: it is compact, built of Purbeck stone. The inhabitants have made their living from stone and sometimes from fishing too, each following as dangerous as the other. Swanworth Quarries still cut Portland stone in blocks for building sea walls; limestone is crushed for roadmaking, and a small quarry at St Aldhelm's Head produces a variety of rocks for specialist use such as repair and replacement of ornamental work in churches.

Worth church, yet another dedicated to the patron saint of sailors, St Nicholas of Myra, like that at Arne, is Norman with traces of Saxon work. The tower was built towards the end of the twelfth century, and the pyramidal roof was raised in 1869. Among the tombs in the churchyard is that of Benjamin Jesty who died on 16th April 1816, aged seventy-nine. He was ". . . particularly noted for having been the first Person [known] that introduced the Cow Pox by Inoculation, and who from his great strength of mind made the experiment from the Cow on his Wife and two Sons in the year 1774". Among the many writers who have commented on Jesty's great strength of mind in not trying it on himself was Treves who, as a doctor, might have guessed that Jesty had already had cowpox and thus realized the possibilities of vaccination.

Worth's pub is named for the quarriers and stonecutters 'The Square and Compass'. In the bar is a portrait of the last man to quarry stone in Winspit. His name, and I quote from Rodney Legg's *Purbeck Island*, was

. . . William Jeremiah Bower—and always called Billy Winspit. He was born in the grey Purbeck stone cottage one hundred yards from his quarry, and it was there that he died, only days from his eightieth birthday, on 9th August 1966. I called two weeks before his death and found him in his garden workshop chipping away at the centrepiece for a stone fireplace. He stopped to sharpen some tools as he had done since the age of sixteen when he was the quarry's blacksmith. Billy Winspit had started quarrying when he was eleven years old, and he looked back to the year of 1907, when pay in the quarries was twenty-five shillings a week, and £11 was the weekly wage bill for Winspit. Till his death, oil lamps gave the only light in the cottage which was without either gas or electricity. The old man told me:

"My father before me worked the quarries like I do, and granfer worked on the cliffs and his father. When I was a boy, father and I worked underground. In the old-fashioned ways you moved the stone out, cut it out and sent it to London in blocks. But that is all finished with now, and I only do a carving job as a part time. Once I had a fourteen-foot boat and went fishing in the summer as well. You couldn't do it in winter as we have some terrific weather here—seas fifty feet high. I have seen the waves come over the cliff into the quarry."

Life at Worth Matravers was always harsh and stony, and there is more authentic village atmosphere in Billy Winspit's memories and the stone dust on the clothes of the regulars in the pub than in the prettifaction of Worth by a duckpond.

Stone and faith combine a couple of miles away in the Chapel of St Aldhelm, named after the first bishop of Sherborne. The chapel is a massive twelfth-century building, only twenty-five feet square inside, standing on a grass plateau at the top of the nearly four-hundred-foot-high St Aldhelm's Head, the most southerly point in the Isle of Purbeck. It is lit by a single small and deep window. There is a central square pier, from which spring four ribs to support the ceiling vaults. The roof is in the form of a pyramid with a low turret that formerly housed a light to guide shipping. There is a coastguard station next door and some cottages nearby, and if they were not there, this would be one of the loneliest spots imaginable.

If Worth Matravers has a heart of stone, Swanage had a stone municipal deposit account. A stone merchant, George Burt, installed the town's first pumped-water system and also brought various bits of London masonry with which to enhance the town, including the front of Swanage Town Hall, which is said to have been designed by Wren but actually was planned by Edward Jarman as the Portland stone façade of Mercer's Hall. Burt saved it from demolition by his uncle's firm Mowlem, and he also brought an archway from Hyde Park Corner and some cast-iron columns from Billingsgate Market. He is remembered most now perhaps for Durlston Castle, which he had built in 1890 as a restaurant, which it is still, with excellent clifftop views. Texts of improving geographical information are incised on the outer walls of the castle, to be read as one goes down through the grounds to the Great Globe, ten feet in diameter, also in Portland stone and equally improving in the care with which the continents are incised, the information spread around it and the stone provided on which visitors can cut their initials instead of on the globe. A good many of the names of countries and much of the information must be unintelligible to most people, so much has changed in the world since Victoria's last decade.

Swanage is a cheerful, confusing muddle of a seaside town and as a town has no place here. One of the best and most amusing, yet fair, descriptions of it is Paul Hyland's:

> . . . the craziest town I know. It has the sublimity of long history, the charm of a fishing village, the ambition and pragmatism of a port, and the calculated grace of a watering-place. Architectural absurdities were imposed upon it by John Mowlem and George Burt, hard-headed men with the avaricious appetites and eccentric tastes of jackdaws. It sports the artistic pretensions of a poor man's St Ives, the garishness of a fun-fair and the red-brick boredom of a retirement haven. It contains modern buildings of flair and style, like the library, as well as block-busting monstrosities like the Mowlem Theatre.

The most rewarding way to approach Studland is to walk from Swanage over Ballard Down or, a longer walk, on the Dorset Coast Path by the Foreland and Old Harry Rocks, where Swanage Bay is separated from Studland Bay. A road rounds Ballard Down to join that from Corfe Castle and enter Studland from the west and join the road over Studland Heath from South Haven Point and the ferry to Sandbanks in the north.

There is not much left of the old village of Studland, but what is modern is pleasant and gathered together under the lee of Ballard Down. The footpath over Ballard Down leads into the churchyard of another Norman church dedicated to St Nicholas, and this approach gives a wonderful sense of discovery to see the church set among old yews, to walk slowly around it, taking in the massive but unfinished tower, Anglo-Saxon basically and with ashlar facings and buttresses added in the twelfth century and another buttress in the fourteenth. There is a squat bell-storey and a saddle roof. It was probably not carried higher because of doubts about both the foundations and the weight. The church was apparently built on an earlier Saxon church which was destroyed by the Danes in the ninth century. That church, probably built at the end of the seventh century, was in turn raised on the site of an even earlier building that may have been a pre-Christian temple. There is a corbel table that helps to support the roof of the nave, and the corbels are decorated with a great variety of grotesque carvings of human faces, animals and symbols which seem almost pre-Christian.

The church is lit by Norman windows on the north and on the south and west sides by windows enlarged in the eighteenth century, while the east window is thirteenth century. But later additions such as these and the eighteenth-century gallery take the background to the Norman arches, decorated capitals and vaulted roof that confirm to the eye that this is a Norman church. The atmosphere, even when the porch is bright with yellow, green and blue rucksacks, capes and plastic beach-toys, and the air alive with the clicking of camera-shutters and polyglot susurration, is one of calm and joyous faith.

Sergeant John Lawrence of the 40th Regiment of Foot lies underground a few yards from the porch. He ran away from the bullying Studland builder to whom he was apprenticed in 1804 and went for a soldier, saw service in South America the following year, was in Spain through the Peninsular War and was wounded at Badajoz. "He also fought at the glorious battle of Waterloo," states his memorial stone. While in the army of occupation he married a French wife, Clotilde Clairet of St Germain-en-Laye, and brought her back to Studland, where in a well-tried tradition of an old soldier, he ran a pub and dictated his memoirs.

This Dorset coast has seen invasion, smuggling, piracy, shipwreck, occupation by soldiers with modern weapons, the development of a new interest in ecology, the preservation of ancient buildings like Studland church and the man-made and man-destroyed Corfe Castle. Here there is Little Sea, a brackish lake hidden from the real sea by sand dunes knitted together by marram grass, among which naturists sunbathe or toss a beach-ball from one to another or to their swim-suited children. To the north, across the harbour water, are the trees of Brownsea, and beyond stretches Bournemouth, as deserted as Studland Heath until Lewis Tregonwell discovered its health-giving attributes in 1810 and grown now to a town of over 150,000 population. Since the reshuffling of UK county-borders, Bournemouth and Christ-church came into Dorset, but they have no place in a book about villages.

Whether you come into Dorset by ferry at South Haven Point, up from Devon through Lyme Regis, down from Somerset and Wiltshire, by sea to Weymouth or Poole, by air to Hurn Airport, or—the way the Saxons came in at the beginning of this book—over Bokerley Dyke, you will find heaths and downs, bare uplands and lush pastures, broad rivers and narrow trout-streams, pebble ridges, rocky shores and sandy beaches, old deciduous woods and new coniferous plantations. I have written a lot about the land-scapes of Dorset, because geology and geography decide settle-ments, industries and types of cultivation, which in turn have created the villages of Dorset in all their great variety. This book is a case of samples to give some idea of the richness of that variety.

Bibliography

Barnes, William, *The Poems of William Barnes*, ed. Bernard Jones (Centaur Press, 1962—two volumes).

Benfield, Eric, *Dorset* (Hale, 1950).

Bettey, J. H., *Dorset* (David & Charles, 1974).

Bond, L. M. G., *Tyneham: a Lost Heritage* (Friary Press, 1955).

Dacombe, M. R., *Dorset Up Along and Down Along* (Dorset Women's Institute, 1951).

Eastwood, John, *The Burton Bradstock Book* (Winterbourne Publications, n.d.)
The Chideock and Seatown Book (Winterbourne Publications, n.d.)
The West Bay Book (Winterbourne Publications, n.d.).

Fägersten, Anton, *The Place-Names of Dorset* (EP Publishing, 1978).

Gardiner, Dorothy, *Companion into Dorset* (Methuen, 1932).

Gittings, Robert, *Young Thomas Hardy* (Heinemann, 1975)
The Older Hardy (Heinemann, 1978).

Hardy, Thomas, (general ed. P. N. Furbank) *The New Wessex Edition of the Novels of Thomas Hardy* (Macmillan, 1974–8).
ed. James Gibson, *The New Wessex Complete Poems of Thomas Hardy* (Macmillan, 1976).

Hutchins, John, *History and Antiquities of the County of Dorset* (3rd ed. 1861–73).

Hyland, Paul, *Purbeck: the Ingrained Island* (Gollancz, 1978).

Hyams, John, *Dorset* (Batsford, 1970).

Kay-Robinson, Denys, *Hardy's Wessex Reappraised* (David & Charles, 1972).

Kerr, Barbara, *Bound to the Soil: a Social History of Dorset 1750–1918* (EP Publishing, 1975).

Legg, Rodney, *Purbeck Island* (Dorset Publishing Company, 1972).

Morshead, Sir Owen, *Dorset Churches* (Dorset Historic Churches Trust, 1975).

Newman, John, and Pevsner, Nikolaus, *Dorset* (*The Buildings of England*) (Penguin Books, 1972).

Royal Commission for Historical Monuments, *Dorset* (HMSO, 1952–76—four volumes).

Taylor, Christopher, *Dorset* (Hodder & Stoughton, 1970).

Treves, Frederick, *Highways and Byways in Dorset* (Macmillan, 1906).

Victoria County History: Dorset (1908–68—three volumes).

Wightman, Ralph, *Portrait of Dorset* (Hale, 1977).

National Trust Properties in Dorset

Houses open to the public

Athelhampton House
Cloud's Hill
Hardy's Birthplace

Open Spaces

Belle Vue Farm, Swanage
Burton Cliff and The Hythe
Cerne Giant
Coney's Castle
Creech Arch
Crook Hill, Beaminster
Fontmell Down
Golden Cap Estate
Hardy Monument
Lambert's Castle Hill
Lewesdon Hill
South Down Farm, Ringstead
Tolpuddle Martyrs' Memorial
Limekiln Hill, West Bexington
White Cliff Farm and Ballard Down
Winyard's Gap
(Further details from the National Trust, Stourhead, Bourton, Dorset.)

About thirty gardens in Dorset are open to the public
(Details from the National Gardens Scheme, 57 Lower Belgrave Street,
London SW1)

South West Way is an association formed to promote the interests of users of the South West Peninsula Coast Path.

(Membership Secretary Mrs D. Y. Lancey, Kynance, 15 Old Newton Road, Kingskerswell, Newton Abbot, Devon.)

Index